Witnessing Whiteness

First Steps toward an Antiracist Practice and Culture

Shelly Tochluk

Rowman & Littlefield Education
Lanham, Maryland • Toronto • Plymouth, UK
2008

Published in the United States of America
by Rowman & Littlefield Education
A Division of Rowman & Littlefield Publishers, Inc.
A wholly owned subsidiary of The Rowman & Littlefield Publishing Group, Inc.
4501 Forbes Boulevard, Suite 200, Lanham, Maryland 20706
www.rowmaneducation.com

Estover Road
Plymouth PL6 7PY
United Kingdom

British Library Cataloguing in Publication Information Available

Library of Congress Cataloging-in-Publication Data

Tochluk, Shelly, 1971–
    Witnessing whiteness : first steps toward an antiracist practice and culture /
Shelly Tochluk.
        p   cm.
    Includes bibliographical references and index.
    ISBN-13: 978-1-57886-725-7 (hard cover : alk. paper)
    ISBN-10: 1-57886-725-8 (hard cover : alk. paper)
    ISBN-13: 978-1-57886-726-4 (pbk. : alk. paper)
    ISBN-10: 1-57886-726-6 (pbk. : alk. paper)
        1. Whites–United States–Attitudes.   2. Whites–Race identity–United States.
3. Race awareness–United States.   4. Anti-racism–United States. 5. Racism–
United States.   6. Interpersonal relations–United States.   7. Responsibility–
United States   8. United States–Race relations.   9. Educators–United
States–Attitudes.   10. Community education–United States.   I. Title.
    E184.A1T63 2008
    305.80973–dc22   2007032646

∞ ™ The paper used in this publication meets the minimum requirements of American
National Standard for Information Sciences—Permanence of Paper for Printed Library
Materials, ANSI/NISO Z39.48-1992.
Manufactured in the United States of America.

Contents

Acknowledgments

Numerous individuals offered insight, support, time, and encouragement during initial stages of this work. Particular thanks go to my formal guides, who opened themselves for full view and whose stories shaped my perspective: Jennifer Obidah, Luis Rodriguez, Michael Meade, Katie Gottfred, Karen Teel, Lorraine Cole, Amanda Perez, Cayce Calloway, Lee Mun Wah, Spencer Brewer, Bob Roberts, Perry Bernard, Shirley Better, Lincoln W., Dave Adelson, and William King. Thanks also to the colleagues who supported this work during its dissertation stage: Helene Lorenz, Elizabeth Nelson, Nelson Rodriguez, and Heidi Gailor-Loflin.

Among those who graciously read, critiqued, and contributed to this work are Traci Dorf, Mary McBride, Nora and Keith Powell, Holly Mosher, Judy Moussa, Katrina Hamilton, Michelle McPeek, Michele Dumont, Anne Wilcoxen, Jackie Fisher, Robin Gordon, Michael Wagner, Pam Muniz, and Ken and Debbie Winters. Without their questions, feedback, and suggestions, this work would not be what it is. To those whose professional advice I turned to in the later stages, a significant debt is owed: thanks to Melanie Bush, Christine Sleeter, Francie Kendall, and Paul Kivel. Their encouragement and example were instrumental in the editing and publishing process. Additional thanks go to the Faculty Development Committee of Mount St. Mary's College for their support.

My deepest gratitude goes to the family and friends who supported me in various ways throughout this endeavor by reading, critiquing, and engaging in continuing dialogues, thereby shaping my life, perceptions, understandings, and this work: Cathy and Larry Tochluk, Julie Chavez, Jennifer Selig, Salina Gray, Aisha Blanchard-Young, Jorge Zeballos, Vance Aniebo, Alex Keeve, Cameron Levin, Sarah Glasband, Hillary Stephenson, Jason David, Clare Robbins, the members of AWARE-LA, and Orland Bishop.

Preface: A Work in Progress

This text requires a preface—a caveat, if you will. When matched against the tremendous need to confront issues of racism and white privilege, this book does not go far enough. If you are one who already sees the fullness of the problem and its links to our various educational, social, and economic systems, the model of *witnessing* proposed here might appear to ask for too little. For folks of color, critical pedagogues, and white antiracist activists, the contents may appear soft and too warmly conveyed for the urgency of the situation. For these reasons, an explanation is warranted.

Fundamentally, the intention here is to start a dialogue and offer a first step for those who are new to the path of perceiving whiteness and its effects on relationships. As such, the text speaks to a particular group of people. The intended audience includes white educators at all levels of practice: teachers, staff, and administrators; their professors, professional development instructors, colleagues, diversity trainers; and other white folks involved in community education implemented through social service and nonprofit groups.

From my experience, I imagine these educators to be people who seek to do good work in the world, who want to be of service to social justice efforts, and who care enough to pick up a book on whiteness in the first place. Within this group, there is much diversity of experience and perspective. Yet one thing is generally common: white folks do not interrogate themselves on what it means to be white on a regular basis. This often results in a lack of both (1) the desire to see themselves as part of a racial dynamic and (2) the skills to navigate the racial terrain successfully.

Since admonishing and shaming white people has not had widespread success so far, this book is an attempt at a different approach. This book offers an invitation that hopefully piques interest and inspires thought. I also hope this book convinces white readers that perceiving whiteness and developing active responses is imperative personally, socially, and politically if we are going to transform our society into a more equitable and just place.

Because the primary intention of this book is to reach out to my white community of educators, I use the pronouns "us" and "we" regularly when referring to white folks in general. However, conversations and experiences leading up to the publication of this book have also let me know that this book is also relevant for people of color. (For those unfamiliar with this term, "people of color" refers to persons of any racial background who are not considered, or do not self-identity, as white.) Due to the differential experiences found within any group, there are people of color who may seek to develop a deeper understanding of the history of whiteness, how white people experience whiteness, and how people continue to struggle against lingering racism after years of work, as well as some action steps we can take as a response.

Also, people of color who see a need to build collaborative relationships with white educators might also find this book useful. To the folks of color, I apologize for the potentially distancing effect my use of the pronouns "us" and "we" might have as the book is read. However, my hope is that readers of color understand that my word choice intentionally places myself within the group of white educators as a way to self-identify with the continued work necessary on this topic and to potentially reduce the defensiveness that so often surrounds discussions of race with white folks.

Additionally, I would like to offer a couple of explanations regarding my use of language. Like Frances Kendall, I too have struggled over whether or not to capitalize the term "white" in order to be consistent with my capitalization of "Black."[1] I capitalize "Black" because most Black folks I know can talk about their identity as Black people. They know what it means for them to be Black, and it is important. They capitalize it and, therefore, I do as well.

On the other hand, most "white" folks I know have no idea what it means that they are white. There is little racial awareness formed around this term, and for this reason, it seems inappropriate to offer "white" the same weight. This is in no way intended to diminish white people's humanity, but simply highlights that our society has not yet asked us to do the work required to form a viable identity around being white. Readers will note that when I speak of Radical White Identity, a consciously formed antiracist white identity constructed within a group of which I am a part, capitalization is utilized. I therefore offer my inconsistency as a challenge to white readers. We should sit with the discomfort of our whiteness being left in the lower case until we work toward an antiracist white identity of which we can truly and appropriately be proud.

My thanks also goes to Frances Kendall for alerting me to the way that my use of terms related to vision—*blurry, blind*, and so forth—as a metaphor related to our needed awareness around race issues might offend.[2] I had never considered that my use of these words betrays my privileged status as an able-bodied person who takes sightedness for granted, yet I too have been unable to find alternate language to convey the points I raise. For this I apologize and remain open to suggestion.

Also, I must confess that absolutely nowhere in this text do I treat the complex issues that face biracial or multiracial people, especially those who are part white. Admittedly, I focus on the easy split: those who are seen as "white" and those who are not. The dichotomy offered between "white" and "people of color" is clearly a vestige of my either/or thinking so reflective of modern, white society. Even the term "people of color" troubles plenty of my colleagues, as it does myself, and yet I find no other way to move forward except to use these imperfect categorizing terms until some new language or approach arises.

Ultimately, the model of *witnessing* invites educators to begin a process, a journey that offers possibilities for an altered way of being that can lead to an effective antiracist practice but without defining an exact goal or destination. The nature of the path requires this open-ended beginning. This racial identity journey involves challenging terrain . . . for everyone. The tone, therefore, reflects the need for each individual to determine how, and to what degree, this information should be utilized and incorporated. This may also be where my own faith enters. I believe that we must leave room for the spirit to move, to guide, and to lead people toward their next steps.

Also important to note, however, is that writing with this tone required me to move through a process of personal healing. Had I attempted to write this text five years ago, the message would have been altogether different. The text would have been less giving, more expectant, demanding, and judgmental. Both the tone and content would have reflected the fact that I was not resolved within myself about who I am as a white person.

For me, part of my journey involved a wholesale rejection of my home community, my culture, and my sense of self. I fell into a troubling pattern that many distressed whites exemplify. Part of that included unwittingly objectifying people of color as I turned to them in escape from my "white" life. I retreated into a world of color, what many describe as "colorful" garb, "colorful" music, and "colorful" people. At that time, I had much antipathy for anything that reminded me of my former, less aware, white self. I found conversations with most white people on matters of race fruitless. I now see that those conversations failed, in part, because they were not in the spirit of two people sharing dialogue. They were arguments, meant to bolster my view of the world and break theirs down.

Years later, I feel more at home at home. I remain unsatisfied with the level of understanding of my white community in terms of racial identity, but I accept my home community as flawed and in need of healing, like most communities. I now find conversations to be spirited moments of engagement and learning. Reaching deeply into myself, I find connecting points. Remnants of former ways of thinking help me to bridge dialogue with those as yet unfamiliar with the strange language I speak. I find myself in dialogues in which the terms *white privilege*, *systemic and institutional racism*, and *white supremacist system* are defined and explored.

Those conversations now inspire this writing. This book speaks to educators because we live in a society where a disproportionately high number of white educators work with youth of color. Numerous texts discuss the various implications this basic fact has on education and our population today. But if I can write from a place of empathetic understanding, utilizing my own process to help encourage other educators like myself to take those first few steps along the path toward deeper racial awareness, then perhaps a larger group might just hold out their hands and join me in that undefined future where well-intentioned folks become perceptive, then angry, then empowered, and finally active against racism. Coming to grips with racial identity is a process. It takes too long and there is no time to wait. I know. That is why we must get as many white people started as soon as possible.

NOTES

1. F. Kendall, *Understanding White Privilege* (New York: Routledge, 2006), xiii.

2. Kendall, *Understanding White Privilege*, xiv.

Introduction

I am an educator with a background in psychology. This simple fact takes on great meaning for this text, as my approach draws upon my training and experience within both fields. Due to this, the reader will rightly recognize that the text sometimes appears primarily concerned with the psychological process people experience as they deal with questions of race and privilege. At the same time, the underlying call is for the growth and development of educators. In this way, although this book is expressly intended for an audience of educators, readers from any professional or academic background should be able to understand and apply its essential message.

A few notes as we begin. First, my use of the term *educator* throughout this text is intentionally broad. This is so because the need to witness whiteness rightly includes everyone within our vast field of education. However, I must first begin by acknowledging the roots underlying the field. Recognizing that there are two viable Latin roots of the English word "education" from which one can take meaning, *educare* and *educere*, I speak to those inspired by either or both. I mean to include all of us who build our practice around *educare*, meaning to train, to raise, to bring up, or to mold. I also want to invite into the dialogue all of us whose practice flows from *educere*, those who intend to draw out and to lead forth.

Whether you see yourself as a trainer or facilitator, whether you hope to instill or inspire, our work will be limited if we cannot see the fullness of ourselves. Also, I must speak to the vast, far-reaching expanse of the field. To my thinking, the field of education involves everyone who promotes learning and growth. Therefore, the term *educator* includes teacher educators, teachers-in-training, teachers' aides, K–12 teachers, administrators, counselors, mentors, professors, student affairs directors, diversity trainers, community educators, health-related service providers on school campuses, policymakers, and inspired individuals seeking to understand themselves and others more fully.

Second, most administrators and veteran teachers know that *we* are the most important instruments we have in our teacher toolkits. All the books, multimedia supplements, and technological gadgets in the world will not offer improved instruction if *we* are not high-quality, perceptive, knowledgeable, passionate teachers/facilitators. In keeping with this understanding, this book is designed to take educators on a personal journey that can radically alter and improve our ability to relate to students and colleagues. My suggestion is that this experience will be more productive if readers approach the text actively, jotting down notes while each chapter is read, forming additional questions for continued dialogue, and journaling as inspired.

Now, with the field laid out before us, I invite educator-colleagues to join me on a journey. Throughout this book, I share my personal experience coming to grips with my white identity, offer the stories of others who have traveled similarly, and put forth a framework that can help move us toward a healthier sense of self, a more successful educational practice, and an imagination of a transformed culture. First, though, I will begin with a bit of my own story.

It was a crowd of primarily Black spectators that first brought my racial being to consciousness. I will never forget the pointing, laughter, and yells: "Look at the white girl!" As a sophomore in high school in the mid-1980s, I was the different one, a minority within a group, for the first time. Eight Black girls and I competed to go to a California State track meet in the 400-meter race. Even though my Orange County high school was very racially mixed (large percentages of Asian and Latino/a Americans), my classes were predominantly white. Selecting mostly white friends and avoiding any direct challenges concerning larger issues of racial identity or justice was easy. For me, racial awareness only existed when I was on the track competing against high-caliber high school athletes, and this was a rare event.

Continued participation in the world of NCAA Division I sprinting brought new issues surrounding race to the foreground. My first collegiate cross-race friendships at UC Irvine were fun, familial, and often flirtatious on the track. The struggles of my Black teammates were acknowledged, but only jokingly and often under the breath. For example, the very real racial profiling struggles they faced were often masked beneath laughing refusals to run behind the white girls on cross-training runs off campus.

"You just can't chase white girls out on the street!" some of the men would yell, half-opposing the distance workout itself, but half-opposing the prejudice they knew went unchecked just a few steps off campus. It was funny, and it was not funny. All in all, the friendships felt real, comfortable, and nurturing. Although we did socialize off the track, these interactions were rather limited and did not continue significantly once the season concluded.

When I later competed for UCLA, the responses to issues of race were dealt with very differently. Discriminatory experiences at UCLA were not discussed softly on the track. Although not a daily focus of attention, when issues did surface, my Black teammates' pain and anger were evident and far from hidden or covered over. There were times when I felt personally implicated just hearing about their experiences. These moments made initial efforts at relationship building a bit strained. But in the end, relaxed friendships formed as the powerful bonds created through mutual experiences of physical trials and competition proved strong. But, again, the relationships off the track were limited and short-lived.

After these collegiate experiences, I existed with a continuous recognition of myself as a racial being and a disavowal of prejudice and racism. But there was still something missing. Why was I unable to maintain these friendships off the track? I still hold deep affection for these men and women who were such an instrumental part of my life. What allowed these relationships to remain superficial enough that they could fall away so quickly once the team completed its activity? I still remain close with several of my white former teammates, so the answer has little or nothing to do with a phase-of-life change. Why was it so hard to translate close interracial experiences into sustained relationships?

Ultimately, within several months of my retirement from competitive athletics, I existed once more in an almost exclusively white world. If the single most important factor in developing friendships is proximity, that we become friends with those who are available, perhaps we can decide that my postcollegiate lack of interracial friendships was just natural.[1] But after all of the interracial experiences that I had had, it felt decidedly *un*natural. Besides, one of my Black teammates and I later taught in the same school district for several years and never made efforts to renew our connection. In the end, after living a *de*segregated life, the return to a segregated life felt like a failure of some kind.

What this speaks to is pervasive. According to the Civil Rights Project report, released in 2002, segregation still marks education, housing, and employment in our society, all of which lead us into segregated social lives.[2] Even when programs exist to integrate these environments forcibly, they are usually competitive and the cross-race individuals often do not have equal status, helping to explain why deep friendships do not frequently develop.[3]

But this cannot account for my experience. My teammates and I had equal status on the track. While we were in competition somewhat, we were teammates first. Overt racism or prejudice did not undermine our friendships. I have to be honest enough to reflect and admit that we simply were not that close to begin with. Something stopped us from fully entering each other's lives such that connections even broke down with those in closest proximity. Whatever this something was, it affected my interest and ability to collaborate with people of color within my own school district.

Looking at it now, I know that part of the problem was my incomplete understanding of myself as a racial being, affected by my own whiteness in ways I did not perceive. At that time, I was unable to hear my Black peers' complaints of racism without requiring them to prove the validity of their experiences. I could not recognize the unequal ground we had traveled to achieve the same positions. Nor was I able to see our difficult moments together as openings for deepening friendship as opposed to causes for rejection. All of this, and more, caused me to pull away.

My relationship to my own whiteness finally became meaningful to me when a significant friendship formed with a Black man I worked with at an urban elementary school. He articulated the ways that my thoughts, feelings, and actions were thoroughly influenced by white privilege. However grateful I may now be for his insight, I assure you that I fought his analysis at every turn. It can seem highly disconcerting and offensive to be told that you are unconscious of what influences your attitudes and beliefs about the world. The insinuation that unrecognized socialization was largely responsible for my thinking and actions struck at the heart of my sense of individuality and freedom. But, unfortunately, as offensive as an idea might sound, it still may be true.

This friend brought me face to face with how the benefits of whiteness shaped my value system, use of language, and perception of the world. For example, I was horrified to realize the offensive and false nature of the judgments I had grown up hearing. I had been influenced by statements like "If I were them I would . . ." when discussing people continuing to reside in gang-infested neighborhoods.

The privilege inherent in judging those struggling, while sitting in comfort, became clear. I had to face the fact that my speech unknowingly betrayed judgments against those with whom I worked at the school site. As I questioned them, I left no confusion regarding my ignorance of the struggles they faced. Adding to that, when I did begin to recognize my errors, my worldview and learned judgments then caused me to respond with pity more often than empathy. A sense of superiority still pervaded my communication style and behavior.

None of this was intentional. Being confronted with my continued failure to eliminate my own patronizing approach, no matter what I did, made me feel either guilty or resistant, depending on the day. Ultimately, accepting that I was acting problematically felt like a rug was being pulled out from under me. I had to reevaluate everything. For quite some time, I felt rather lost in the world and clung to those who appeared knowledgeable about these subjects. I became a student of my Black colleague, sometimes unhealthily subservient, sometimes fiercely defensive.

After several years of discussions, challenges, and tears, I now see my racial self as incredibly significant and meaningful. I also see how being white means more than what I determine it to mean. Its historic significance lives on within me whether I perceive it or not. My whiteness affects my teaching practice, my relationships with colleagues, and my ability to collaborate with parents in more ways than I could have imagined. But through questioning that experience, I also have developed a healthier sense of self and recognition of how privilege plays a role in my life, relationships, and community.

During those years, I came face to face with a variety of discomforts and pains related to being a white person in the United States, a dis-ease

I now believe to be reflective of a collective white experience. I spent several years trying to find solace in teaching students of color in an urban school district and doing community work with people of color until one day, while attending a meeting at the Community Self-Determination Institute in Watts, one of the staff members turned to me and said something like this: "You know, we're really glad you're here, and we like you and all. But we are working with our own people. We can do this. What we really need is for you to go and work with the white people."

She went on, but my mind was already spinning in several directions, understanding deep down what that really meant for me. Her suggestion essentially asked me to face my biggest fear, talking to white people about race. To be truthful, that was most likely not the first time somebody said that to me. I would wager that it was simply the first time I was ready to hear what it implied, that I needed to take another step on my journey of racial identity development, one that would lead me home to really heal the inner pain I was avoiding and ignoring.

So, finding myself incompletely recovered from my initiation into seeing whiteness, I began to ask some questions. What should the next phase of my racial identity development look like? I realized that for quite some time I had been seeking validation from people of color to help me see myself as a worthy person in the world. My sense of self had relied upon the Black teachers at my school site, who said I was not a "regular" white person. I recalled the satisfaction I felt when the Black counselors and administrators called me an "angel" for my work. When some of the Latino/a parents and I spent time together, I felt valuable because of the "service" I could provide.

Recognizing how much of my so-called service was tied to my need to feel good about myself, I began to wonder how many other white educators out there were living a similar experience. Further, how can white educators like me leave the guilt behind and exemplify a healthier way of being? How can we dedicate ourselves to working towards equity without letting go of our sense of self? These questions became a project with a larger, formalized research focus.

Within this process I looked for models, deciding that I would do in-depth interviews to locate answers. I chose to interview pairs of cross-race friends because I wanted to hear how race, particularly whiteness, played a role within a sustained, long-term relationship. Ultimately, I wanted to talk to people who had done significant personal work with each other and had experienced deep conflict and/or transformation.

I rightly imagined that these people's experience might translate into wisdom that would help me do two things. First, I hoped to learn what it would take to better form and sustain collaborative relationships with the people of color in my life. Second, I hoped their experience would help me understand how to create a positive sense of my racial self so that my work did not involve my seeking validation from people of color.

Admittedly, the concept of *witnessing* offered in this book had not yet occurred to me. Rather, this model emerged out of the process of collecting, analyzing, researching, and interpreting the interviews for the project. Because of that, I do not know what the participants would have said about the concept I put forth in this book.

This book incorporates pieces from the larger project, highlighting white educators of various types who have begun to see their own whiteness. During interviews, they discuss their struggles and the way race issues continue to affect their cross-race friendships. The interviewees talk about how they see whiteness and where they continue to find white privilege and racism lingering within their psyche. The stories of their struggles demonstrate a variety of paths with varying levels of challenge. But, collectively, I believe their stories illustrate a process that can lead toward greater understanding for people who care about equity, improved cross-race relationships, and a life that subverts dominating whiteness.

To find the white people, I searched where whites often do not go successfully: within friendships with people of color. I purposefully looked for people of color who would be intensely aware of race issues, those who actively work to educate people regarding issues of race and/or their community's healing. I asked for a lot. Both the white person and the person of color talked to me about personal racial identity, perceptions of whiteness, enduring cross-race friendships, and continuing struggles with race issues.

Although wanting most to hear from whites because they would be models for me, I had long ago learned that people of color are usually more keenly aware of white privilege and its effects. Therefore, the original research highlights the perceptions of both the white folks and their friends of color as equally as possible. In this book, however, the white folks receive increased space in terms of their introductions and backgrounds, as their particular journeys can help white educators see our possible paths.

Among others, this book includes several community educators, such as Chicano poet Luis Rodriguez and his friend, mythologist Michael Meade, as well as a diversity trainer, Lee Mun Wah, producer of *The Color of Fear*, and Spencer Brewer, his white friend who helped make the film possible. The book also includes antibias teacher-trainers Jennifer Obidah and Karen Teel, coauthors of *Because of the Kids*, as well as educators with a background in speech-language development, such as Lorraine Cole, the CEO of the YWCA USA, and her white friend Katie Gottfred, founder of LEAP Learning Systems, a nonprofit organization advancing language development within the Cabrini Green housing project in Chicago.

During the years that I spent interviewing, researching, and analyzing data related to the questions I had generated, I also participated regularly with a growing movement of people in Los Angeles called AWARE-LA, Alliance of White Anti-Racists Everywhere-Los Angeles. The dialogue space provided by this group was essential in clarifying my thinking and strengthening my resolve that I am not the only one experiencing distress over what it means to be white in the United States. I am not the only one searching for a way of being that promotes a healthy sense of self while simultaneously working to increase the capacity to be effectively active in equity efforts.

AWARE-LA promotes the development of a *Radical White Identity*, an identity I have been working to create for myself. We recognize that work toward a solid, effective antiracist practice must include the creation of a healthy white identity. Working toward this also involves training ourselves to better recognize and respond to the racism and white privilege that are enacted in our daily lives . . . essentially, *witnessing*.

Deserving note is the fact that although AWARE-LA did not set out to recruit educators, our group attracts teachers from many different arenas. Whether we work in elementary or high schools, on college campuses, or serve as community educators, many of us see that our willingness to struggle together with this issue has translated into positive impacts within our educational communities.

It has now been over a decade since my first crying fit in the parking lot of an elementary school campus where I refused to acknowledge that my being white had anything to do with anything. After much consideration, I now stand convinced that the future of our country depends on white educators being able to turn within, into the depths of our being, focus on our whiteness for a time, and perceive its effects on our deepest psyche, our teaching practices, and our collaborative relationships. We must face our deepest shadow, our country's historical legacy of white supremacy. While uncomfortable to admit, its memory lies within us, embedded.

Ours is a collective history so deeply ingrained that it cannot be wished away, consciously put aside, or dismissed. Healing lies in the courageous move to interrogate our racial legacy and understand its continued manifestations. Only when we develop the capacity to name the effects of white privilege can we begin the work of investigating to what degree our relationship with our whiteness requires alteration. White educators must be able to bear witness to the overt and subtle ways that issues of race and dominating whiteness continue to emerge in our daily lives with students, colleagues of color, and community partners, and how they affect policy decisions, health-related services, diversity trainings, and reform initiatives.

The purpose of this book is to encourage white people—those who identify as European Americans living in North America, specifically—to investigate our sense of self from a racial point of view in order to create more intimate and honest relationships with ourselves, others, and the world in general. As uncomfortable as it may become, we have to keep our eyes focused on ourselves. We have to keep whiteness squarely in sight.

One thing white people are really good at is shifting a conversation on race to focus on other groups. As soon as a finger gets pointed at us, many of us point somewhere else and expect the conversation to move in that direction. We shield ourselves reflexively, often without real awareness of the implications. This is precisely the type of dominating whiteness that we need to start noticing. Our tendency to shift focus away from ourselves is very strong. We have been getting away with it for so long that it appears normal. For that reason, this book will keep the finger pointed at white people.

The history of race in the United States is so tragic that each group requires its own healing process. Although true that there are many similar consequences of oppression for groups of color in general, each group also has its distinct needs based upon its differential history. Some call it ethno-specific healing work. Fortunately, there are many people out there working to uplift and heal their specific communities. Joy DeGruy Leary is but one example. Her work on *Post-traumatic Slave Syndrome* discusses the ways that African Americans require healing from their trauma, both past and present.[4]

Dr. DeGruy Leary's work is thought-provoking and inspiring. As an African American woman deeply committed to the healing of her community, her insight is precise. Although targeting her Black community, all readers can benefit from her work. I know I am grateful that my Black teacher-colleagues introduced me to her work. Dr. DeGruy Leary's work not only expanded my vision regarding the trauma experience by the African American community, but it reinforced my conviction that white people also need to focus on our own healing, not only for our own sake but for our country as a whole.

For these reasons, my work speaks primarily to white educators, although I hope it will be useful for readers of all backgrounds. I recognize that white folks have developed ways of being due to our history in this country from which we need to heal and that, as educators, we play an important role in shaping the beliefs and attitudes of those in our surroundings. There is no reason to believe that different groups require the same healing process. That would make about as much sense as a doctor giving the same medicine for all maladies. The white experience has been different, and therefore the process through which we must pass must also be different. For white people, as the group that has held dominant status, we are less in touch with how race affects us. For this reason, our first step is to identify the ways our whiteness emerges. Our first step is to become witnesses to our whiteness.

NOTES

1. L. Festinger, S. Schacter, and K. Black, *Social Pressures in Informal Groups; A Study of Human Factors in Housing* (Oxford: Harper, 1950).

2. "Race, Place, and Segregation: Redrawing the Color Line in Our Nation's Metros," *Civil Rights Project*, 2002, http://www.civilrightsproject.harvard.edu/research/metro/three_metros.php

3. M. R. Jackman and M. C. Crane, "'Some of My Best Friends Are Black . . .': Interracial Friendship and Whites' Racial Attitudes," *Public Opinion Quarterly* 50 (1986): 459–486.

4. J. DeGruy Leary, *PostTraumatic Slave Syndrome* (Milwaukie, OR: Uptone Press, 2005).

Part I

DIS-EASE IN THE WHITE COMMUNITY

Chapter One

Naming the Problem

I offer my students an uplifting view of the world. I talk about how racism is unacceptable in our society. I teach about how we outlaw discrimination and that more and more people are transcending race. In fact, I explain that race has no biological reality. Focusing on our ethnicity is therefore a much better way for us to talk about, and appreciate, our cultural differences. Self-identifying as being white simply reinforces old problems of division, so I make sure my students know that I am colorblind. I just see us all as part of the human race.

There was a time when I spoke using this language. I have plenty of colleagues who continue to describe their approach to race using these terms. Admittedly, this orientation sounds like the right and healthy approach to most white folks and some people of color. The trouble is what many of these statements ignore and deny. The trouble is what is left unexplored and unsaid. The reality is this: There is a deep dis-ease regarding race residing within much of the white community.

White people in general are ill at ease over issues of race, and we are not very skilled at naming the true nature of the problem. We are confused by its complexity, and our discomfort arises in our multiracial classrooms, schools, collaborative relationships, and meetings whenever race becomes the focus of a conversation. Many of us choose a colorblind, transcendence-seeking optimism that ends up stifling honestly difficult dialogue about the very real racial dynamics that continue to play out in our interactions. The strategies we use to avoid dealing with race, unfortunately, often allow us to behave offensively without awareness. What we need are witnesses who can help sound the bells of alarm and raise a voice in the interest of improving our ability to create healthier, more successful, and productive educational experiences and institutions.

CAN I GET A WITNESS?

Have you ever been a witness? Witnesses see a situation clearly and speak out about wounding events. Can you recall a time when you found yourself in the midst of a situation where you needed to speak out? Was someone's safety or emotional well-being hanging in the balance? What did you do? If I were in a serious traffic accident, I hope a witness would be present to call for help. Without a witness, my injuries might prove unnecessarily fatal. If assaulted, I hope a witness would be present to disrupt the event and describe the perpetrator. Without a witness, my search for justice might go unrealized. Events that take place in the shadows might require concerted effort to witness. A scream in the night hopefully can bring someone running, someone close enough to see and interrupt the problem.

If I am ever in a situation requiring me to witness a trauma-filled situation, I hope that I will have the courage to be present and speak the truth of what I perceived. Depending on the circumstances, I might be frightened myself—but I can only imagine what turning and running would do to my sense of self. I think my own soul would suffer if I attempted to justify turning away. Ultimately, choosing to disconnect from the situation at hand would damage my own spirit.

Depth psychology, the study of the unconscious, shapes my perspective. In a class on trauma, one of my mentors spoke of "percepticide" to describe the ways that we kill off our own perceptions when we feel that we are in a dangerous situation.[1] Although it is easy to imagine that we would shut down in the face of a lethal threat, we can do this even if the situation is not life threatening. When we fear that we will be socially punished because people in our immediate surroundings cannot tolerate hearing about what we see, we often silence ourselves and shut down parts of our psyche.

Like a student who runs to tell a teacher something, only to be dismissed, we only say "Yeah, but . . ." in protest so many times before we turn away and stop trying. We become numb and disconnect from aspects of ourselves. What we know becomes exiled, and over time that information becomes unavailable as we move through life.[2] This idea is not new. Frances Kendall offers a somewhat related idea in her book *Understanding White Privilege*. She speaks of white folks "anesthetizing" themselves to avoid guilt and other confusing feelings, and refers to Charles Mills' explanation of "structured blindness and opacities."[3]

Regardless of what terms we use to describe it, this type of dissociation can also stop us from creating or maintaining emotional connection with others. If I am not fully seen, why should I see you? If my injury and perception does not receive attention, why should yours? If I have shut myself off from my own pain, shouldn't you do the same? In other words, when we are not able to witness or be witnessed, we end up with splits in our psyche that keep us disconnected from both ourselves and other people. Of course, our attempts to avoid painful emotional states are understandable. Unfortunately, once we split off from the aspects of our lives that bring us pain, we disown and reject them, casting them into the shadows of our psyche.[4]

This book argues that there is a scream to which educators must respond, a traumatic situation that for many of us remains obscured in the shadows. We need people to come running because there is a deep distress to which we must bear witness. Repeatedly turning away has created deep injury. Undoing this damage requires us to face the painful situation and become clear-seeing witnesses.

RACIAL IDENTITY IN THE SHADOWS

I teach in a teacher preparation program at a small, liberal arts Catholic college. My job is to prepare teachers to work with the ethnically, racially, linguistically, and culturally diverse student body within the greater Los Angeles area. Although my classes are diverse, there are a good number of white students. An exploration of how race, ethnicity, gender, religion, education, and citizenship status can affect our perspectives on the world always begins one of my courses. The one thing I can count on is that at least one white student will hesitate when filling out a worksheet section related to race. More often than not, white students reveal discomfort naming "white" as the racial placement.

Bearing witness to that discomfort is important in order to determine corrective action. Unfortunately, racial identity for white people is a very blurry topic and we are not very good witnesses of our own whiteness. Our relationship with race involves a great deal of anxiety, and we ignore our racial identity for some very understandable reasons. But this neglect allows the ways race affects us to remain within the shadows of our unconscious.

As we leave our relationship to race unexplored, unquestioned, and untreated, our whiteness becomes analogous to the far side of the moon. We never see the mysterious far side that scientists tell us appears far more battered and beaten than the visible side facing the Earth. White educators often act out of our unexplored whiteness and then feel injured when our attempts at overcoming racial issues in our practice fail. Witnessing whiteness involves not only shining a light into our shadows and facing the damage our history of race continues to do to our psyche but also clarifying our individual relationship to race and our racial identity.

Fortunately, mythology can offer us something to take with us as we journey into our racial shadow. A primary figure linked with the dark moon is Hecate. Much can be narrated and debated about her attributes and abilities, and the multiplicity of her characterizations can be instructive. Each aspect can offer guidance as we move forward. First, Hecate is often seen as the hag, a witch practicing evil. As a bearer of uncomfortable truths, she offers unwelcome light emanating from the shadows. This text assuredly offers uncomfortable truths regarding white folks' relationship to race. So, in the minds of some readers struggling against descending into what remains hidden, the image of the hag—a harping woman continuously poking and prodding—might arise.

On the other hand, Hecate is also the fairy godmother stirring up brews for magical transformation. She represents the wise mother holding deep wisdom. She is the ruler of the crossroads, asking us to consider that the messiness of our lives is also the raw material used to create soul. For those of us willing to descend into the depths of our own unconscious, these images remind us that becoming more attuned to the hidden sides of ourselves increases our wisdom and can help us make better choices as we reach new crossroads in our journeys. Inviting the image of Hecate to join us can be helpful because the uncomfortable truth is that white folks have neglected the consequences of race for such a long time that we can hardly define our own discomfort.

CLARIFYING OUR VIEW:
DEFINING OUR TERMS

Let us start by naming our distress. Speaking generally, white people are uncomfortable being called white, naming ourselves white. But, admittedly, we are not at ease with anything having to do with race. So we have to start there, acknowledging that this mess called "race" is problematic at its core. Without time to sort through the overwhelming collection of evidence, I will simply say what many already know: It is true that race has no natural, biological reality.[5]

Of course we see physical differences among people from different environments. Yes, we turn to science to help us understand these differences—but science cannot find any coherent and absolute way to locate race. Yes, many of us have been taught that certain physical characteristics go together with a certain race. But when we look closely at the subject, we end up confused if we try to pinpoint where many people fit within racial categories. Variety outweighs consistency. Ultimately, we humans made up the concept of race as we tried to increase both our understanding and manipulation of our world. In other words, race is *socially* constructed. Because of this, our experience of racial identity holds to no absolute physical markers or experiences.

That said, regardless of the false nature of racial categories, the concept of race holds great social force. Our society uses race in spite of some people's disavowal and often treats us differentially as a result. Race has truly gotten under our skin, into our psyche, lingers within the layers of our unconscious, and continues to require attention. To begin honestly, we must discuss what may be, for white people, the most challenging aspect of any discussion of race. We must deal with the terms *racist*, *racism*, and *systemic white supremacy*. We must also confront the fact that some people might ask us to associate those words with ourselves and our actions.

Understandably, these words can appear inflammatory and many white folks shut down as soon as they are spoken. We see ourselves as essentially good-hearted people doing the best we can within a society deeply impacted by the wounds of our country's past. These terms are especially difficult to relate to for educators who dedicate long hours to a diverse body of students, working hard to support the achievement of all.

Our resistance arises, in part, because individually we avoid behaviors historically considered racist. To be a racist, to be associated with racism and a system of white supremacy, is tantamount to saying that we represent the worst of what the United States has to offer. Being a racist means that we are mean-spirited, closed-minded, and lack essential goodness. Imagine a list of negative attributes one might use to criticize, a set of characteristics that inspire a defensive reaction. Consider the emotional reaction you might have if labeled that way. For most whites, the label *racist* will spark a more defensive reaction than almost any other slight. I would certainly rather be called narcissistic, greedy, or insensitive than be called racist. For this reason, we have great difficulty withstanding any conversation that asks us to consider ourselves related to that term.

But if we do not at least investigate and understand how we have developed opinions about what the term does or does not mean, we do ourselves a disservice. For example, close your eyes for a moment and imagine a racist. What is the image that forms in your mind? Take a moment and write down a few descriptors. Some might have a picture that looks something like a Southern or Midwestern rural or small-town person who drives a truck and wears a baseball hat. This was the stereotypical image I grew up ingesting.

Others might imagine a conservative lawmaker who enacts policies that disproportionately benefit whites. Still others might imagine a social liberal who advocates for differential treatment of people based on race. These are just a few of a thousand possible images that different people might have. The big question is, how many of us imagine ourselves when we think of a racist? If I were a betting person, I would wager that precious few of us see ourselves in that category.

The problem with this is that our images can amount to psychic finger-pointing that results in a personal distancing from the issue. Imagining only a neo-Nazi or member of the KKK as racist psychologically cuts us out of the problem. This book argues that we *all* are part of the problem of race in the United States and we *all* can be part of the solution. This includes well-educated folks who already see themselves working toward social equity. There is more to see. This also can include many people of color, though white people and our relationship to the problem is the focus of this book, since we *all* have been negatively affected by the social conditions of our country. Everyone who lives in this country has a stake in healing our relationship to race and its effects if we are ever going to be able to move past it. *Everyone.*

However, we still need to define what is meant by the term *racism.* For the sake of brevity, this chapter offers an abbreviated analysis from a couple of more thorough sources. In short, racial prejudice and racism are not interchangeable concepts. The first few pages of Beverly Daniel Tatum's bestseller *Why Are All the Black Kids Sitting Together in the Cafeteria?* discusses the difference between the two ideas.[6]

According to Tatum, *racial prejudice* is a preconceived judgment or opinion based on insufficient knowledge. Tatum argues that we all have prejudices by virtue of living in a society offering a preponderance of misinformation about different groups. We might consciously reject overt prejudices, but very often prejudices remain due to misunderstandings, an incomplete knowledge base, or isolated experiences.

Racism, on the other hand, involves a system that offers advantage based on race. White people might consciously reject prejudice, yet we are often completely unaware of how the structure of our society continues to advantage whites over other groups. In this view, racism is not necessarily about the belief system one holds as much as racism involves the systemic inequity maintained through both individual and institutional means.

In *Institutional Racism,* Shirley Better defines and compares *individual racism* and *institutional racism* and illustrates how each relates to beliefs, attitudes, practices, and structures.[7] To offer just a few of the ideas presented, on the individual side of racism a person might accept social and economic inequality as acceptable, hold an attitude of blindness to racism, utilize negative verbalizations, and follow both conscious and unconscious behavior patterns that reinforce inequity. Although this is just a sample of what Better offers, the list illustrates that not all aspects of individual racism are necessarily conscious. Individual racism can involve following customs and patterns that white folks consider race-neutral but that actually uphold social and economic inequity. This book offers illustrative examples throughout of how we might individually perpetuate inequity without realization.

On the other hand, institutional racism includes the maintenance of white-skin privilege, segregation, and formal and/or informal politics, practices, and procedures. Overall, this is what some people are talking about when they refer to *systematic dominating whiteness*, *systemic white supremacy*, or *a system of supremacy of whiteness*. Essentially, each of these terms calls us to notice the basic fact that white people, and our social norms and patterns, continue to wield controlling power within our social, economic, political, and educational structures in ways that maintain inequity. True, as individuals we may not have created these structures. True, we might even disagree with how racial inequity continues. But the fact is that we are related to these systems of inequity because our continued existence within them usually supports the status quo.

Our ability to notice *systemic*, *institutional* racism expands with our consciousness regarding unintended *individual* racism. The model of witnessing our whiteness described in this text depends on increasing our ability to notice both individual and systemic forms of racism and dominating whiteness. But in order to even begin to do that, we must be willing to fathom that our lives are not as far removed from the concept of racism as we hope.

WHAT DOES IT MEAN TO BE WHITE?

Just as the term *race* poses difficulty, the term *whiteness* is similarly troublesome. As part of the social construction of race, whiteness suffers from all of the same confusions as race in general. The concept is not clear. What do we mean when we say that someone is white? Are we simply talking about skin color? Skin color is actually a poor predictor of whether or not someone is considered white and anthropologists now generally agree that race itself has no biological reality.

In fact, the American Anthropological Association recently put out a "Statement on Race" to reflect the thinking of most contemporary scholars.[8] Within the statement, they note,

> In the United States both scholars and the general public have been conditioned to viewing human races as natural and separate divisions within the human species based on visible physical differences. With the vast expan-

sion of scientific knowledge in this century, however, it has become clear that human populations are not unambiguous, clearly demarcated, biologically distinct groups. . . . Historical research has shown that the idea of "race" has always carried more meanings than mere physical differences; indeed, physical variations in the human species have no meaning except the social ones that humans put on them.

So, what is whiteness? From my experience, the question provokes a tilt of the head and a furrowing of the brow in the majority of white people in predominantly white communities. "What do you mean?" comes with a queried look. Upon further prompting, a great many of us respond that being white means nothing. If anything at all, being white may be described as being either just normal or neutral.[9]

If some whites consider whiteness as being normal, then the question becomes normal how? Is whiteness a way of being in the world? Is there a white culture? Some say yes, some say no. If yes, what does that culture look like? For many, white culture is an amalgamation of a variety of variables that any particular person may or may not exemplify. Some of these include skin color, a position of racial dominance, the ability to avoid issues of race, the primacy of individualism, the achievement of middle-class economic success, and often a residentially, socially, and/or socioeconomically segregated life.[10]

And yet we occupy so many social positions that each individual's experience necessarily varies. My conception of whiteness is surely different from that of someone coming from a different region or socioeconomic class. My experience, having grown up in a middle-class suburb with white-collar, college-educated parents, is undoubtedly far different from that of someone from either a rural town or a working-class, urban area. Even so, the general concept of "white culture" remains widely used. The term "white culture" means something to a lot of people. Taking a step back and considering to what degree each of us fits into that picture is helpful. Later chapters will investigate both how our country's history shapes these meanings and how they continue to be enacted and perceived.

Viewing whiteness as a process, as suggested by Ruth Frankenberg, can be helpful. Whiteness is not a thing that can ever be fully captured and nailed down.[11] Whiteness is irregularly experienced and dynamic, always shifting and changing. This perspective helps me understand why there are moments when I see whiteness so clearly that I am ready to dedicate years of my life to making it visible for other people and then only a day later the meanings of whiteness practically disintegrate in front of me, seemingly too fragmented and illusory to grasp. Now that I have been party to this dissolution a sufficient number of times, I know that it will only be a matter of time before my perception of my whiteness reconstitutes.

An important aspect of our blurriness over our whiteness is that fact that whiteness is simply invisible to many of us. Some authors use the analogy of a fish in a fish bowl in an effort to help us understand. Does a fish notice the water in which it lives? The idea is that white people are accustomed to living in a world dominated by whiteness. We are saturated with the whiteness in our social world. Our position has sustained us in ways that we do not perceive.

Another approach is to use the analogy of handedness.[12] In a world dominated by right-handed people, we of the dominant group rarely perceive that our world has been created for our benefit. I recall arriving late one day to a college class and sliding as quickly as I could into the first available seat, which happened to be along the left aisle. I was a bit put out as I tried to pull up the collapsed writing desk, finding it on what I considered the wrong side! I had unwittingly sat in the few seats that catered to left-handed people and I sat rather uncomfortably for the rest of the class period.

If you are right-handed, have you ever found yourself mistakenly picking up a pair of left-handed scissors? Did you even know they existed? I did not know until I began working in a kindergarten class as an adult. In any case, my perception of the writing desk as on the *wrong* side illustrates how white people often experience situations that are not designed specifically for us as problematic.

When our normal, daily experience includes items and services oriented toward our needs, it is a real surprise to be in spaces that do not cater to our preferences. In this way, many white people take things for granted that people of color recognize as benefits of being white. Peggy McIntosh's well-known article "White Privilege: Unpacking the Invisible Knapsack" offers a list of advantages, both significant and minor, that she receives because she is white.[13]

One day at a conference last year, Dr. McIntosh described how she developed the list. After making a prayer asking for guidance in her ability to understand racial disconnections more clearly, the examples came to her in the middle of the night. She awoke and hurriedly wrote them down, convinced that in the light of day they would be irretrievably lost to unconsciousness. Even she, noted for her ability to perceive the privileges of whiteness, admits that she struggled to keep them in mind.

We all can use some help in perceiving what has been left unspoken, and therefore unnoticed, for most of our lives. Thankfully, many educators have been doing this work for some time and offer their realizations as helpful aids. There are even those who have used Dr. McIntosh's work as inspiration to highlight how white privilege emerges in school situations.[14]

For white educators practicing in diverse environments, however, the water in the fish bowl can become visible fairly quickly. We are faced with mirrors that remind us that we are perceived as part of a white group. In these circumstances, the dis-ease of naming our whiteness can take on a different feeling. This is where the majority of my white colleagues and students fit in. They live in a multiracial environment in which the political and historical associations with whiteness are readily understood. Being white means being an oppressor. Whiteness symbolizes our history of slavery, the genocide of the Native American populations, racism, and the Ku Klux Klan. Whiteness is bad. To claim whiteness is to associate oneself with irreconcilable damage to humanity. Being white is shameful.

No wonder that the white community, in general, is not at ease with its own whiteness. At best, being white is just normal or neutral. At worst, whiteness aligns us with a shameful history to which we do not want to be connected. Sometimes both occur at the same time in the same person. We might feel that being white has no effect on our thoughts, behaviors, or our teaching practice, but we recognize that our students and/or their parents might see us as representing negative aspects of U.S. history.

When I felt this way, my reaction was to be both saddened and angered at feeling simultaneously misunderstood and under fire. Top that off with the proposal that we are part of a white culture. Seeing our white selves as part of a culture of whiteness automatically throws us into a collective that may offer us little of which we will be proud. I understand why our resistances go up at this point. Not only is our individuality at stake, but so is our fundamental ability to see ourselves aligned with goodness. Used to seeing ourselves as decent, good, hard-working people, this whole idea can catapult us into a fight-or-flight reaction. For this reason, focusing on our whiteness can feel like an attack on our sense of self.

White folks in general have several common responses to this perceived threat to self. Each of these can involve an effort to reframe our understanding to avoid alignment with racism. Each of these can also allow us to deflect our need to give meaning to our whiteness. Each of these can also create difficulty in our relationships with students, parents, colleagues, and community partners. Collectively, these responses involve turning away and leaving our racial identity very blurry, which renders us incapable of truly witnessing the dis-ease we face.

RESPONDING TO OUR DIS-EASE: LOOKING AWAY

Our avoidance of our whiteness can manifest in several different forms. We can deny the continuing effects of race and its categorizations, move toward ethnicity, become colorblind, and believe that we transcend race altogether. Important to acknowledge is that we can take up one or all of these approaches with the best of intentions. For many of us, the flight from the discomforting meanings of whiteness is not made consciously. We are not aware that we are distancing ourselves from the problem of our whiteness instead of working toward a solution.

The following approaches sound good, feel good, and follow a thread of logic that we believe will move us closer to equity and justice. It is precisely the feel-good nature of them, however, that disguises causes for concern. The nettle of race we are in is not so easily disentangled. These approaches disguise the ways that race continues to affect us all. Only if we allow ourselves to see the shadow side of each of these avenues might we begin to see a different path that will not simply cover over our symptoms but lead us toward the type of long-lasting, substantial healing that can transform our teaching practice, collaborative relationships, and educational institutions.

Equal Protection under the Law

One way we allow our view to remain blurry and evade the need to look at whiteness is to point out that our country has outlawed racial discrimination. For whites who live in relatively segregated spaces or who have little intimate, social contact with people of color (especially those from different class backgrounds), it is not that hard to assume that racism has been eliminated from most people's lives. Discrimination is against the law, right?

I was fortunate to grow up in a home completely absent of racial slurs. In fact, I do not recall my parents ever bringing up the subject of race. My friends and I never talked about race. My friends' parents never used race language. When my Black teammates began calling my parents "Mom" and "Dad," to include them in the larger family of sprinters during my freshman year in college, I think my parents smiled more broadly than when I performed well in a race.

My teachers did not seem particularly discriminatory either, except if you count Mr. C., my high school government teacher who used to bellow at our newly arrived Vietnamese English learners when they could not comprehend his questions and directions. I remember his classroom vividly because it was perhaps the only time that I truly acted out in a class setting, challenging him on his cruelty. Truthfully, however, I did not interpret his behavior as being racist; I just thought he was mean. He had been mean to me too, calling me "tough luck, Tochluk." Besides, he was only one person, and he was the exception to the rule. At least that is how I perceived his behavior.

All in all, I experienced very little that I would have termed discriminatory, and I didn't know anyone who espoused racist beliefs. I grew up learning about equality and the Civil Rights Movement. Everybody in my world advocated equal treatment for all. Because of this, I walked in the world thinking that racism was not much of a problem.

The trouble is that when we focus on legal race neutrality and are not open to the possibility that both personal and institutional racism still exist, we cannot even hope to be able to identify existing racism. We thus give up our chance of making any additional positive change. In *Colored White: Transcending the Racial Past*, David Roediger explains that one of the greatest barriers to the continued fight against racism is the neoliberal *and* neoconservative view that issues of race are in the past.[15] Those who bring up the issue of race are now often considered the trouble since so-called race-neutral policies are now widely in effect. Many argue that if we would just stop talking about race that people would be able to move past our racial history.

One problem with concentrating on race-neutral language is that we often do not perceive how race is a factor in the way we look at social and economic issues and policies. For example, Roediger explains that when a governmental program benefits a predominantly white, middle-class population, such as home mortgage tax deductions or subsidies for high-way construction that benefit white suburbs, those policies are seen as race neutral. On the other hand, when a program significantly benefits people of color, such as public assistance, those programs are often seen as race specific even if they are universal in policy. Those programs are then seen in racial, often pejorative, terms.[16]

Roediger goes on to describe how although some might explicitly avoid speaking of race, there are those who make wordless racial appeals and offer coded messages by linking nonracially identified ideas with visually racial representations. This effectively denigrates people of color and links them with issues such as welfare reform, job-training programs, criminality, and sexual promiscuity.[17] For example, a January 1995 *U.S. News & World Report* cover included pictures of seven women to illustrate its article on welfare. Six of the seven women were women of color, most were Black, and only one was white.[18]

It is through this type of linkage of image with issue that the stereotypical image of a welfare recipient has become a Black woman in many minds, even though approximately one-third, or more, of all welfare recipients were white throughout the past two decades.[19] A more in-depth discussion of this issue can be found in Michael Brown's *Race, Money, and the American Welfare State*.[20]

White educators swim within this swell of media images and social and political outlooks just like the rest of our country's population. Yet when we ingest those images and perceptions uncritically, we can unwittingly act out of them when engaged with our own students, their parents, and our colleagues. Our relational patterns can easily betray the prejudices that our social conditioning engenders, and to imagine that they have no effect because we have outlawed discrimination is to seriously underestimate the power of unconscious psychic processes.

Essentially, our seemingly race-neutral policies continue to betray clear signs of racism, and we often unconsciously accept skewed and selective information from our media outlets. We would do well to realize that there are many factors that play into which stories are told in the media and how images and words are associated. But when we are unconscious to the differential attention paid to different groups and racist portrayals, then we are unable to do anything to stop the problem. That is just one way that we become party to its continuation. If we cannot even see racism in action, then we cannot be witnesses who call for change. If we cannot see how prejudice affects our deep psyche, we can do nothing to stop privilege and racism from emerging in our relationships with students, parents, and colleagues.

Let us take an example from the media to check our ability to witness racism in action. Do we take notice that African American women who go missing receive scant media coverage while a veritable media blitz takes place when white women are in danger?[21] Sure, rich or famous women of color might have the social and political power to receive attention—but what of those without money or power? Most of the white women receiving coverage are neither rich nor powerful, yet they receive plenty of attention.

Once we notice this pattern, we have to ask ourselves, are we outraged? If not, why? Does this issue appear insignificant? If it does, imagine that it is your daughter, sister, or wife missing and you cannot get the media interested in running the story. This disparity of coverage is no small matter. The degree to which the media pick up a story can have life-and-death consequences. Local media attention can generate important leads in a time-sensitive situation. National media attention might also influence the degree to which local authorities call for additional aid.[22]

We might consider how differential media coverage affects education today. To what degree have our perceptions of our students' abilities and motivation for learning been shaped by the media? Does media reporting skew our view regarding the accomplishments of students of color? Only if we are aware of these racist practices can we raise our voices and call attention to the matter, letting news sources know that we see this as a problem.

Another example of how racism emerges in subtle and often unnoticed ways is the now-famous differential language used to describe victims of Hurricane Katrina. One aspect of differential coverage became widely known after Yahoo's image pages put news photos and captions near enough to each other for a comparison to be impossible to miss.

In case you did miss it, though, the Associated Press published a photo of a young Black boy wading through floodwaters with food. The caption read, "A young man walks through chest-deep flood water after looting a grocery store in New Orleans on Tuesday, Aug. 30, 2005." Within a similar time period, Agence France Press published a photo of a white couple similarly wading through floodwaters with food. The caption read, "Two residents wade through chest-deep water after finding bread and soda from a local grocery store after Hurricane Katrina came through the area in New Orleans, Louisiana."

We have to question ourselves here. Do we more easily identify with other white people and therefore offer a more understanding view when white folks are in a dire situation? Are we more inclined to consider a Black person as acting criminally even in similarly dire circumstances? Is it possible that we fail to question when people of color are characterized negatively because we are emotionally removed from their lives? How often does this happen unfairly without our recognition? And how often does this differential sensitively affect our relationships with students, parents, faculty, and community partners of color?

Although many forces combine to create these discriminatory practices, it is likely that the great many white people involved in their creation do not play their role consciously. I would venture to say that the majority do not perceive themselves as acting on prejudices. Those of us who passively receive the media images and messages many times are not even aware that these differential treatments are taking place. But this does not excuse us from seeing the problem and recognizing that we play a role in its continuation. It is exactly because of our lack of consciousness that we need to train ourselves to become witnesses to discrimination. Our sensitivity must increase, because only when we can see racism and name it can we put voice to our internal sense of justice and begin to call people to account when they choose to highlight subjects differentially, consciously or not.

Let us keep in mind that these issues go largely unnoticed by white people because of our dominant racial position. We do not see our lives impacted by racism, and therefore we are usually less sensitive. By and large, however, people of color see these injustices, recognize their linkage to a long history of maltreatment, abuse, and neglect, and are justifiably angered. A few years ago, I sat with Dr. Shirley Better and invited her to participate in my investigation of cross-race friendships. We talked at length about what I wanted to do and my approach.

One of the things Dr. Better said that day that particularly struck me went something like this: "Do not be fooled. The majority of middle-class Black folks are angry too. We might have learned how to be successful in the white world and we might be very pleasant in our interactions with you. But we are angry about how racism continues, and you don't even see it." Hearing her say that made me stop and think. How many times have people of color tried to let me know what they experience? How do I respond in those moments? Might this have something to do with whether or not they feel close to me, able to really tell me what is on their hearts?

I have to admit that I still struggle with my almost knee-jerk reaction to hearing a person of color claim that he or she has suffered discrimination. For example, one of my teacher-friends of color might say, "You know, I went to the district office and that white woman ignored me because I am. . . ." My mind almost immediately begins racing and I begin to ask questions. One of the first questions is, "How do you know it was because of race?" A close second is, "How do you know it was not because of . . . ?" I start to imagine all of the possibilities of what might have happened in that white person's head that have nothing to do with race. I am quite sure that I am not the only white person who does this, judging from what I have heard from people of color on this issue.

There are a couple of reasons why white people do this that deserve attention. First, many white people are raised with the idea of being the "devil's advocate." We often respect the role of "the questioner" who pokes holes in someone's argument. I know that I do this same thing to my white friends and colleagues about all sorts of issues. Questioning is something I do. I question. I know some folks of color who have also been raised to do the same thing. But there is also another factor.

When a person of color suggests that a white person has acted in a discriminatory fashion, I start imagining myself in that white person's place. Very subtly, when I ask questions about the situation, I am looking for how I might have acted if I had been that white person, how I might have been misperceived had I been there. Admitting that the white person in question might have been racist somehow seems to implicate me.

Without realizing it, I put myself in the psychological position of defending myself as I defend the white person in the situation. Not so subtly to the person of color, I engage in a battle to make sure that any discriminatory act experienced be provable in order to protect my sense of self and the world. Regardless of intent, these two combined characteristics—the devil's advocate position and the psychological defense of myself—create an infuriating experience for the people of color trying to share their story.

We can better recognize the problem with this if we take an example from our own experience. Whenever I start speaking about our need to work against racism, I invariably find a white person just itching to tell me the story of the one time when he or she was subject to a prejudicial act. I remember one moment especially clearly. A gentleman who had heard of my work approached me to make sure I was aware that racism is a problem that affects every group and that we should not just concentrate on white against people of color racism. He went on to narrate the one time, *the one time*, a person acted discriminately against him. An African American coach would not let him play the position he wanted on the football field and he recalled that this was because he was white. This experience had to have happened at least twenty years prior to our conversation.

This is not to diminish the pain of this individual who felt so slighted by his coach. Believing that you lost an opportunity because of your racial placement is understandably distressing. Many of us might be able to reflect on some moments where our whiteness was used against us in some way. But we would do well to think about how often this has happened and the degree to which the impacts did or did not alter our life paths.

True, just one instance of racial discrimination can be felt so strongly that feelings of hurt and anger still emerge quickly within conversations twenty years later, even when there were only minor effects on our life's achievements. But imagine enduring consistent racist acts over a lifetime and throughout one's family history. Living in a world fraught with discrimination can shape a person and define perspectives about the world. Racism is painful in a way that time does not always heal.

That many educators have worked hard to bring an end to racist policies and practices must be acknowledged. Unfortunately, we cannot take it for granted that seemingly race-neutral legislation translates into social equity in either our wider society or at our individual school sites. In our large context, media, whether intentional or not, can offer us views of people who discriminate and the media's focus and approach can have life-or-death consequences. In our local contexts, we are not immune from the various ways that our ingestion of racist information embeds itself in our unconscious and emerges in our educational relationships.

If we cannot accept that racism continues to exist and that we have a role to play in ending it, then we will continue to deny the experiences of people of color, dangerously pouring salt in already painful wounds. Certainly, if we continue a pattern of self-defensiveness around the issues of our whiteness, always nervous about being associated with anything perceived as racist, we will remain resistant to a fuller investigation, one that undertaken might just allow us to more consciously witness and name racism when it erupts.

Race Is Not Real

Another way that whites try to solve the problem of race while unwittingly falling victim to its effects is by reminding themselves and others that race is a social construction. We can then take the position that we simply are not white. I admit the logic here appears flawless and goes something like this: Race is an idea constructed by humans. Race is not biologically real. The whole concept of race is false. Anyone can see that my skin is not actually white. Rather, I can more accurately describe my skin tone as olive, tan, or some shade of pink. Therefore, I am not white.

I remember using this logic myself on numerous occasions. I have had graduate school professors use this approach, one who proudly held out his arm one afternoon to show me that, yes, in fact, his skin truly is olive colored. A dear friend of mine proudly tells the tale of her preschool-aged son grappling with language one day and coming up with the word "toink" to describe her skin tone, interpreted as a combination of tan and pink. My friend uses this story to highlight that she understands the false nature of race language. She is not alone.

Many of us reject racial whiteness as a personal identifier when we are ready to say that we disagree with the divisions that race perpetuates, the false categorizations that do not offer exact, accurate self-reflection. We do this believing that we are striking back against prejudice and racism. Through this argument, we hope to demonstrate that we will not be fooled into continuing a fundamentally flawed system of naming.

Deciding that we are not white allows us to scratch racial identity off of our already crowded to-do list. We can move on with our lives, imagining that issues of race are taken care of as far as it relates to us. Sure, there are plenty of people who identify with race and prejudiced viewpoints—but we are no longer part of the "race problem" because we are not part of the race. Those of us taking on this approach generally are philosophically opposed to prejudice, so we do not see ourselves doing anything that would cause distress in anyone from another group.

Unfortunately, there is also a subtle implication in this approach that often goes unnoticed by white people, but it is hardly lost on a good number of people of color. The implication is this: If we reject being called white, we also reject the idea that we are connected to a broader, white culture. Let me say it again in a few different ways.

If we are not white, then whiteness becomes meaningless for us. If we are not white, then there is absolutely no reason why we should concern ourselves with what people of color have been saying for generations about the features of white culture. If we are not white, then we have nothing to gain by investigating how our country's history of racism shapes us. If we are not white, then conversations about our unwitting participation in perceived racism in our classrooms, on our school campuses, or in communities of color are irrelevant. All of these statements become possible when we take our whiteness off the table.

Our claim that we are not white is true, but only as long as we are talking specifically about skin color in its most literal form. The problem is that whiteness is related to a lot more than fair skin and we cannot deconstruct its effects by simply walking away from race. True enough, the idea of deconstruction might strike fear in anyone even remotely familiar with academic, postmodernist thought. For many, this approach leads one down a never-ending rabbit hole where nothing is real, no value judgment can be made, and existential trauma ensues. I am familiar with this hole. Just like Alice, I have been captivated at the wonders. I have also found the critique. Navel gazing ourselves to death is possible, and we could spend time analyzing our whiteness but never linking our new understandings with real movement or action in the development of our educational and relational practice or wider efforts for social justice. That is not helpful.

Distancing ourselves from our discomfort with racial identity by claiming that we are not white betrays our hopes. Although we hope that the distance excuses us from being a part of the problem of race, our denials do not stop us from being treated as white. Philosophically rejecting whiteness does not stop us from escaping racial profiling. We will never have to deal with the frustration of being passed over by cab drivers due to our race. We will never be mistaken for gardeners when working in our front yards. We are also less likely to be harassed by gang members near our inner-city school sites than our male faculty of color, who are frequently asked to identify the set to which they belong.

Worse, in our lack of investigation, we cannot recognize that benefits come with our whiteness. We remain blind to the myriad ways that our whiteness opens doors for us. We also do not stop enacting the whiteness that has embedded itself within us through years of social conditioning. Our expectations of respect, attention, and courteous service from all people we encounter are experienced as normal. Then, as we remain unconscious of the ways we receive unearned benefits, we act in ways that are thoroughly infuriating to people of color in our surroundings. Later chapters will more fully explore privileges that come with whiteness and the various ways lingering racism emerges without conscious intent.

Ethnicity Replaces Race

Another response to the challenges presented by the concept of race, and whiteness in particular, is to shift our attention toward ethnicity. There is something really important about this move toward a return to our roots. As a later chapter will discuss, our assimilation story has left many of us without a rooted sense of self. The loss of our ethnic heritage and culture plagues many within the white population in this country. For that reason, we do need to attend to our ethnicity. Knowing more about the cultures we come from, the traditions that supported our forebears, and the lineage they represent can offer us a grounding that we not only deserve but also psychologically require. Ethnicity offers us a way to identify with something other than whiteness, which can seem rather hollow, false, and negative.

One of my African American friends first encouraged me to explore this side of myself during a period when I was struggling against my whiteness. I began to ask my parents questions concerning where, exactly, my great-grandparents came from in Germany, Italy, and Russia. Being that I look very much like my mother, I have held her up as a role model for years, and because she is full German, I looked most closely for areas where I could connect to my Germanic heritage.

I went through all of my grandparents' old items, searching for remnants of cultural artifacts that might connect me to my ethnic heritage. A strange thing happened as I searched through my maternal grandparents' old trunk. I found that all of the artifacts were Chinese. My grandparents had spent a few years living in China prior to World War II and these were my grandmother's prized possessions. A hand-carved Chinese trunk that I have at the foot of my bed today was one that she brought back with her in the 1930s. There was nothing German to be found.

I was going to have to get creative with this search, and less concrete. As I questioned my mother, I learned that it is a cultural tradition in Germany to eat salad at the end of the meal, as opposed to at the start, which is the norm in the United States. There is my German tradition. My family eats salad last! Looking deeper, I can recognize a certain discipline and order in the way I live my life, a particular rigidity that I can associate with Germanic culture. As anyone who has traveled in Germany knows, the trains there leave on time. Now, there is something that fits. I suppose I can call that my cultural heritage.

On the Italian side, there is far less, unless you count that I make good lasagna. Admittedly, however, it is meatless and I made up the recipe myself. I imagine my far distant great-great-grandmother would be less than impressed. During this period of time, I also came extremely close to changing my last name, Tochluk, back to its original Russian form, Tochalenko.

My sense of self benefits when I feel connected to something ancient, like when I read old Germanic fairytales and feel somehow related to them. I will continue exploring my ethnicity as I move forward, searching for fragments of a culture long lost to my family—for the truth is that my cultural connection is lost; I am not German. That culture is too disconnected. My Germanness was traded in long ago for the benefits available in this country for European immigrants able to fit in to the white group. Feeling connected with my ancestry is essential, but I cannot kid myself into believing that I share the same culture as contemporary Germans. I do not.

At the same time that this process of reconnecting with our heritage is essential, there simultaneously is a problem. The downside is not that we search for rootedness; the downside is that whites' uncritical movement toward ethnicity can act as a disguise that masks multiple issues. Omi and Winant's book, *Racial Formation in the United States*, concentrates on the politics of race.[23] In exploring the valuable contributions that an acknowledgment of ethnicity can offer, they also express concern that ethnicity language often functions as a new form of race language.

Essentially, Omi and Winant argue that there are many different ethnic groups, such as Japanese Americans, Korean Americans, and Chinese Americans, who are simply called Asian American by most people in the United States. The authors suggest that even though we would like to think that these specific ethnic categories allow people to retain their ethnic identities, the use of the broad category, Asian American, is "clearly a racially based process" because "the majority of Americans cannot tell the difference between members of the various groups."[24]

In other words, the idea that we are avoiding the vestiges of race through a turn toward ethnicity is illusory. We have simply replaced the old, objectionable race terms for new terms such as European American, African American, Asian American, Latin American, or Native American. In our effort to deal with our country's diversity, we continue to collapse people into groups that closely mirror the parameters of the old racial categorizations.

One problem with this disguise is that the language of ethnicity allows us to escape the negative associations with race without acknowledging the very real effects that our history with race continues to have on our perceptions. A focus on ethnicity allows us to more readily ignore our country's history of racism and its continuing effects. For example, seeing various groups within the country as ethnicities allows us to evaluate each group's assimilation into American society against that of the early European groups.

Oftentimes, white people will recall our own family history in efforts to understand and evaluate the experience and "progress" of other groups. We often justify the oppressions of some groups as we recount tales of discrimination suffered by our immigrant family years ago. White educators in a faculty lounge might say something like this: "All of our ancestors went through the process of coming to the United States and figuring out how to fit in. All groups struggled when they first arrived and gave up aspects of their heritage, and most had to learn a new language. So, why can't this group move past it like mine did?"

We see this emerge most readily when we discuss the achievement gap between different ethnic/racial groups in regards to standardized testing, high school graduation rates, and college admissions statistics. We also tend to start pitting one group against the other, such as the well-known problem of holding up Asian Americans as "the model minority," without attending to groups' differential histories.

A deep problem with this is that however long European Americans search within our family histories, we will never find an appropriate comparison with those who remain hyphenated Americans in our social consciousness. European immigrants become Americans when they blend in. People who have long been considered members of races other than white based on physical features do not blend in. They remain racially typed, and the fact that this alters their assimilation experience is pushed to the side with a narrow concentration on ethnicity. White people find some groups blameworthy for not fitting in and assimilating appropriately while their differential position goes ignored. Essentially, we blame those who have been most victimized by racism.

Admittedly, this is challenging in no small part due to our efforts to answer to the wishes of the various groups who prefer terms of ethnicity to the language of race. For many of us, the shift to ethnicity language is made in concert with requests from people of color. It might therefore feel inappropriate to criticize a focus on ethnicity. Because race is a fabrication, there are plenty of people who simply cannot locate themselves within race's ill-defined categorizations. Ethnicity simply makes more sense.

Since each racial or ethnic group living within the United States has a substantially different historical experience, we all have different needs. For example, many of my Latino/a students struggle to place themselves racially, and statistics from recent U.S. census reports suggests that an important factor associated with whether or not Latinos/as consider themselves to be white is socioeconomic status.[25] This question of what it means to be white is a complicated one with which each group that has been able to claim the privileges of whiteness has to grapple. A later chapter will discuss more thoroughly how legal rulings helped shape these meanings and contradictions.

White folks who cannot fully recapture a lost cultural heritage, like myself, often experience a real sense of loss. Sure, there might be subcultures of whites who feel attached to what they see as a particularly American culture, like those who would claim a "Southern" culture. However, many of us find ourselves looking at other groups and longing for the connection we imagine they feel with their roots, their homeland, their culture. Many white folks can be heard saying, "We don't have culture. They have culture."

Even if African Americans do not choose to reconnect with their African ancestral culture, many white folks generally imagine that Black culture in the United States is rich with meaning. Many of us then travel and bring other group's cultural artifacts home with us. In my familial home, for example, we have puppets from Indonesia, figurines and baskets from Africa, a rug and bedspread from Guatemala, and carvings from Mexico. For a long time, I saw my inclinations toward tourism as evidence of my openness and respect for other cultures, having no idea how much it also betrayed my inner sense of loss.

In the mid-1990s, I attended a performance put on by the UCLA Drama Department. In one main hall, individual artists each had a roped-off section of space. Each enacted a cultural way of being. There was someone representing Santeria, another enacting a Middle-Eastern culture I cannot remember. And then I saw her, the white woman. I stood transfixed in front of the white female artist. She sat on a chair on a square stage four feet above the crowd in a glass case. She wore a delicate white dress and was holding a bag from Pier 1 Imports. She admired the exotic artifacts from lands abroad one after the other.

I stood transfixed for several minutes, trying to sort out the emotion rising in me. There was something very discomforting about seeing her that way. I recognized that woman. She was me. Or at least, she had been me. She was my mother. She was my grandmother, perhaps to some lesser degree. I felt that, that blandness, that plainness, that whiteness. I felt her whiteness as a lack, a loss. I felt this loss in my bones. I could barely move as I was reminded of how I loved what other cultures have precisely because I know the emptiness that results when tradition is traded in for whiteness.

I know that I am not alone. I hear the same sentiments too much from other white people. If anything, this is one of the truest hallmarks of whiteness that I have yet encountered. There is a hole within many of us, created when our families gave up our culture in order to be successful in the United States. Of course, there are plenty of people from other groups and cultures who also travel, collect artifacts, and shop at Pier 1 Imports. However, the collection of objects is not the important point. What struck me most was the deep, underlying pain that I hear emerge from many white people as they discuss what it means for them to feel connected to another culture.

At this time, with what I now see, there is nothing about that setting that feels coincidental: the glass separating the woman from the audience, the stage that put her on a pedestal, the center, privileged position within the room, and the way her presence commanded attention. Even given that secure foundation, she exuded a sense of loss, of being lost, adrift in the larger world . . . captured by the glass case.

The various meanings of this type of whiteness are very real for me. I see how when I am able to witness these features of my whiteness and acknowledge them that I gain the power to alter my relationship to them, to alter my relationship with myself. In this way, I am better able to navigate the world. I am better able to relate to my students of color. I can admit to what they already know about whiteness. We can share in a conversation of complexity that seeks not to make it all okay, but grounds us in the understanding that we exist together without those particular barriers to our communication.

But most whites are not able to have those conversations with students and colleagues if we hide within our focus on ethnicity. Instead, there are coping strategies many whites use, either consciously or unconsciously, in order to deal with the feeling of ethnic loss. (Please note that coping strategies are not necessarily healthy.) Although not an exhaustive list, some of the most frequent forms include:

- Identifying ourselves with our lost heritage to whatever degree possible (such as claiming that we are German, even when we have little to no relationship to Germanic culture)
- Emphasizing other identities (such as our gender, religion, joining a subculture, etc.) as a more defining aspect of our lives
- Identifying with other cultures, taking on beliefs and/or practices from other groups
- Focusing on relationships with people of color
- Embracing mainstream American culture and its value systems

Each of these coping strategies can feel like it enhances our sense of self and helps us find grounding and connection. But each has a downside when we utilize the coping strategy to escape confronting our white identity. Further, unfortunately, depending on how enacted, these strategies are often offensive to marginalized groups. Unhealthy manifestations of the above coping strategies can include:

- Denying our relationship with collective white America
- Uncritically appropriating cultural practices and behaviors from other groups with little consciousness regarding their deeper meanings
- Using people of color for the "culture" they bring into our lives
- Creating needy relationships with people of color wherein we seek validation and/or escape from the white community
- Holding up American culture as a product of diverse contributions without acknowledging the role of exploitation and the ways in which groups benefited differentially

Unfortunately, so many whites have trampled people of color as we ran away from our whiteness that many people of color are highly suspect when whites demonstrate an interest in their culture and participate in traditional ceremonies and practices or wear their cultural symbols and dress.

Educators might want to consider how this might play out in schools. I

recall wearing an African *lapa* (a type of wraparound skirt) to school for
several years while hoisting a *djembé* over my shoulder. On one hand,
some faculty of color perceived me as a cool, white teacher who was
"down" with African culture and who ensured that my Black students
were able to see something of the beauty that comes from their heritage.
Not only that, but it was recognized that the motivational level of my students increased when they knew that they could play the drum during
breaks. Their academic performance improved and so did our relationship. In this way, I was doing my best (given what I knew at the time) to
be culturally responsive.

On the other hand, for other fellow faculty members and parents of
color, my use of those cultural forms did not always sit easily. My behavior, in some ways, was looked at suspiciously. Some people were attentive
to whether or not I was trying to escape my need to relate to my home
community. For those who questioned me about this, I am grateful. Had I
not been open to hearing their concerns, surely I would have increased the
damage done by centuries of *appropriation*, the exploitation of another
group's culture for another's benefit. Not only that, I would have missed
an opportunity to clarify my understanding of my use of cultural artifacts
that do not come from my familial heritage.

If we can understand that our cultural exploration or adoption is often
warily perceived as related to appropriation and a history of oppressive
behaviors, then we can more effectively explain our intention to people of
color. If we can avoid becoming defensive, we might be able to hear the
concerns of people of color, then be offered the opportunity to explain the
respect we have for the cultural tradition or faith. Further, we can enter a
discussion about how our interest in a particular culture is related to our
own sense of cultural loss. Even more helpful is an ability to discuss how
we understand our approach in terms of our relationship with our own
whiteness and the benefits that have traditionally come with membership
in that group.

Overall, the more we understand ourselves, the reasons for our actions,
and how our cultural explorations might be perceived in relationship to
an oppressive history, the more we are able to navigate our way through
challenging conversations, to build authentic relationships with our students, colleagues, and community partners, and to break down the

wounds built up over years of injury. Perhaps even more important, we might be able to avoid enacting a disrespectful form of appropriation.

To sum up, white people benefit greatly from a healthy investigation of our ethnic heritage. Researching and reconnecting can help us deal with the loss many of us feel because of our assimilation into whiteness. We run into trouble, however, when we focus narrowly on ethnicity as a way to escape grappling with our race identity. If we remain unclear about our own whiteness, then we do not perceive the negative, unhealthy aspects of the coping strategies that we use to help us manage the cultural loss we feel. We then both ignore the effects of historical and contemporary racism and offend people of color.

We Don't See Color

Choosing colorblindness is a fourth way that we distance ourselves from our discomfort with whiteness. This is not to say that we *intentionally* use the term as a distancing technique. Most of us say that we are colorblind as an assurance to others that we are *not* prejudiced. I learned this type of language as a child when my teachers would say something like, "I don't care if you are yellow, purple, blue, or green." I know that when I used the term *colorblind*, my intentions were positive. I wanted to let people know that I treated everyone equally. I remember feeling good when saying that I did not pay any attention to race, feeling that being colorblind was an attitude that aligned me with progress and humanity's evolution. I felt that being colorblind moved us away from our history of racism and toward a future of equity.

My understanding of this term completely changed after reading Ruth Frankenberg's book *The Social Construction of Whiteness: White Women, Race Matters*.[26] Reading her analysis of white women's use of the term, I recognized myself in some areas and saw differences in others. But the subtle implications of the term that she described altered my perspective. I was so shaken that I asked people of color in my social and work circles if they, too, saw into that language what Dr. Frankenberg outlined. Indeed they did, and I have not used the term *colorblind* to describe my perspective since.

There are three basic problems with using the term *colorblind*. First, the entire idea of colorblindness is a lie. Of course we see color. Of course we perceive different skin tones and the physical features most commonly associated with racial categories. To tell ourselves differently denies reality. Colorblindness is a complete fabrication. Alone, this argument might appear unimportant, calling up a response such as, "Sure, I *see* color, but what I mean is that a person's color doesn't *mean* anything." This moves us into the second area of trouble with colorblindness.

When we say that we do not see another person's color, what we essentially are saying is that a person's racial placement is meaningless in our social environment. Being colorblind also means that we do not see the ways that a person of color experiences the world differently than does a white person. Worse, being colorblind implies that since we do not see differential experiences, people of color will likely have to convince us that race continues to matter in their lives.

In essence, when we say we are colorblind, we end up saying, "Race doesn't matter to me, and therefore it should not matter to you." That being the case, the alignment with colorblindness builds a shield to protect us from considering how lingering, unconscious prejudices might play out. Essentially, claiming that we are colorblind can stop us from being open to dialogues with our students, colleagues, and community partners who experience and/or perceive racial injustice.

Finally, white people tend not to speak of being colorblind when speaking of interactions with other whites. Colorblindness really only comes up when we speak of how we see, or do not see, people of color. We are essentially saying that there is something about people "of color" that should not be seen. This implies that there is something negative about being associated with color and that there is no value in being recognized as a person of color. In essence, we are saying, "I don't hold this part of who you are against you." Although there are many people of color who use this term to denote that they do not hold our whiteness against us, there are far more who reject the colorblindness approach for the above reasons.

In addition to offending people of color and denying and dismissing their experiences, choosing colorblindness also has one glaringly negative ramification for white folks. Being colorblind truly keeps us blind, blind to ourselves. Our whiteness, already a rather blurry topic, moves from being uncomfortable and out of focus to being purposefully invisible. As we refuse to see the color in someone else's life, we refuse to see the whiteness in our own.

Our philosophic refusals to see our racial identity as significant does not translate into a psychological overcoming, and issues of race continue to affect us, as later chapters will illustrate. We do have an option, however. To use Ruth Frankenberg's words, we can become race cognizant, or race conscious. We can develop a clear vision of how race impacts our lives and the lives of others, so that we can move toward honestly witnessing the ways our whiteness characterizes our practice.

We Transcend Race

A final way that we turn away from our whiteness is when we say that we transcend race. This is perhaps the most deeply felt approach because when we see ourselves as "beyond race," we align our belief system with our sense of spiritual being. It does not really matter to which faith community we belong. From this perspective, we focus on what is most inherently meaningful about our lives. We very often search for what "resonates" with us, that which rings true and feels right, that which fits with our individual experience of the world. Race, as a fabricated concept itself, understandably does not fit with our deep sense of self.

I know that my core—my spiritual self, my soul—transcends race. The deepest and most essential aspect of who I am in the world is not related to race. Personally, I can still hold this to be true and simultaneously recognize that my current manifestation, my current physical form, exists this way for a purpose. To my way of thinking, the learning that my spirit/ soul requires on this planet, in this time/space pattern, is related to me being a white woman.

For me, my spiritual self is connected to my physical form. I see my job as needing to learn as much about existence in this context as possible. For that reason, although I completely understand the personal nature of the transcendence approach and the intricate role spirituality plays in our sense of self, it is worthwhile to offer our idea of transcending race up for questioning. Just because our deepest spiritual nature is not related to race does not mean that our socialized behaviors in the world are not.

For many white people, our belief that our experience of the world transcends race also comes with additional values. For example, many of us who are dedicated to transcendence as a broader ideal also have a sense of spirituality that manifests as a deeply felt connection with all people and things. This sense of connection can translate into a desire and push toward creating community, wholeness, togetherness, or oneness. Spiritually oriented folks are oftentimes committed to expanding consciousness, continued growth, and becoming more compassionate people in the world as well.

Although paradoxical, our efforts toward racial transcendence can sometimes thwart our ability to truly live out those spiritual goals. For instance, in some ways similar to the earlier mentioned approaches, transcending race can sometimes mean remaining unaware of how racial identity affects our way of being in the world. But if part of life's effort is to be more connected to others, then being less aware of how our whiteness plays out seriously jeopardizes our chances of truly coming together with other individuals. How can people tell us about how the racial dynamics in our schools and communities affect them if we refuse to acknowledge that race remains significant in people's lives?

Additionally, in an odd sort of way, transcending race can become a tool for reinforcing individualism more than a way to find deeper connection with others. Let me offer an example to illustrate this. A good number of years ago, I fell in love with a Black man. Although this gentleman considered dating me, he ultimately decided that it was not a good match. Much went into that decision, but what I remember most was how race played a role. He argued that being with me would be painful for the Black women in his life due to the way that white women had been represented as the epitome of womanhood throughout our country's history. Added to that was the history of Black men being persecuted for even looking at, or speaking to, a white woman, which eventually turned white women into prizes to be won—trophies, if you will—in the minds of some Black men.

The man knew many women who readily dialogued among themselves about how this history lived on, and he refused to add to their hurt. He recognized that the effects of that history are not over, and he was careful to recognize how his behavior in the world would impact others. From what was reported, this same consideration is what prompted Denzel Washington to refuse to kiss Julia Roberts in the film *Pelican Brief*, if I recall the magazine story accurately.

At that time, I could not see why the injury to Black women was important, or more correctly, I did not want to care about what this man saw and what Black women would feel. I could not grasp why what someone else thought about our potential relationship made a difference. I recall saying things like, "We can't be responsible for their feelings." "Why should we be punished for something we were not a part of?" "Why can't we just be beyond race?" Even though I thought I transcended race and was ready to be in relationship with anyone, that very belief caused me to become insensitive to the effects my actions would have on others. I was only concerned about myself.

The point of this is not to say that interracial dating is wrong. People will always follow love when truly deep and powerful. Love does not, and should not, know racial boundaries. However, sensitivity is in order. Transcending race should not mean refusing to acknowledge how our actions affect others. The very least required of us is to expand our awareness and understand the issues and perspectives involved. Besides, if we are going to function well in a diverse world, the ability to sensitively explain why we make the choices we do, in full awareness of the complexity of the situation, the better able we will be to really connect with those who might otherwise feel betrayed.

The last aspect of the transcendence approach that can prove troubling is how the effort to raise one's consciousness can sometimes become twisted into a view of oneself as more evolved than another. In reference to the above situation with my failed attempt at building an interracial relationship, I can imagine having said something like this: "We should not have to worry about those who are still stuck in race thinking. We are more conscious than that." The belief that those who see race and racism and feel its injury are less evolved, less conscious, and therefore less worthy of consideration completely contradicts efforts toward community, oneness, and compassion.

Still worse, within white people this approach can unwittingly reinforce the historically racist views of evolution that held that whites are the most evolved manifestation of humanity. This can affect how we interact with our world. If the majority of whites choose transcendence, and the majority of people of color call out for its visibility in efforts to hold whites accountable for continuing racism, who is more evolved? Whose perspective receives attention? Essentially, in white folks, the idea of transcending race can unintentionally perpetuate a sense of superiority that can prove exceptionally damaging when people of color and whites come together in dialogue and community building.

This is not to say that moments of transcendence are impossible. My participation over the past decade in multicultural and multiracial groups, conferences, and events put on by community educators leaves me grateful for the many incredible people who offer their hearts to nurture others, regardless of differing backgrounds. Certainly, I have witnessed countless moments of true acceptance and understanding, ceremonies and dialogues where race fell away and only the human spirit remained.

That being said, those moments become possible when people have a deep resolve to ensure that their way of being in the world takes care not to injure another. In my circles, that has meant that community educators producing the events and conferences explicitly treat issues of race, placing their effects in the center of the room and asking participants both to acknowledge the trauma and the perpetuation of racial wounding and to hold themselves accountable for their actions, be they conscious or unconscious.

Similar to the other ways that we evade the discomfort of our whiteness, transcending race fails us in our efforts to demonstrate rejection of racism and prejudice. As with the previous four approaches, transcending race also asks us to remain ignorant as to how our whiteness plays a role in how we think and behave. Holding ourselves as beyond race can cause us to ignore the pain of others and see ourselves as more evolved than those who talk about the continuing effects of race on our lives. Lastly, the idea of being beyond race can have negative effects within efforts toward community building within classrooms and schools unless we build the capacity to bring race into the dialogue and work it through on the way to deeper connection.

FROM BYSTANDER TO WITNESS

The methods most white folks use to avoid facing our dis-ease about being white do not work terribly well. Yes, our various approaches can satisfy us on the surface, make us feel as though we are on the side of right, and offer us some good-sounding arguments for why we no longer need to focus on race. Unfortunately, the shadows masked emerge the moment race enters the classroom, faculty lounge, school site, or meeting space and we find ourselves disconnected from those who speak of continuing problems. We quickly become defensive and resistant, unable to withstand the critique that we continue to be related to the problems. But we can do things differently. Instead of turning away from our whiteness, we can turn the other direction. We can face the dis-ease. We can clarify our vision.

Trauma theory can help us understand the needed shift. Within any traumatic situation there are several positions we might inhabit. We know each of the positions fairly well, as we play each role at different times throughout our lives. We can be the perpetrator, victim, bystander, or witness. When we are the perpetrator, the cause of the trauma, justice then generally involves us being held accountable in front of the community. When we are the victim who suffers the brunt of the trauma, then care and attention is required to heal from the situation.

As a bystander, we might stop to look at the situation, but we are not involved in the remedy. This is in contrast to the witness. If we witness, we see the situation clearly enough to speak out. Continuing to turn away from the way race affects us places us either in the perpetrator or bystander position. We cannot interrupt racism, either someone else's or our own, if we cannot see how racism manifests in a systematic fashion. We do not have to remain blind, numb, and dumb to how race affects our teaching practice, our relationships with our colleagues, and the wider community. Instead, we can begin to witness.

NOTES

1. H. S. Lorenz and M. Watkins, "Silenced Knowings, Forgotten Springs: Paths to Healing in the Wake of Colonialism," *Radical Psychology* 2, no. 2 (2001), http://www.radpsynet.org/journal/vol2-2/lorenz-watkins.html

2. H. S. Lorenz and M. Watkins, "Depth Psychology and Colonialism: Individuation, Seeing Through, and Liberation," *Quadrant* 33, no. 1 (2003): 14.

3. Kendall, *Understanding White Privilege*, 85.

4. Lorenz and Watkins, "Silenced Knowings."

5. M. R. Mahoney, "Segregation, Whiteness, and Transformation," in *Criti-*

cal White Studies, ed. R. Delgado and J. Stefanic (Philadelphia: Temple University Press, 1997), 654.

6. B. D. Tatum, *Why Are All the Black Kids Sitting Together in the Cafeteria?* (New York: Basic Books, 1999).

7. S. Better, *Institutional Racism: A Primer on Theory and Strategies for Social Change* (Chicago, IL: Burnham, 2002).

8. American Anthropological Association, *Statement on "Race,"* May 17, 1998, http://www.aaanet.org/stmts/racepp.htm

9. B. D. Tatum, "Racial Identity Development and Relational Theory: The Case of a Black Woman in White Communities," in *Women's Growth in Diversity: More Writings from the Stone Center*, ed. J. V. Jordan (New York: Guilford Press, 1997); J. H. M. Vanderryn, "A Qualitative Analysis of the Meaning of Being White American," PhD diss., University of Colorado, Boulder, 1997.

10. F. W. Twine, "Brown-skinned White Girls: Class, Culture, and the Construction of White Identity in Suburban Communities," in *Displacing Whiteness: Essays in Social and Cultural Criticism*, ed. R. Frankenberg (Durham, NC: Duke University Press, 1997), 239.

11. R. Frankenberg, Introduction, "Local Whitenesses, Localizing Whiteness," in *Displacing Whiteness: Essays in Social and Cultural Criticism*, ed. R. Frankenberg (Durham, NC: Duke University Press, 1997).

12. Better, *Institutional Racism*, 16.

13. P. McIntosh, "White Privilege: Unpacking the Invisible Knapsack," in *Peace and Freedom* (Philadelphia, PA: Women's International League for Peace and Freedom, 1989).

14. R. A. Olson, "White Privilege in Schools," in *Beyond Heroes and Holidays: A Practical Guide to Anti-Racist, Multicultural Education and Staff Development*, ed. E. Lee, D. Menkart, and M. Okazawa-Rey (Washington, DC: Network of Educators on the Americas, 1998), 83.

15. D. R. Roediger, *Colored White: Transcending the Racial Past* (Los Angeles: University of California Press, 2002).

16. Roediger, *Colored White*, 60.

17. Roediger, *Colored White*, 40–41.

18. C. Crass, *Beyond Welfare Queens: Developing a Race, Class and Gender Analysis of Welfare and Welfare Reform*, 2004, *Infoshop*, http://www.info shop.org/texts/welfare.html

19. Z. F. Parvez, "Women, Poverty, and Welfare Reform," *Sociologists for Women in Society*, 2002, http://www.socwomen.org/socactivism/factwelfare.pdf

20. M. Brown, *Race, Money, and the American Welfare State* (Ithaca, NY: Cornell University Press, 1991).

21. Eugene Robinson, "(White) Women We Love," *Washington Post*, June 10, 2005, A23.

22. Mark Mennott, "Spotlight Skips Cases of Missing Minorities," *USA Today*, June 12, 2005.

23. M. Omi and H. Winant, *Racial Formation in the United States* (New York: Routledge, 1994).

24. Omi and Winant, *Racial Formation in the United States*, 23.

25. S. Moore and R. Fields, "The Great 'White' Influx." *Los Angeles Times Online*, July 31, 2002, http://www.uwm.edu/%7Egjay/Whiteness/latimes article.htm

26. R. Frankenberg, *The Social Construction of Whiteness: White Women, Race Matters* (Minneapolis: University of Minnesota Press, 1997).

Chapter Two

Facing the Dis-Ease

"You are not helping him," said Mrs. Washington. "You come in here and think you're helping. Well, you're actually hurting him. Giving him so many chances with no consequence is only teaching him that he doesn't need to take responsibility for his actions. Allowing him to talk back to authority like that is going to get him killed someday," she continued. Mrs. Washington kept talking, explaining, and instructing me about my insufficient understanding of the ramifications of my approach to her community.

I had wanted so much for Dustin to give that speech. After the abusive parental relationship he had survived and the difficulties he had experienced in the foster homes, I wanted desperately for him to stand in front of the whole school as a leader and to feel successful and loved on graduation day. But he kept breaking rule after rule. I kept giving him extra chances, wanting him to feel a sense of the unconditional love with which I had grown up. I felt deeply that I could not give up on him. Because of this, I did not want to take away his opportunity to deliver his speech even in the midst of the acting-out behaviors.

Being unaware of the subtleties of how my whiteness informed my thinking and actions, what I completely missed was the way that my needs influenced how I saw my students and what I thought was best for them. At that time, I was just starting to recognize the way my race and class positions had shaped me. Looking at these issues had aroused some very deep feelings of shame and guilt in me. Seeing for the first time the way that being white had benefited me, I began to see the relationships with my students as my opportunity to make up for the societal inequity I saw around me.

I saw myself as being in service, dedicated to being there for the students no matter what. This work with my students would be my redemption, the thing that would make my life, and the privileges I had received, absolvable. This was my payback. My dedication to my students would make my whiteness okay. Seeing Dustin up on stage would have made *me* feel like a good, worthy person.

Implementing the rules and disallowing him to make that speech would have seemed a testament to *my* failure to inspire him. Giving Dustin repeated chances offered *me* additional chances to feel successful. Did I realize that at the time? No. Was I able to see that my lack of a solid racial identity was the underlying cause for my problematic approach to my students? No. Was I willing to hear Mrs. Washington tell me why my overt behavior was damaging? Thankfully, yes.

It is no wonder that white folks want to be colorblind, return to our ethnic heritage, and do away with the concept of race through transcendence. Facing the dis-ease of whiteness does not eliminate confusion. My relationships and teaching practice actually seemed to get *more* difficult when I began to face my whiteness. Those initial struggles came about because I no longer knew how to be myself. As it turned out, learning to witness my own whiteness required me to develop a new sense of myself in terms of racial identity. Without this foundation, my teaching practice suffered and so did the students.

WHAT ARE THE OPTIONS?

Beverly Daniel Tatum describes how none of the well-known models of whiteness inspire white folks to invest in a sense of racial identity.[1] There are essentially three models with which large numbers of white people are familiar. The most common model is the *White Racist*. There may still be plenty who fit this category, but few who want to claim it.

Second, we have the *Unconscious White*. This model refers to those of us who are oblivious to the effects of race and say, "Being white doesn't mean anything." This model, by virtue of essentially naming ourselves as ignorant, is hardly attractive, even though this is the category where most of us rightly fit. In our efforts to escape our discomfort, we often do, in fact, remain rather unconscious and ignorant about what it means to be white. We might see social inequity and strive to do good work in the world in response, but we do so without allowing that our racial identity should hold meaning. The unconscious white does not face the dis-ease.

Alternatively, there is the *Guilty White*. This model describes those of us who recognize our connection to the shameful aspects of our United States' history. My years at the elementary school in Inglewood, California, and the relationships formed there prompted me out of an *unconscious* position into one where *guilt* predominated. The idea of the guilty white also closely aligns with the commonly used put-down attacking the "bleeding-heart, liberal do-gooder." This characterization fits with Mrs. Washington's critique of my approach to my students at that time. Perhaps for this reason, even liberals shun this model wherein guilt and shame are the basic motivators for educational justice work.

What do we do when our options appear so limited? For those of us who see the effects of past injustices at work in the twenty-first century, we might want to be part of correcting the situation. Keeping an eye on our disastrous history understandably inspires guilt and shame in many of us. The question becomes, what do we do with that feeling? Do we turn around and flee? Many do.

However, many of us also turn to community service efforts so that we can feel good about our work in the world, knowing that we are trying to do at least something to make up for the history from which we benefit. Certainly, this had a lot to do with my dedication to my students and teaching practice. We want to face the effects that white privilege has had on people in our country, but our relationship to this work remains strained. Our lack of resolution, our incomplete recovery from the guilt, can follow us and create problems even in our efforts to face our dis-ease.

ADVERSE CONSEQUENCES OF AN INCOMPLETE RECOVERY

When we see that racism continues, we often dedicate ourselves to work toward improved race relations and increased social justice through our educational practices. We recognize that current social ills are rooted in an unjust past and present, and we offer ourselves—and the influence we can have in our school sites and communities—as part of corrective actions. Yet we often experience difficulty in the multiracial world of teaching, public service, and advocacy. Two common challenges are our lack of confidence and our overconfidence.

On one hand, when we enter multiracial schools and meeting spaces, we often take with us our own discomfort with our racial selves. Especially for those of us who have only recently begun to recognize the ways that the more subtle forms of racism emerge, our earlier lack of sensitivity can turn into an awkward oversensitivity. Where once we never noticed race (or at least claimed not to), increased awareness makes issues of race appear ever-present. Race consciousness is at its height and we can often feel paralyzed while trying to figure out how to behave in order to subvert the racism in the room while not appearing racist by concentrating on race in the room! What will the person of color think? What if I say the wrong thing? Our deep sense of guilt over our history and our current ineptness damages our ability to relate.

As I moved through this phase of awareness, my new sensitivity created anxiety that worked against me when trying to develop relationships with people of color. My lack of confidence in myself as "a person who sees race" kept me from feeling comfortable and confident in my behaviors and opinions. I needed a supportive network to help me work through these questions, but there were no whites in my surroundings who understood what I was going through. There were no whites in my circles who could help me work through these anxieties without asking me to return to the previously discussed strategies to deny the impacts of race.

There were no whites who could help me see where my thoughts and behaviors *were*, in fact, problematic. There were no whites who could simultaneously challenge me to keep digging deeper into my behaviors to find trouble spots *and* help me develop skills to better communicate cross-racially. There were no whites who could both hold me accountable for the ways lingering prejudices emerged in my teaching practice *and* hold me up as a valuable person in the world who legitimately struggles. In part due to the absence of white models, I turned to people of color on campus for help.

White folks turning to people of color is a well-known pattern. People of color become the supportive networks we turn to in order to feel better about ourselves and/or be prompted toward further growth. Sometimes this can be really beneficial, with the white folks learning much and improving their efforts to educate for social justice in ways that the people of color also value. On the other hand, helping white people see what has previously been invisible to us usually also involves them working through our resistance and denials. This takes a great amount of dedication and effort and can leave our colleagues of color feeling overburdened and exhausted.

Questions from people of color such as, "Why do I have to be the one to teach you about yourself?" or "Why should I have to fix the problems your people set in motion?" are common. Although people of color will likely continue to regularly offer insight, acceptance, and nurturing, white people need to develop the skills to take on some of this work. White folks need to develop the capacity to help each other grow, encourage each other to take next steps, and find a way to become *appropriately* sensitive to race issues.

My belief is that the majority of white folks in this country are well-intentioned people who are disturbed by the inequity in our society. Taught to question "How can I leave this world better than I found it?" many of us battle against grim forces such as poverty, homelessness, disease, illiteracy, and so forth. We donate resources, volunteer, and engage in philanthropy whether as part of, or in addition to, our teaching practices. We visit unfamiliar communities, offering our specialized service. But we consistently run into trouble when engaging in this work with people of color.

Whereas white people can experience a *lack* of confidence when first coming to awareness of race issues, we can also be *over*confident if we join social causes while seeing racism as existing only outside of ourselves. In other words, we can be *over*confident when it comes to our ability to interact with our students, colleagues, and communities of color and offer ourselves in service if we do not see how our being white affects us and how it might be associated with adverse effects. Our guilt translates into a sense of purpose, sometimes a *mission*, and gets us into the door, but our fragile sense of self as white people can keep us resistant to the growth required for effectiveness.

When white folks go into communities of color without sufficient awareness, we can fall into three interrelated traps: we take on a savior

complex, enact a superiority complex, and feel sorry for those with whom
we work. These three tendencies arise together so much of the time that
teasing them apart proves challenging. For the sake of clarity, the following sections describe each of the three in isolation, along with some
adverse effects, yet the reader may quite rightly see these elements
infused within each other.

The Savior Complex

The savior complex refers to a pattern wherein white people see our participation in a school or community organization as essential. Sarah Sentilles speaks of her relationship to this attitude in her book *Taught by
America*, in which she describes her two years teaching in Compton as
part of the Teach for America program.[2] I experienced something similar
when teaching elementary school in Inglewood. Like Sarah, I also began
teaching students without sufficient training or materials. I began my first
year teaching having never taken a teacher education course and with a
set of twenty second-grade reading books for the twenty-seven fifth-grade
students in my class. I too learned to scavenge for math books, desks, and
chairs. I recognized the systemic problems Ms. Sentilles describes.

I also recall feeling the following sentiments early in my tenure at the
school. "I can't leave because then who would they have? They need me.
I'm better than anyone else they will get to come work here." Michelle
Pfeiffer's character in the movie *Dangerous Minds* could have been my
model. I was the white woman who would single-handedly lift up the students and offer them what their community could not. Dedication and perseverance on my part would allow these extremely bright young students
to overcome the adversity they faced.

Seeing the racism in those ideas took awhile, recognizing that regardless of my efforts, the truth was that I was just one more well-intentioned
white girl who showed up in the community intending to make a difference, knowing virtually nothing about the people who lived there and
lacking the skills necessary to educate the students successfully. I was
well meaning and hard working. But I was still part of the problem.

In a moment where Ms. Sentilles describes her sense of belonging
within the Compton community, she admits that, "I belonged—and at the
same time, I didn't belong. I had been sent to Compton, not invited. I was

dropped into that community, a colonialist, a missionary believing I carried something Compton needed, when so many had come before me." She describes the learning that she gained from her time spent in Compton, how it changed the entire trajectory of her life, and how she feels a continuing sense of accountability to those who live there.

These aspects of her story resemble my own in some ways. I, too, must see myself as part of a system that allows the most inexperienced young teachers, usually white, to work in areas with the highest need.[3] We enter these positions believing that our good intentions will make up for our lack of skills and cultural knowledge. They do not. We enter believing that we are essential in the success of those we touch. We fool ourselves. We touch lives, yes. But, if we concentrate on glorifying our areas of success, we neglect the systemic change we rightly should work toward.

Additionally, when our approach incorporates the idea that another group needs us for their betterment, we overestimate the value we bring to the situation. We ignore or justify the effects of our inexperience, saying things like, "At least I am here. Without me, they would be worse off." The list could go on. Our mission can be read as missionary, and like those who descend upon another's land without sufficient cultural knowledge and respect, we can do real damage as we neglect cultural mores and unintentionally offend, thereby rendering our work less effective.

The Superiority Complex

The savior complex often goes hand in hand with a sense of superiority. When we approach our teaching in communities of color with a sense of superiority, we are all too often unconscious of how people of color read our lack of humility as enactments of privilege and racism. For example, in our work as community educators and advocates, we often move toward leadership positions before gaining sufficient knowledge of the community's members, concerns, and contexts.

Even without this vital information, we sometimes believe that we know what the community or organization's goals should be and what needs to be done to achieve those goals. We can also be unconscious of our tendency to take over the direction of conversations in staff and faculty meetings. In other words, we take up valuable time and space without dedicating enough time to listen, to learn, and to gain the skills required for success within the community.

When white folks begin to display one or more of these tendencies, some people of color might offer a challenge. Depending on the person involved, this might be our only chance to demonstrate our willingness to grow in the situation. If we are unable to explore to what degree our whiteness plays a role in our behavior, we are likely to show resistance and invalidate the concerns raised. When we do this, the people of color involved might, if we are lucky, continue to pester and prod until we respond favorably.

Far more likely, however, is that people of color pull back and turn to each other for support. An often unspoken, yet palpable, tension then usually arises. During moments of informal socializing, people of color will retreat from those who have slighted them and will coalesce, leaving white folks to themselves. This sequence of events can happen without anyone even consciously recognizing the dynamics in play—individuals seeking support from those they believe will understand them.

Generally speaking, regardless of which group is in the majority, the white folks feel left out and excluded. White people get together and try to figure out why the people of color sit together and avoid in-depth conversations or socialization with us. At this point, we usually resort to blaming the people of color for what we see as "their divisiveness," completely missing that we likely played an essential role in creating the sense of discomfort that put the separation in motion.

We wonder, "Why are we not fully accepted? What did we ever do?" If we dare to ask, we might receive another opportunity to name the oppressive behaviors we continue to enact. But we might not. Either way, something is required of us that unresolved guilt or ignorance sometimes makes difficult for us to offer. We must offer an open mind, open to the possibility that our intentions to "help" have brought with them rather pernicious forms of subtle racism. We might already feel bad enough deep down. Admitting to lingering, albeit unconscious, racism might send us over the edge, so we often avoid that conversation. We keep working together, but the divide between people produces a tension that can become the "elephant in the room." Understandably, this can impede efforts to create educational programs and community events.

Beyond the tensions among staff and faculty, however, the divisiveness is often readily apparent to students, parents, and community members. In this way, the racial dynamics bleed into the work. The people of color involved see white people trying to "help" and "save" them, seeing into our behavior an attitude of "we know best." We also may not appear willing to consider that we might enact racism in the process. There are many ramifications of this process, including the degree to which the students, parents, and community feel drawn to participate in the programs developed. Thus, a concrete consequence is poor program attendance and a resulting decrease in the school or organization's effectiveness.

The adverse consequences of a perceived sense of superiority on the part of white people increase exponentially when power differentials exist. The key difference here is the reduced likelihood that white folks will be challenged and brought to awareness of their missteps. Take the parent-teacher conference, for example. But first, let us admit up front that lousy parents exist everywhere. Some spoil. Some neglect. The list is long. But we need to talk about teachers, white teachers, who meet with parents of color.

We need to talk about white teachers, like myself, who enter communities of color armed with solid educational backgrounds, a set of values that serve us well in U.S. middle-class society, and the intent to see our students succeed. When success does not happen, our sense of ourselves as their saviors tarnishes. We anticipate the parent-teacher conference, relishing the idea of getting the parents to support our efforts and becoming a two-timing system to hold the student accountable. We realize that we need help. In fact, we cannot single-handedly propel all of our students to success. The whole "It takes a village" idea feels more real.

Unfortunately, very often this hoped-for collaboration does not happen. Even though I had some lovely relationships with my students' parents, I had very low attendance rates on conference day overall. This frustrated me to no end. In hindsight, I can understand that some of the parents' resistance to meeting with me had to do with me and the teachers they met with previously. One way I participated in the problem included offering unsolicited parenting advice.

I told parents what they ought to do if their children did not complete homework, and so on. I did this without asking the parents how they felt we could be partners. No visits home occurred. Although I began each year promising myself I would make phone calls for good behavior and send home positive notes, within two months that became a low priority. I became the bearer of bad news and with a slap in the face to go with the message I conveyed.

Admittedly, this topic raises many issues and there are many dynamics that enter that have to do with class, culture, age, educational background, language, and so forth. Each could be discussed extensively. But race also emerges. When I offer parenting advice to a parent *without asking if there is interest in my viewpoint*, I position myself as the powerful holder of knowledge in the situation. Some parents are vocal enough to remind teachers of their boundaries, but many are not.

Similar to the above community organizing description, parents of color might simply walk away. My students' parents never challenged me concerning behaviors perceived as racist. But, looking back, I certainly exhibited some subtle racism. Not every day, and not with every parent. But my success, or lack thereof, had something to do with me. My first few years of teaching were the most challenging. Had I had the where-withal to seek counsel and inspect my approach to parents, my sense of aloneness in the struggle would have lessened and I would have improved more quickly.

Since that time, I have learned that at the same time that I experienced a lack of attendance, there were teachers of color *at the same school* who did not experience the same issues I did. These teachers of color went to the homes. They interrogated and overcame their own fears and anxieties. They created parent-teacher events. The parents came. They reached out respectfully before trouble emerged. Their students achieved more than mine.

Without the appropriate openness to investigating how I carried myself in the situation, my sense of having superior knowledge kept me blind to the ways that I contributed to the further disintegration of the parent-teacher relationship. I am sure that in many cases future teachers suffered the effects. Parents who felt mistreated upon leaving my classroom certainly entered the next teachers' classroom with less enthusiasm. As a pattern, this is devastating, especially considering that 40 percent of public school students in the United States come from communities of color while 90 percent of the teachers are white.[4]

The dynamic described also can be tailored to fit any number of scenarios educators face when communicating with parents or community members. The only way to break this pattern, already entrenched in many institutions, is for us to be able to really be honest and talk about concerns over racism openly, discussing earlier experiences and offering ourselves as ready to receive feedback. As long as power differentials exist, this will remain a struggle, but we have to start somewhere. We would do well to remember that we are the factor upon which we exert the most control.

Sympathy Gone Awry

A third problematic element within our approach to students and parents of color involves our deeply felt sadness in seeing people living in challenging situations, when our sympathy turns into pity. In the absence of intimately knowing the individuals who live in the community—their strengths, joys, and valuable personal resources—we can act in ways that disempower. With intent to become models for others and demonstrate how our way of being offers a road to success, we often:

- Approach communities of color in ways that neglect some valuable, available community resources
- Disparage or ignore beloved aspects of culture present in communities of color that inspire pride and joy
- Continue the process of cultural loss in new generations by using our positions of authority to highlight our sense of what it means to be a valuable person, not recognizing that we simultaneously ask people to think less of those they love
- Remain entrenched in a well-researched cycle of low expectations that emerge subtly even when we consciously intend to serve all community members[5]
- Create enmeshed relationships where our sense of value and goodness depends upon the success we inspire in the community of color, leading us to relate in ways that undermine relationships of equality

Each of the above issues presented emerges differently depending upon the context. Honest exploration and self-questioning is the only true way to know to what degree each of us individually enacts these problematic behaviors.

In the interest of offering a concrete example, however, let me tell you about one more rather common error we white folks make when we feel sorry for the members of the multiracial school communities we enter. White liberal teachers in the inner city, even those already trained at top institutions, can be real trouble. There is one thing we do that has become a joke: We completely fail to see that strict discipline and nurturing can go hand in hand, and that each of them is essential for success.

I walked into an inner-city school with a couple of degrees in psychology already under my belt. Beyond academic learning, I was extremely concerned for the emotional well-being of my students. My liberal attitude backfired. (Recall my earlier experience with Dustin as a prime example.) The guilt I carried over my own privileged background, mixed with the sadness I felt for the students living in conditions I could not imagine surviving, combined to make me too soft, inconsistent with consequences for misbehavior, and unable to see *my* need to offer students opportunities, even when students failed to meet criteria. In short, my guilty conscious and my pity led me to teach students that they were not accountable to high expectations and personal responsibility.

The book *Because of the Kids*, by Jennifer Obidah and Karen Teel, expands on this discussion, offering many examples of how a well-meaning white teacher can be party to the disengagement of students of color due to a lack of race consciousness.[6] Clearly, my intent was to promote success. But it took really giving African American teachers like Mrs. Washington to point out to me how my approach was very "white" and would actually do the students a disservice. They educated me lovingly. But I struggled.

I struggled, in part, because I approached my work in a community of color with an unhealed sense of self. My work acted as a salve for my deeply penetrating guilt and shame. My unresolved understanding of who I was as a white person and what that meant for my behavior in the world allowed me to make numerous missteps that undermined my positive intentions. I intended to be of service, be helpful, and to some degree I certainly was. The fact that some of my former students continue to stay in contact with me is a testament to that. But there were also, perhaps even more, moments where things did not go as well.

In order to become more successful, which I believe I did over the course of my years of teaching, I had to give up a number of assumptions and look closely at myself. First, I had to stop seeing the image of the racist as some evil bad person out there, disconnected from me. Second, I needed to find supportive people to help me discover the subtle ways that racism continues to live deep within my psyche. Third, I had to admit that my work was as much about myself, and my need to heal, as it was about those with whom I worked. Although that might seem an overstatement, recognizing the way guilt and unresolved anxiety concerning my whiteness sabotaged my work actually released me to become a more *appropriately* confident person engaged in more effective work, able to make more honest and intimate cross-race relationships.

When white folks feel guilt and shame in response to the confrontation with our country's relationship with race, we can become unsure of ourselves. Unless we can create a positive sense of our racial selves, our educational efforts will likely involve neediness, prompting us to seek validation from people of color. I remember taking solace in statements from people of color that I am "a different kind of white person" or "not really white."

But in seeing ourselves as not really white, we see ourselves as outside of the problem and therefore we are often also less able to hear the critical feedback we need in order to enact a more successful teaching practice. When we develop a white racial identity that offers us a healthy sense of self, then we can move from being validated into being accountable. To do this, we need a different model of what it means to be white. Fortunately, many people have been working on these ideas for some time now.

WORKING THROUGH WHITENESS

Two approaches that push people beyond the *Racist*, *Unconscious*, and *Guilty White* are fairly well known within antiracism circles. The first is the model of the *Abolitionist*. The abolitionist begins with the understanding that race is a social construction and, therefore, racial categories have the potential to be deconstructed, dismantled, and done away with. In some ways, this approach is similar to the "race is not real" approach that we can use to avoid looking at the problem of our whiteness.

The abolitionist position differs, however, because it calls on white people to become "traitors to their race." Abolitionists believe that "the key to solving the social problems of our age is to abolish the white race, which means no more and no less than abolishing the privileges of the white skin." They hold that "the defection of enough of its members to make it unreliable as a predictor of behavior will lead to its collapse." One of its guiding principles is that "treason to whiteness is loyalty to humanity."[7] This model asks us to look at how white skin offers benefits and then refuse to participate by giving up those privileges. We are to find our sense of self in our essential humanity.

Unfortunately, becoming aware of, and resisting, skin privilege is an incomplete strategy. Practically, resisting the benefits of skin privileges does nothing to stop others from perceiving and treating us preferentially in ways we cannot control. We also can only resist something that we consciously recognize. This model can allow powerful unconscious elements to slip by undetected and remain unworked. We require a deeper and more long-lasting look at how whiteness is embedded in the deepest layers of our social and cultural unconscious. This process takes time. With the majority of white people still utilizing the approaches that turn away from our whiteness, a model that asks us to break race down without spending significant time interrogating the subtleties of our whiteness appears premature.

A second alternative is the model of the *White Ally*. Beverly Daniel Tatum describes how this model can offer white people a hopeful alternative and aid in the integration of white identity.[8] The term *white ally* is most often used to describe white people purposefully and actively working in ways that oppose either individual or institutional racism. A white ally traditionally takes responsibility for lingering racism and continues to explore ways to combat white-skin privilege. Commonly, the white ally model appears as synonymous with a white antiracist activist. White allyship also tends to involve an advanced, comprehensive analysis of the interrelated nature of systems of oppression and active efforts to support various movements for social justice.

Certainly, there have been white people working against oppression for hundreds of years in this country and, more recently, there are many white critical pedagogues who have joined in teaching for social change in schools. But Tatum indicates that information about how to become a white ally remains difficult to find. She discloses that she used her own white friend Andrea, with whom she co-wrote an article on cross-race friendship, as a model of a white ally within one of her college courses.

She argues that the white ally is a figure that needs modeling and publicity.[9]

When looking through the various models of whiteness available, the racist, the unconscious white, the guilty white, the abolitionist, and the white ally, the model of the white ally suffers from the fewest critiques. That is not to say that there are none. One criticism involves the tendency to use the noun "ally" as a label. Some argue that the term can be taken to mean that once someone achieves the status of an ally that the person has reached a sufficient level of consciousness across the board and can discontinue internal work. For this reason, I tend to speak of doing effective ally work as opposed to becoming *an* ally.

Another criticism concerns how the term "ally" generally refers to white folks taking on activism work for the sake of people of color. Many raise concerns that actions done for the sake of another are less dependable. These critics remind us that continuing actions against racism are essential, but that white folks must find a personal stake in the work. Thankfully, this is being done. One example specifically targeting educators comes from Gary Howard's work, *We Can't Teach What We Don't Know*.[10]

Howard outlines and describes three different "orientations" to white identity: the fundamentalist, integrationist, and transformationist. Of his three orientations, the transformationist approach is clearly aligned with the white ally position. It involves practitioners deeply interrogating their whiteness, analyzing dominance comprehensively, feeling responsible without guilt, challenging Eurocentric perspectives, and challenging and dismantling white dominance. Without doubt, this work should be read by practicing teachers in order to learn more about phases of racial identity development and to better understand issues of whiteness and its relationship to school reform efforts. However, for me personally, I know my practice has also benefited from additional work offering me a broader picture than simply the elements related specifically to schools.

I feel fortunate to be part of the Alliance for White Anti-Racists Everywhere, AWARE-LA, currently based in Los Angeles, that is working to advance an approach to racial identity called *Radical White Identity*. This approach to white racial identity also aligns with the ideals inherent within the white ally model. AWARE-LA uses the term *radical* to highlight our interest in going deeply to the roots of the challenges we face.

The fourfold exploration the Radical White Identity requires and the way it locates white folks as meaningful stakeholders in efforts toward social justice offer a sense of hope and inspiration. Within this approach, our antiracism efforts are not *in service of* people of color, they are part of our own effort to shed the socialization that has led to us behaving in ways that support and maintain the oppression of others. In this way, our sense of ourselves as being fully human is realized when we work toward educational, economic, social, and environmental justice.

Although space does not allow for a full and detailed description to be offered here, developing a Radical White Identity essentially asks individuals to devote concentrated time to exploring (1) our ethnic roots so that we can appropriately deal with the effects of our assimilation process, (2) our history of privilege and the systems that have oppressed people throughout our country's existence, (3) the way privilege works in concert with our other multiple social identities, and (4) our individual and collective potential to work against racism, oppression, and the enactment of skin privilege.

Doing this work with other white folks, we are building what we call *Radical White Community*. Essentially, this is the community I lacked when I began to struggle with my new understanding of race. Within this community are people who can help me see privilege and racism more clearly, motivate me to continue constructing a healthy and effective antiracism practice, and support me to keep moving forward in times when I fail. One important aspect of this group is that it welcomes people who are new to the ideas as well as those who have been working in antiracism efforts for many years. In this way, AWARE-LA hopes that a healthy white identity can begin to be formed even as we take our first steps toward ally work.

A FOUNDATION FOR
ALLY ACTIVITY: WITNESSING

From the earlier discussion regarding the potentially adverse consequences of guilt on our educational practices, we can see that there is good reason for the general discomfort among white folks regarding consciously forming a white racial identity. Whiteness does not have a positive list of associated meanings; when we turn to face race issues, we often struggle. Our unresolved angst can keep us blind to the subtle ways in which our best efforts are destructive for our students and relationships with parents and community members. If we continue working on race issues, we come across two models that offer promise, the abolitionist and the ally. At least here there is support for our need to keep an eye trained on whiteness and a promise of a better, more complete sense of self.

As I began to face what it means for me to be white and tried to find a healthy sense of myself as a person committed to antiracism within my teaching practice and my life in general, each of the previously discussed models somehow left me wondering. I like the ultimate goal of the abolitionists, but my psychological training just will not allow me to ignore how deep the problems lie. The white ally is a laudable model, one that I work toward as I build my Radical White Identity, but it is one that I still feel uncomfortable claiming sometimes.

Developing an effective white ally practice still feels like a goal on most days. I know what most folks of color expect of an ally, and I continue to struggle to become as consistent and skilled as that requires. Throughout all of this, what seems unacknowledged is what a massive leap it takes to move from being in an unconscious or guilty phase to becoming effective in ally work. There is so much to learn. Creating a clear vision takes time. Developing the skills to proficiently move into activism requires a sophisticated analysis.

White folks need a positive, supportive foundation if we are going to collectively investigate our own whiteness. We need a model dedicated to inner psychological work leading to altered behavior. We need a model that starts with the development of a racial identity that helps us increase our perception. In order to dismantle white dominance, privilege, and racism, we must be able to clearly see their manifestations.

The model of *witnessing* proposed and described in this book is just such a model. My hope is that developing the skills to witness helps people construct a foundational bridge on the path to becoming proficient at ally work. To my thinking, Sarah Sentilles began to witness while teaching in Compton. She writes,

> I struggled while I was teaching in Compton. When I stopped teaching, I struggled harder still. I didn't know what to do with what I had experienced.

I asked myself, again and again, "How must my life change in response to what I have witnessed?" My conversion, my awakening to the understanding that I am accountable and responsible for what is happening in Compton and in places like Compton across this country, devastated me. But it also liberated and empowered me. If I am accountable and responsible, then what I do matters.[11]

What we do matters. How we *witness* matters greatly. Becoming adept at witnessing our whiteness involves more than a simple decision to see race as meaningful. Witnessing asks us to create an inclusive vision of ourselves and our communities.

We need to recognize our interrelationship with those in our country from whom we have separated ourselves. We have to leave behind our view of ourselves as rugged individualists, on our own, disconnected from those living far from us or differently from us. Recognizing our interconnectedness, we can no longer ignore our obligation to play a role in ridding our society of racial injustice. We cannot remain bystanders, casually gazing at the trauma in front of us, nor can we afford to remain blind, perpetuating racism unwittingly.

Witnessing involves creating sufficient insight to imagine and support becoming active in racial justice efforts both within and outside of our classrooms and school sites. Witnessing means knowing that we remain unhealthy as long as we are unconscious perpetrators and bystanders to racial injustice. We discuss each of these necessary elements in chapter 9. Ultimately, witnessing requires us to know that our society remains unhealthy as long as we do not recognize our white privilege and do not give voice to the ways that racial injustice continues to create dis-ease and distress in all of us. We witness for ourselves, our children, and our country's future.

This idea of witnessing our whiteness comes out of my reading of Kelly Oliver's philosophical book *Witnessing: Beyond Recognition*, which describes how witnessing holds two meanings simultaneously.[12] Extrapolating from the definition as given in the *Oxford English Dictionary*, Oliver notes that witnessing involves "*eyewitness* testimony based on first-hand knowledge, on the one hand, and *bearing witness* to something beyond recognition that can't be seen, on the other."[13]

In other words, we have to see with our own eyes *and* bear witness to the experiences of others that we cannot see on our own. In this double meaning, there is a "tension between eyewitness testimony and bearing witness, between historical facts and psychoanalytic truth."[14] Basically, this requires us to recognize that although seeing what is in front of our eyes is an essential aspect of witnessing, we have to also allow that the experience of trauma does not always correlate exactly with the degree of danger present in a situation.

For example, if you take a walk along a mountain path late one evening and trip over something long and thin in the road, you might run in terror from what you have every reason to believe is a snake. Your experience that evening, the trauma you felt in that moment, will not be lessened when you discover the following day that the snake was a rope. In other words, psychological truths hold meanings of lived experience that objective, historical facts cannot always verify. When our intent is to increase healing, arguing over fact can actually invalidate psychological experience and pour salt in wounds. So our witnessing is not simply about determining the facts of a situation. Bearing witness involves being present to the experience of another person.

Facing our whiteness also means facing our past. Oliver argues that, "forgetting the past through the double oblivion of forgetting what has been forgotten almost guarantees that we will repeat rather than work through racism."[15] Seeing the links between past and present are essential for us to work through racism. In light of this, developing the ability to witness begins with knowing the legal, political, economic, philosophical and social histories of whiteness. In the next chapter, we focus on the historical construction of whiteness. When we understand how white identity developed, linking our present with our past, we can begin to notice for ourselves the ways that we might be unwitting participants in the perpetuation of racism. We take on this investigation because we are in distress, we are dis-eased by our connection to whiteness, and this lack of personal healing affects our educational practices.

NOTES

1. B. D. Tatum, "Teaching White Students about Racism: The Search for White Allies and the Restoration of Hope," *Teachers College Record* 95, no. 4 (1994).

2. S. Sentilles, *Taught by America: A Struggle of Struggle and Hope in Compton* (Boston: Beacon Press, 2005).

3. This pattern continues to emerge each semester as my students do their demographic studies on public schools within California. Although recent legislation has increased the number of credentialed teachers in classrooms, my students regularly find that suburban, affluent schools continue to report more stable, experienced teaching staffs, whereas inner-city schools serving minority populations continue to have more turnover and less experienced teachers, exceptions notwithstanding.

4. B. Bigelow, B. Harvey, S. Karp, and L. Miller, eds., *Rethinking Our Classrooms*, vol. 2, *Teaching for Equity and Justice* (Milwaukee, WI: Rethinking Schools, 2001).

5. Association for Supervision and Curriculum Development. *Closing the Achievement Gap: A Vision for Changing Beliefs and Practices*, ed. B. Williams (Alexandria, VA: ASCD, 2003), 100.

6. J. E. Obidah and K. M. Teel, *Because of the Kids: Facing Racial and Cultural Differences in Schools* (New York: Teachers College Press, 2001). This is a good text for examples of how a well-meaning white teacher can be party to the disengagement of students of color due to a lack of race consciousness

7. RaceTraitor.org, available at http://racetraitor.org/

8. Tatum, "Teaching White Students about Racism."

9. Tatum, "Teaching White Students about Racism."

10. G. Howard, *We Can't Teach What We Don't Know* (New York: Teachers College Press, 2006), 104.

11. Sentilles, *Taught by America*, 192.

12. K. Oliver, *Witnessing: Beyond Recognition* (Minneapolis: University of Minnesota Press, 2001).

13. Oliver, *Witnessing: Beyond Recognition*, 16.

14. Oliver, *Witnessing: Beyond Recognition*, 16.

15. Oliver, *Witnessing: Beyond Recognition*, 131.

Chapter Three

Uncovering a Hidden History

Mrs. Pearson, my fifth-grade teacher, stands out as the most impassioned of my early educators. She loved early U.S. history, the story of the Pilgrims' survival, Williamsburg, the Founding Fathers, and the colonists' fight for freedom and independence. In the spring of my fifth-grade year, in support of my teacher's work, my mother took me to visit Washington, D.C., Williamsburg, and Mount Vernon. That experience left me valuing the people who survived those early days with little technology and few medical advances. Both my parents and my educators oriented me toward that which inspired pride in our country, concentrating on historical figures with whom I could most easily identify, those who looked like me (even if most were men). My tenth-grade U.S. history class offered me more of the same, albeit without Mrs. Pearson's passion.

The limits of my education now stand out in several ways. First, the shameful aspects of our history played a minor, almost tangential role in my education. A few pages here and a few pages there, the bulk of the text focused on heroic tales of overcoming by European colonists, immigrants, and settlers. Second, those few pages offered a sanitized view of the tragedy infused within our country's beginnings. Slavery was presented as a blip in the colonial experience, and the details of the extensive and inhumane treatment of African Americans throughout our country's history (not just during slavery) were largely left out. The takeover of Native American lands were offered as westward expansion, not the genocide of indigenous peoples.

Third, the small amount of information offered did not grab hold of my psyche and push me to investigate further, most probably because the negatively affected groups were not part of my day-to-day experience. For that, I am responsible. As I got older, I could have known more. I chose to orient my attention elsewhere.

Thankfully, multicultural educators today are increasingly expanding curricula, locating and producing supplementary texts and media, and offering diverse points of view in order to move away from the type of Eurocentric education I received. They are responding to the needs of their diverse body of students, often offering both a critical analysis as well as ensuring that students see themselves represented within history along with their rich cultural traditions and important contributions to our country. Yet multicultural education is not without its detractors and, sadly, it remains sporadically and superficially implemented in general.

Unfortunately, many teachers continue with a sanitized or Eurocentric approach, concentrating on what they consider to be positive historical themes. These teachers often argue that incorporating too much of the shameful aspects of our past is destructive. Although we might tell ourselves that we do this in order to offer students a hopeful, optimistic, connected, confident stance in the world that will allow young people to more easily relate to one another, we would do well to admit that this orientation largely serves white folks by allowing us to retain a sense of self as coming from a positive and heroic history. This also helps us avoid the troublesome dialogue that comes whenever race enters the conversation. This will remain an underlying, and driving, issue as long as white educators remain uncomfortable discussing race.

Most relevant for the focus of this book, however, is that although the educational texts I have been exposed to included various European immigrant groups' struggles to find success, not one page of those texts discussed the history of Europeans developing a white identity and how that history informs today's society. Discussions with others have convinced me that my experience is common. But my experience has also convinced me that we need to know the history of whiteness so that we can better understand how this particular aspect of our past plays out in our contemporary lives.

Along with knowing the history of oppression of various groups within the United States, we all need to learn about the creation of the white race. Even though its direct and inescapable relationship with racism makes the development of white identity a subject we prefer to leave in the shadows, white educators' ignorance over our own group's development hinders our efforts at moving through, and potentially past, the dis-ease we have regarding race issues.

Let us not imagine that this investigation is in any way novel, however. Scholars of color have been looking into issues of whiteness, its historical roots, and psychological consequences for many decades. Some essential historic and contemporary researchers include W. E. B. Du Bois, Frederick Douglass, bell hooks, and Gloria Anzaldua, among a long list of others. Important to recognize is that the relatively newly developing field of "whiteness studies" rests on the shoulders of these early voices. Without them, few of us would have known where to begin. Thankfully, their work paved the way for this text as well as the various works that I draw upon to formulate a thread of thought that might help us move forward.

A first step involves exploring how the experiences of the earliest colonists and what occurred throughout the 1700s and 1800s have contributed to the way we live our lives in the twenty-first century. If we form a deeper understanding of the invention of the white race and how whiteness has been created, maintained, challenged, and changed over time, then we are not destined to live out the influences of the past, and we can find a more solid ground on which to stand and from which to move. Through this investigation, educators can develop a perspective that clarifies our relationship to whiteness, offers insight into our cross-race experiences with students, parents, faculty, staff, administrators, and community partners, and sheds light on some of the education-oriented issues we currently find debated in the public sphere.

Before we delve into this history, though, I need to say up front that this chapter does not pretend to offer a comprehensive view of U.S. race history. Thorough studies of the history of racism and its manifestations in our country are easily obtained elsewhere.[1] This chapter also only begins to discuss the complex nature of white racial identity formation. Equally, volumes exploring this subject already exist.[2] This chapter offers just one perspective, one orientation that holds a particular truth.

From my background in depth psychology, I understand that any historical analysis is created as much out of the present and future as from the past. Each author brings an orienting view, a paradigm, an axe to grind, or a wish to the subject. Acknowledging that every historical tale is in some way a work of fiction, in my view, makes the offering more honest.[3] With this in mind, the value of this offering will lie in its ability to resonate and make sense. Also, reminding ourselves how variable any individual's experience of whiteness can be might prove helpful here, as each of us will form our own conclusions regarding the degree to which the history of whiteness impacts our contemporary lives.

Lastly, each section within this chapter draws extensively from particular works that I have found invaluable in understanding the various aspects of this complicated history. Although generally frowned upon, in two areas I do quote these authors' secondary source materials in order to both admit when I am following the logic thread of the works cited and make use of the most essential voices referenced. That said, my efforts here are to present an overview of the disparate works to which I have been exposed that, when put together, offer a point of view I consider helpful.

There are several aspects of our hidden history that this chapter explores. First, when, how, and why was the white race invented? Second, when and why did European Americans take on a white racial identity? Third, in what ways is the development of a modernist perspective associated with whiteness? Fourth, how did science play a role in this history? Fifth, how did legal rulings help define the parameters of whiteness in the United States? We then use the answers to these questions to inquire into how this history lives on in our educational institutions today.

THE INVENTION OF THE WHITE RACE

The history of how the white race developed receives scant attention, and when the history is discussed, there is disagreement. True, as the first English explorers encountered West Africans, they began to use the word "black" in their descriptions of African people. Although an exaggeration of the actual appearance of the African people, the language used highlights the powerful impact that the difference in skin color made upon the English.[4]

Yet the use of the word "black" to describe Africans did not inspire the English to see themselves as part of a separate race called "white." Yes, they used the terms "white" and "black" to describe humans' complexions, but early theories regarding the differences in skin color involved explanations related to environmental factors, such as exposure to the sun.[5] Yes, the English most certainly compared themselves to Africans using color symbol terminology in such a way that the English saw themselves as godly, pure, and infused with light—in short, finding themselves superior.[6] Christianity's scripture and symbols certainly played a significant role in European people's justifications for denigrating, abusing, and enslaving African people.

But this was *not* the beginning of the word "white" as used to delineate a race of people. Early uses of the term "race" generally referred to differences between populations that are now considered ethnic, such as language and cultural characteristics. Examples include the "French race" or the "Russian race."[7] The idea of a white race would take quite some time to develop.

Some might consider this line of thought splitting hairs. We have one group of people oppressing another group for whatever reason, an age-old us-versus-them, power-and-control situation. What difference does it make whether or not that oppression included a race-based analysis? For those from traditionally oppressed populations, the only important difference worth discussing might be the level of extreme inhumanity characterizing the European slave trade as opposed to other forms of ancient slavery.

But for those of us who are part of the dominant group, those of us who have been convinced that white racial identity emerged as soon as Europeans encountered Africans, the idea that the white race was actually constructed later in colonial history makes a big difference. Finding out to what degree our own ancestors were duped into an exploitative system marked by white supremacy for the benefit of the powerful and wealthy can actually open the door for us to begin to see the impacts of this system more clearly and work toward its dismantling.

Theodore Allen's text, *The Invention of the White Race*, cites, agrees with, and refutes many classic history texts on race.[8] He weaves a particularly provocative and compelling thread, arguing that the invention of the white race involved an effort to manipulate European Americans into remaining divided from other groups.[9] The story goes something like this: First, the existence of slavery in the early British colonies was not necessarily an oppression based on race. When the African population was first enslaved in the colonies, the colonists had not yet begun to think of themselves as part of a white race.

To understand how slavery could exist without the race construct already in place, we have to recall the short-lived 1547 slave law in England that made slaves of unemployed Englishmen who would not work for simple board.[10] If the English were not above enslaving their own, it is not necessary to attribute the origins of slavery in the colonies to a racial factor. Interestingly, when the 1547 Act was repealed in England within only a few years of its enactment, it was largely due to the unseemliness of Christians owning other Christians.[11] In 1600s Virginia, the Africans were not Christians. No doubt, Africans were considered other and "less than"—but this did not mean that Europeans thought of themselves as a separate, white race. They thought of themselves as God's chosen people.

Second, in the colonies' earliest years, African Americans held a legal position somewhat similar to that of the European American indentured servants. Examples exist of African American families who possessed bond-laborers themselves in the early 1600s, at times owning, buying, and selling European American bond-laborers.[12] In Northampton County, Virginia, in 1666, almost 11 percent of rural Africans Americans owned land. In that same year, 17 percent of the European Americans owned land.[13]

While some African Americans were experiencing lifetime servitude, European American chattel bond-laborers were also subject to severe oppressions that included extensions of servitude, extreme punishments, and rules barring family development.[14] This is not to argue that the experiences of European Americans equaled those of African Americans. African Americans were regularly treated more harshly than their European American counterparts. Accounts from the early 1600s suggest that lighter sentences were given to European American servants than African American servants who tried to escape their bondage.[15] Also, whereas European American servants were legally guaranteed freedom upon finishing their terms, African Americans purchased to be slaves had no such guarantee.[16]

The point, though, is that European American bond-laborers were treated increasingly harshly by the mid-1600s. They were kept in servitude for longer periods of time than they had been previously, and this situation resulted in significant social tensions. Class antagonisms between proletariat and bourgeois classes heightened. This resulted in the disintegration of the buffers that normally allowed English societies their stability and social control.[17]

The increasing exploitation of the European American bond-laborers was part of an effort by landowners to retain as much of their unpaid workforce for as long as possible. In Maryland, this effort even involved a law in effect from 1664 to 1692 that held that any free woman "who married an African American lifetime bond-laborer was bound to serve" the man's master for the duration of the man's life. This law inspired owners to foster marriages between European American women and African American men so that their progeny would add extra unpaid labor.[18] Consistent with this effort was the push toward hereditary, lifetime bond-servitude for African Americans.[19]

Whereas some previous judgments affecting African Americans in the colonies remained consistent with English common law, the 1660s witnessed some important changes.[20] One such alteration enacted by the Virginia General Assembly in 1662 discarded the English common law practice *partus sequitar patrem*, descent through the father,[21] for a new practice holding that "the condition of the child follows the condition of the mother."[22] This change helped open the door for lifetime, hereditary bondage for African Americans in the colonies, wherein any child born to a bondswoman automatically would be considered enslaved for life.

Another change negated the English common-law custom outlawing holding Christians as slaves.[23] In 1667, the General Assembly decreed that baptism into Christianity would no longer alter the conditions of a person's bondage, eliminating a way that African Americans might otherwise gain freedom.[24] Further developments during that time period included a 1670 change wherein "the Virginia Assembly made it illegal for African American planters to buy 'Christian' bond-laborers, limiting them to the purchaser of persons 'of their owne nation.'" Additionally, "the purchase price for Africans was half again as much as that for Europeans."[25] The significance of this history lies in the fact that there was a shift in approach during the latter half of the 1600s toward people of African descent. Whereas laws once treated both Europeans and Africans somewhat similarly, new judgments increased the differential treatment markedly.

Laws allowing increased oppressions for bond-laborers led to increasing levels of discontent.[26] Adding to the tense situation was a large increase in numbers of African slaves stolen and purchased directly from Africa at that same time. The large numbers of discontented and enslaved workers raised questions of management within the colonies.[27] The time was ripe for a rebellion. Who would control the increasingly exploited European American bondsmen and African Americans experiencing life-time hereditary servitude? Who would help manage and enforce this increasingly inequitable and strained social system?

A rebellion would come within a decade. By 1676, laboring-class workers, both free and bond, of both European and African descent, fought side by side during portions of Bacon's rebellion. These workers came together based on a common desire to see an end to the type of capitalism existing in the colonies that concentrated wealth in the hands of the plantation elite.[28] Those fighting the rebellion sought an end to unpaid labor and an increased "opportunity to become independent farmers." In essence, they fought for upward social mobility.[29]

The wealthy, landowning elite recognized the threat this posed, realizing that if the system of capitalist agriculture, which was dependent upon lifetime hereditary slavery, was to last, the ruling elite would need to induce "a new birthright" for all European Americans, both free and bond, an identity that could set them apart from people of African descent and enlist them as supporters of lifetime hereditary slavery.[30] This new identity was "white." Soon after Bacon's rebellion, enacted laws began utilizing this new terminology.

The creation of this new white identity involved the Virginia General Assembly, which deliberately fostered contempt between free whites and African Americans and Native Americans through a series of white-skin privilege laws.[31] One 1691 law forbade owners from setting African slaves free. Another 1691 law banished whites caught intermarrying with non-whites, a marked alteration considering that previous decades saw the encouragement of these unions to increase unpaid, bond labor.

The 1705 Virginia Codes offered additional privileges to white servants. These included a ban against beating or whipping a Christian white servant and a definition of dues owed to white limited-term bond-laborers of corn, clothes, and a gun. As well, the new codes denied rights to free African Americans. This included the confiscation of livestock raised by African American bond-laborers who had previously been allowed to raise livestock on their own account.[32]

The Act of 1723 further imposed a system of racial oppression with new laws against free African Americans. These included, among others, disallowing any free African American the right to hold public office, banning free African Americans from testifying against a white person, instituting a policy of public lashing for any African American acting violently against any European American, "excluding free African Americans from the armed militia, and forbidding free African Americans from possessing any gun, powder, or shot, or any other weapon whatsoever, offensive or defensive."[33]

Additionally, to ensure that even if these divisive techniques did not prove sufficient for whites to stay apart, the act included a provision such that whites "found in company with any [illegally congregated] slaves" would be either fined or receive lashes.[34] This effectively created a system of *racial* oppression throughout the colony whereby rights were now based on race, rather than bond or free status.

After an exhaustive look at the circumstances leading up to Bacon's rebellion and the repressive and divisive legislation enacted following, Theodore Allen agrees with the conclusions of Edmund S. Morgan regarding the white-skin privilege laws, that

> The answer to the problem [of preventing a replay of Bacon's rebellion] . . . was racism, to separate dangerous free whites from dangerous slave blacks by a screen of racial contempt. In this way, he emphasizes, the [Virginia] Assembly deliberately did what it could to foster contempt of whites for blacks and Indians.[35]

Further, Allen agrees with Philip Bruce, who states that

> Toward the end of the seventeenth century there occurred a marked tendency to promote a pride of race among the members of every class of white people; to be white gave the distinction of color even to the agricultural [European-American bond-] servants, whose condition, in some respects, was not much removed from that of actual slavery; to be white and also to be free, combined the distinction of liberty.[36]

Finally, Wertenbaker is also quoted as coming to a similar conclusion that "Every white man, no matter how degraded, could now find pride in his race. . . . Moreover, the immediate control of the negroes fell almost entirely into the hands of white men of humble means."[37] From this we find that being part of the "white race" involved a status of being free, Christian, nonslave, and of pure blood, one who might also be a voter, holder of public office, judge, juror, or witness in a trial.

Although European American bond-servants continued to experience little opportunity for social advancement, being given the distinction of being white, and therefore, free, allowed a pride among the newly constructed white race to develop such that by the early 1700s, "the bourgeoisie had drawn the color line between freedom and slavery, and established white supremacy as article one of the Anglo-American constitution. Only European-Americans, as 'whites,' were thereafter to be entitled to the full rights of the free citizen."[38] Being white allowed even the poorest of whites to feel a sense of self-pride and hold power over anyone considered not white, enacting violence without fear of reprisal. Even with this, since a primary feature of capitalism is the "tendency toward concentration of capital ownership," many poor would-be planters moved to the frontier, a lateral mobility, claiming their readiness to "take lands from the Indians in the name of 'a white man's country.'"[39]

In sum, this perspective holds that racial whiteness was intentionally developed by the wealthy and political elite as a way to separate low-wage, or no-wage, laborers from each other in an effort to protect the interests of the still-growing capitalist system through the introduction of both (1) white-skin privilege laws and (2) more severe laws further limiting rights and freedoms for African Americans and Native Americans. In other words, in the late 1600s and early 1700s, laboring-class European Americans were offered a privileged status to keep them from uniting with African Americans and Native Americans in a fight against economic exploitation.

The result of this, over time, was the inculcation of white identity to such a degree that by the mid-1700s, European American workers were claiming white-skin privileges for themselves.[40] Laws offering job preference to whites, such as a 1750 law in South Carolina stipulating that handicrafts tradesmen could not teach African Americans their trade, further solidified the economic value of white skin.[41]

The economic gains that came with white racial membership help explain why other European immigrants, such as Irish workers, who were not yet seen as white, struggled to be accepted as white during the 1800s by siding with anti-abolitionist and white supremacist political move-ments.[42] Lastly, even with the abolition of slavery, demands to limit or deny nonwhites from competing for employment, essentially appealing to "white race solidarity" remained a strong feature in U.S. politics.[43]

Ultimately, this argument suggests that white racial identity did not emerge simply in response to Europeans trying to investigate their world and understand its diversity. Whiteness as a racial construct was deliber-ately invented for political and economic purposes. Yet there is certainly more to the story than the colonists being manipulated by the powerful and wealthy. Additional issues must be considered.

A NEW IDENTITY: BECOMING AMERICAN, BECOMING WHITE

The development of a white identity involved more than offering Euro-pean Americans economic and social privileges. The development of a new racial identity also included creating defining characteristics and norms. To some degree, the development of this identity interpenetrates and infuses the economic pressures previously discussed. Yet additional assimilation pressures also contributed to the development of a white, American identity.[44] (See notes for a discussion regarding the use of the term "American.")

Philip Cushman's work *Constructing the Self, Constructing America* offers a psychological analysis that dovetails with the political discussion offered in the previous section.[45] Essentially, Cushman's work offers the psychological underpinnings that allowed the economic and political tac-tic of racial division, described by Allen, to take root during the 1700s and 1800s. The first hint of this is his argument that capitalism and racism were "aspects of a fledgling immigrant nation searching for its identity— part of an attempt to configure the self in a time of rapid and disorienting socio-historical change."[46] Put simply, the early colonists, by and large, sought new lives in a land with little familiarity and rapid change. These new lives, built around capitalism and racism, required a new identity.

Of primary importance is that the early colonists' disorientation involved an economic crisis that also brought about a moral crisis. Let us recall that many of the early colonists held a religious view valuing the humility of a "self" working as part of a communal whole. But this moral way of being did not support the growing capitalist system. In order to survive within the system, the colonists had to shift from believing in the ideal of a communal self to adopting a more individualistic, ambitious self.

The colonists needed to see God as expecting his followers to become personally ambitious, fending for themselves and their families, acquiring wealth, increasing in knowledge, and seeking material possessions.[47] Due to the pressure to fit into the capitalist system for survival, the communal self lost favor rather rapidly, but the creation of a coherent vision of what it meant to be an American took some time to develop.

Over time, the increase of urbanization, industrialism, secularism, and immigration within the colonies exacerbated the colonists' identity crisis. Since the colonists and new immigrants had either moved away from something unwanted, or landed in a sociocultural atmosphere that made their prior way of being impractical, they all needed a new and cohesive identity that would allow them to better survive.

The variety of groups from Europe settling simultaneously in the American colonies created a situation in which no communal identity existed within the United States in its early years. To deal with this absence of a common identity, American society developed a "negative identity," a way of seeing the self, a way of determining the correct way of being by determining what was "other than American." This other then became the justification of the white self, solidifying what it meant to be white by illustrating what being white was not.[48]

What it meant to be white was constantly reinforced through the images of what it meant *not* to be white. There is ample documentation of the negative images created to dehumanize and make fun of different racial groups in American history from the country's origins. Native Americans and slaves became two readily available images against which the European colonists and immigrants contrasted themselves. Images used to ridicule the Chinese in California and the Hispanic populations in the Southwest were also used at various times and in various places as contrasts while European immigrants became white.[49] The American self thus became a white self as negative portrayals of disparaged and oppressed groups defined what was un-American and, therefore, not white.

The minstrel stage was but one avenue used by European colonists to negatively characterize African Americans during the 1800s as a way to strengthen white self-identity. These images served as the contrasts against which Europeans learned to see themselves. Commonly, African American men were portrayed as lazy, stupid, absurd, corny, clownish, jolly, flashy, and comic. African American women were portrayed as crude, unclean, and very sexual. Their marriages were shown as being controlled by the women, as the men were perceived as worthless. As audiences composed of European Americans watched these portrayals, they learned that being white meant the exact opposite of what it meant to be Black.[50]

We can also look at early American literature to locate the construction of the American, white self. Toni Morrison, in *Playing in the Dark: Whiteness and the Literary Imagination*, discusses how African and African American characters within white American literature helped whites to define what it meant to be white. She proposes that

> Africanism is the vehicle by which the American self knows itself as not enslaved, but free; not repulsive, but desirable; not helpless, but licensed and powerful; not history-less, but historical; not damned, but innocent; not a blind accident of evolution, but a progressive fulfillment of destiny.[51]

Further, Toni Morrison offers two themes she sees as paramount to the psychology of white America that run throughout early American literature—specifically, the mythologies of innocence and autonomy. The concept of "newness" as related to characters within American literature is significant, and can be read as a sense of innocence, "without pollution, corruption, illness, or evil."[52] Our early literature demonstrates our construction of the "new man" of the world within the writings, a construction dependent upon establishing what was different. The maintenance of white innocence within this context depended upon the maintenance of Black people as disgraced, dirty, soiled, sinister, and wicked in some respect.

We can also read the themes of autonomy and freedom as efforts to support "individualism." Those with freedom and autonomy are white within early American literature. The characterization of the new man being innocent, free, and individualistic supported the development of the newly constructed white identity, and in countless pieces can be contrasted with the un-free, un-autonomous characters that rarely displayed a white face.

A similar dynamic allowed white Americans to characterize Native Americans in negative terms in order to support an idealized way of being. Thus, Native Americans were found to be heathens, savage, ignorant, lazy, dishonest, and worst of all, communal, as they lived in a way that worked against capitalism and were seen as lacking bourgeois values.[53] To remedy this, during the 1870s Congress created a plan to "save" Native Americans by "civilizing" them, which essentially meant creating separate individuals through the breakup of tribal units and reconstructing its members.[54]

While much else could be said about the interactions between the Native American populations and white colonists and settlers, the important point for the sake of this discussion is that the Native American way of being was not only other, but it was wrong, according to white Americans. The correct way of being an American meant to take on the values of the white American self, a self that was independent and personally ambitious, and who accumulated wealth.

By disparaging other racial groups, whites could more clearly identify their own attributes. Some of the primary characteristics attributed to being white can be seen by looking at the significant white bourgeois class that had developed after more than a century of colonial experience. The small communities of Puritan, or other, settlers had given way to large cities with varied and diverse sections. The turn away from communalism was all but complete, and capitalism was the dominant economic paradigm.

The bourgeois white American self that developed by the 1800s was characterized as individualistic, hardworking, moralistic, frugal, able to postpone gratification, able to tame nature through hard work, and used others' labor for personal advancement. What was considered acceptable was rigidly defined.[55] White Americans valued emotional reserve. To have a lack of entrepreneurial ambition, initiative, inhibition, or individual competitiveness was to be ill. High levels of sexuality, communalism, fear, hopelessness, confusion, and mysticism were looked down upon.[56]

And yet, this identity needed continued strengthening, and new immigrants required indoctrination. Ultimately, in the midst of rapid socioeconomic change, the pressures faced by European colonists and immigrants prompted the creation of a rather rigid and isolated white American self. This self was contrasted with the other groups found in America for the sake of a cohesive community of white people with a similar set of values.

The common value system born from negative views of others held great value for white Americans. Ultimately, the contrast allowed the white American self to hold a positive sense of self-worth. But additionally, and extremely important for this text's discussion, the disparagement and stereotyping of other racial groups as wrong, ill, and worthless also masked the shadows that came with a rigid and restrictive way of being. Finding all devalued characteristics within the community of the other allowed our European ancestors to protect themselves from acknowledging their own wishes to push back against the productive, individualized, rigid white self. Most likely without consciousness, newly created whites projected their own unacceptable thoughts and desires onto nonwhite groups.[57]

For example, with productivity at a premium, any thoughts deemed lazy were pushed off onto another group: "We are not that way, only those 'others' are lazy." In this way, the negative images of others, produced and consumed through such vehicles as the minstrel stage, can be seen as European American's attempts to deal with the "illnesses" faced by many whites, the shadows of the newly formed culture, illnesses such as "personal rigidity, loneliness, isolation, and lack of imagination, humor and creativity."[58] In other words, white Americans soothed their own distress by relishing in negative portrayals of others, in effect focusing blaming attention elsewhere instead of acknowledging that their constricted way of being can have negative effects.

Important to consider is how the white qualities developed during the colonial period mirror the generally accepted values of contemporary white society. The description of the white American self fits me fairly well. My family prizes independence and individual freedoms to a great degree. Conversations with my cultural elders taught me that logic trumps empathy, and I admit that I am often emotionally distanced from what occurs around me. All the while, I learned to work hard, follow a strict moral code, and postpone gratification so that larger goals could be achieved.

I also value frugality and absorbed the cultural idea that what some call "exploitation" is what my ancestors saw as "paying one's dues" in order to offer me a better future. Productive is the word most often used to discuss how I walk in the world. To be competitive and ambitious has always felt required. I cannot even fathom how much the stories of heroes and heroines—individuals fighting against the odds for the sake of their dreams—have influenced me.

Yet this approach has in many ways left me somewhat isolated. I follow the prescribed plan more often than I create my own, and creativity is hardly one of my strong suits. My cultural matrix has bred a particular type of perfectionism in me that I constantly struggle against. Why do I have such a hard time taking a break, letting go of my work ethic for even a short time? Why do I have trouble acting silly or letting myself dance with abandon? Why must I always see myself as a model of propriety? As with other issues raised within this text, years of conversations with other white people have convinced me that I am not the only one who struggles with these concerns.

Let me be clear. The point here is not to devalue all of what people call American values. As someone thoroughly entrenched within them, there is much about my way of being that I prize. But there are two serious issues worth considering. First, many of our current American values are the same as those used to construct the white identity in early American history. Some of our American values are the same ones historically used to disparage others. In essence, our American values are also the same values we constructed as identifiers to mark what it means to be white. Second, taking on the traditional white American identity involved splitting off aspects of our psyche and projecting unacceptable feelings and thoughts onto others. In other words, some of our American values are the same values that led to rigid norms from which we still require healing.

Additionally, this discussion of what it means to be white in America today would be incomplete without recognizing the cultural loss that many whites feel. True, each European ethnic group has its own particular history in this regard, and some groups gave up more of their cultural identity than others in their assimilation process. However, descendants of European immigrants often no longer retain a deep sense of ethnic identity and culture apart from being American. Even though this shift from ethnic European to American might have played out differently for each family and for each generation, we can recognize that something was given up when we became white. As we gave up one cultural way of being, we took on another.

For some of us, in taking on a white self that could not value many aspects of being in the world, we became exiled from ourselves. Many of us suffer from a lack of experience. We no longer fully understand what it means to have a communal, interdependent attitude. (This is not to romanticize. There are shadows to every way of being.) But for all of its benefits and privileges, there is something that has been sacrificed in our assimilation into the group called white. Many in today's culture feel it as an ancestral loss. To some, it suggests that something more soulful has been replaced with materialism and consumerism. To others, it is the loss of community traditions that do more than preserve familial and personal rituals.

There is no doubt that this history is complex and that whiteness now holds multiple connotations. As educators, however, knowing something of where we fit into this matrix is essential. We can then see the links between our past and current trends, such as the large numbers of white youth seeking an escape from rigidity and isolation by turning to communities of color. We can also begin to deconstruct the ways that some educator's assumptions that previously contrasted groups should simply fit in to contemporary U.S. school systems without systemic change ignores the way so-called American values remain linked with whiteness for many people.

Fundamentally, this perspective can help us understand that our historical construction of a white identity continues to complicate what it means to be part of American society and remains a salient issue for many of our students, parents, and colleagues of color who may have very different relationships to the terms "American values" than white folks. To quote William Faulkner, "The past is not dead; it is not even past."[59]

A DISCONNECTED WORLDVIEW

Admittedly, the development of racial whiteness, although invented in the United States, did not occur in a vacuum. Even though I find the political, economic, and psychological perspectives previously discussed essential, we can gain additional insight when we include the way in which larger philosophical shifts impacted the development of white identity. Briefly, the idea is that the modernist worldview and its associated meanings are often considered white. Richard Tarnas offers a compelling and thorough description of the development of the modern, Western psyche in *The Passion of the Western Mind*.[60] Where our discussion of white identity crosses paths with Tarnas' work is in the movement from the classical and medieval Christian worldviews to the modern perspective that took place throughout the time period of European exploration, colonization, and exploitation, from the 1500s through the 1800s.

Several distinguishing changes occurred during the shift to the modern perspective worth noting. First, instead of the world being alive with spirits and divine forces with which humans can relate, the modern universe is a naturally regulated, impersonal phenomenon whose secrets can be learned only through scientific, rational inquiry. *Science* and *rational thought* begin to rule. Second, in the modern world the objective world is separate from the subjective mind, and both are seen as operating on different principles. The modernist view holds that the objective world can be studied and offers factual knowledge, while the subjective mind is associated with emotion and holds far less value. Enter the increased value of *objectivity*.

Third, this shift in world perspective altered humanity's view of the self. Fundamentally, by the 1800s, the direction and quality of the modern character

> reflected a gradual but finally radical shift of psychological allegiance from God to man, from dependence to independence, from otherworldliness to this world, from the transcendent to the empirical, from myth and belief to reason and fact, from universals to particulars, from a supernaturally determined static cosmos to a naturally determined evolving cosmos, and from a fallen humanity to an advancing one.[61]

With the advent of the modern view, the human subjective experience lost its value. The rational, objective, scientific mind became the hallowed vehicle for understanding the world and one's place within it.

The modern view encouraged the autonomous, separate self. The modern awareness became complex and productive as it increasingly found power and authority in independent judgment and human achievements as opposed to religious structures. The modern view also made it possible to utilize power to exploit during imperialistic voyages, industrializing efforts, and the secularization of society.

The modern perspective, encouraged by the scientific, democratic, and industrial revolutions, developed simultaneously throughout Europe and in the American colonies. Take a moment to note that many of the characteristics described earlier, as part of the American colonists definition of the white self, found their base in the modern character: the reliance on the individual, autonomous self; the move toward the capitalistic acquisition of material wealth; and the value of rationality and logic. Recall that Cushman's analysis of the moral crisis affecting the colonists required a new way of seeing what God wanted in a congregation. This crisis reflects the larger worldview shift with its focus on science, rationality, independence, and the exploitation of nature and its peoples as machines.

If we can see this admittedly complex, but interwoven, relationship between the modernist perspective, the creation of a white racial identity, and the political decisions that put a system of white supremacy in place within the American colonies, we might be able to see how for many people, the modernist perspective is practically synonymous with being white. If we keep in mind that "the entire western intellectual canon [developed during the modern era] is defined and privileged by a more or less exclusively male, white, European elite,"[62] then we can see how Western became associated with white.

For many, as Western nations and peoples gained power over others, pushing the modernist perspective across the globe and dehumanizing indigenous peoples for their supernatural belief systems, modern became synonymous with Western. In this way, for many people, since Western equals modern and modern equals white, then white equals Western. Clearly, this perspective raises immediate concerns as its breadth sweeps any person of color who holds a modern worldview into the large unfixed zone of whiteness. Yet this is precisely what some believe to be true, and therefore it is worth looking at these associations and meanings in order to better understand this viewpoint.

As the modern philosophical paradigm still holds a dominant position in much of our twenty-first-century society, the connection of modernism and whiteness as intrinsically related has serious implications for how white people experience the world and how people of color either do or do not relate to the white, modern worldview. As would be expected, this also has important implications for classrooms and curricula, which we will discuss later.

UNDER THE COVER OF SCIENCE

The earlier-discussed political, economic, social, and philosophical developments intertwined to prompt the invention and development of the white race. Capitalist desires to amass wealth combined with the moral crisis, asking new colonists to find a new way to relate to the social, religious world. Religion, political policies, and propaganda combined to help whites see themselves as superior to other groups, fostering a new, white American identity. These are our hidden histories, absent from most educational texts. These various factors are the roots—the foundations, if you will—for those who would put forth theories of racial difference beginning in the mid-1700s.

To make the point more clearly, the theories of race that became popular in the mid to late 1700s did not begin race thinking in the United States. Instead, they operated under the banner of science to build on what had already become widely accepted views among Europeans in the United States.[63] Racial difference theories are hardly hidden. Many of us continue to learn about these now-discredited theories as part of our history of science. Even though these theories cannot be considered hidden, we turn to these fictive, pseudoscientific justifications for racial oppression very briefly in order to highlight how these theories maintained a white racial identity characterized by white supremacist ideology.

Dr. Joy DeGruy Leary discusses the false nature of racial classification theories and how they helped whites reduce their own psychological anxiety regarding treating groups of people as less than human in her text *Post Traumatic Slave Syndrome*.[64] In short, she discusses how the racial classification of humans began with Carl Von Linnaeus in the mid-1700s, well after racial oppression developed within the United States, with the extension of his taxonomic system of plants and animals.[65] His text, *Systema Naturae*, offered a system based on a color criterion with humans described as white (Homo Europeaus), black (Homo Afer), red (Homo Americanus), or sallow (Homo Asiaticus). This text also offered opinions on the moral and intellectual capacities of each group. Dr. DeGruy Leary refers to Haller's *Outcasts from Evolution* to detail the differential descriptions.

> Linnaeus describes Homo Americanus as reddish, choleric, obstinate, con-
> tented, and regulated by custom; Homo Europeaus as white, fickle, san-
> guine, blue-eyed, gentle and governed by laws; Homo Asiaticus as sallow,
> grave, dignified, avaricious, and ruled by opinion; and Homo Afer as black,
> phlegmatic, cunning, lazy, lustful, careless, and governed by caprice.[66]

Linnaeus' classification system opened the door for later researchers to offer their own systems. One such researcher was Johann Friedrich Blumenbach, whose *On the Natural Variety of Mankind* grouped humans into five categories: Caucasian, Mongolian, American, Ethiopian, and Malayan. In this classification system, group membership derived from a combination of color, hair, skull, and facial characteristics. Dr. DeGruy Leary uses a quote from Haller's *Outcasts from Evolution* to illustrate the ridiculously subjective and fictive nature of this theory. Regarding Blumenbach's research on Caucasians, Haller writes, "He took the name from Mount Caucus because its southern slope cradled what he felt to be the most beautiful race of men."[67]

In 1908, after a century and a half of research on racial typology, A. H. Keane's *The World's Peoples: A Popular Account of Their Bodily and Mental Characters, Beliefs, Traditions, Political and Social Institutions* located all humans into four tight categories.[68] This framework retained the same color-coded system as Linnaeus' original work, white, black, red, and yellow, and used the terms Caucasic, Negro, American (Amerind), and Mongolic. In addition to this furthering of previous authors' work, this text continued with more detailed descriptions of the mental characteristics of each group. Overall, the descriptions offered of each group mirror the already prejudicial views held by whites, views developed as part of a European's indoctrination into white identity.

The fact that these theories today appear absurd to those of us who recognize that they simply reflect the previously existing pervasive racism can make highlighting them appear unimportant. However, race theories played a key role in many legal decisions that helped shape the racial makeup of the United States today. The courts used these theories as they determined who was or was not white, shaping our sense of what it means to be white in America.

PRIVILEGE AND CITIZENSHIP:
WHITE BY LAW

As detailed in the earlier section on the invention of the white race, laws discriminating between Blacks and whites helped set the foundation for racial oppression and the development of white racial identity in the colonies. But later legal history can help us understand exactly who fit into the white category. Ian F. Haney Lopez, in *White by Law*, documents how the courts decided who would be defined as white—and therefore who could become a naturalized citizen—in the United States.

Reviewing this history astounded me. My education left me woefully ignorant as to how the legal system helped shape our understanding of whom we consider white, who could be naturalized as an American citizen, and how those decisions were made. This brief look also adds support for those who argue that our country purposely connected being American with being white.

Recall that the Virginia Codes, enacted in 1705, outlined a privileged system for Europeans in an effort to create a separate group of people who would claim whiteness as an identity. By 1790, the conception of the "white race" was strong enough for the passage of the Naturalization Act, which made being white a prerequisite for U.S. citizenship.[69] For the next 162 years, an immigrant's ability to naturalize depended upon the applicant's race. Let me say this more clearly: From 1790 until 1952, U.S. naturalized citizenship was restricted to whites.

The only exceptions to this rule were, first, the post–Civil War 1870 alteration that allowed persons of African origin to naturalize in order to accommodate the newly freed slaves. In other words, following 1870, the right to naturalize as a U.S. citizen required the applicant to be classified as either white or Black.[70] The second exception involved Native Americans whose citizenship was enacted in "piecemeal fashion, often tribe by tribe" until 1924.[71] Third, "the basic law of citizenship, that a person born here is a citizen here, did not include all racial minorities until 1940."[72]

Throughout the 162 years that naturalization depended upon racial classification, the courts heard 54 cases and struggled to decide who would be white. Of those 54 cases, only one did not involve the applicant claiming to be part of the white race, highlighting how immigrants easily perceived the social value of whiteness. Throughout those cases,

> applicants from Hawaii, China, Japan, Burma, and the Philippines, as well as all mixed-race applicants, failed in their arguments. On the other hand, courts ruled that applicants from Mexico and Armenia were "white," and on alternate occasions deemed petitioners from Syria, India, and Arabia to be either "white" or not "white."[73]

The court records reveal that what made someone white could never be nailed down and fixed.

Overall, decisions drew from four distinct rationales: (1) common knowledge (popular speech or use in literature), (2) scientific evidence (theories of racial difference), (3) congressional intent (searching within the statutes for clues as to earlier intention), and (4) legal precedent.[74] Similar to the previous discussion on creating a new white identity, the key to knowing who was white depended on defining who was not white. Added to this was the legal statutes' wording that membership to the white race was the key to citizenship, not the applicant's European descent.[75] Decisions were made on a case-by-case basis, often utilizing racially prejudiced personal characteristics to denigrate those denied citizenship and label those considered not white as inferior.[76]

For the most part, within the early years of these prerequisite decisions, the common knowledge and scientific evidence rationales tended to support each other.[77] The pattern of immigration also reveals that during that time, citizenship questions largely revolved around those who were more easily distinguished white or Black.[78] The "one drop of blood"[79] rule, which renders anyone with known African ancestry as Black, was in effect. Since only whites were allowed to become citizens, anyone of mixed-race was denied citizenship. This led to some odd decisions, however. For example, one court case in 1854 categorized a Chinese man as Black in order to justify disallowing his testimony against a white man accused of murder.[80] Decisions such as these allowed the courts to protect the value of whiteness, further defining and protecting white identity.

Yet cases heard between 1909 and 1923 demonstrate a divergence between the science of the time and popular understanding, which led to contradictory results and rationales.[81] During this period, six decisions relying on scientific evidence allowed naturalization, while seven decisions relying on common knowledge did not. The explanation for this involves some courts' reliance on theories of race, which at that time conceptualized Caucasian as a broader category than what was commonly considered white.[82] For those courts, racial categorization did not hinge on skin color. This is in contrast to the courts that rejected the equaling of Caucasian and white and discredited the science of race.[83]

The contradictory decisions came to a halt in 1923, however, when the Supreme Court heard two cases within that same year, *Ozawa v. United States* and *United States v. Thind*.[84] Briefly, Ozawa was a Japanese immigrant who argued that his skin was white. He offered a letter outlining his dedication and service to the United States and, by any standard, he would have appeared the epitome of assimilation. But the Supreme Court rejected skin color as the sole test to determine race. In this case, the court ruled that Caucasian and white were synonyms and that the Japanese, not being Caucasian, could not be white. Ozawa's application for citizenship was denied.[85]

However, Thind, an Asian Indian, argued that he was Caucasian, and therefore was white. Here, the Supreme Court denied the link between Caucasian and white and used common knowledge to deny him citizenship.[86] This set in motion a program to strip other Asian Indians of their previously granted citizenship.[87] According to Lopez, "Comparing the rationales put forth in Ozawa and Thind suggest that the Supreme Court abandoned scientific evidence explanations of race in favor of those rooted in common knowledge when science failed to reinforce popular beliefs about racial difference."[88] The reliance on common knowledge over science would continue thereafter. Important to highlight is how science can be held up as objective evidence when supporting racist ideology but struck down when challenging popular conceptions.

With such a fundamentally racist approach, one might wonder what might have prompted this program of racial discrimination to change. Issues surrounding World War II can be seen as those that pushed the United States to change its white prerequisite policy.[89] Consider this: With Hitler's policies enacted in Germany in 1935, Germany became the only other nation besides the United States to use race to restrict naturalization. The hypocrisy of the United States embracing the very racism that it purported to be fighting overseas was visible to international allies. To avoid charges of racism, Congress enacted reforms in 1940, with complete reform by 1952.[90] Naturalization would no longer be tied to an applicant's race. This does not mean, however, that the country of origin became meaningless.

A significant point to gain from knowing this history is that the predominance of white citizens in the United States is no accident. Not only did the naturalization laws favor whites in becoming U.S. citizens, but the enactment of racial quotas for immigration were also conscious attempts to retain the racial status quo in the country.[91] For example, the National Origin Act of 1924 included a temporary quota system limiting the number of Eastern and Southern Europeans allowed into the country.[92] This law set aside 50 percent of available slots for British citizens, excluded Asian immigrants, and heavily restricted Jewish immigrants. Even refugee status did not make a difference, with the United States turning away thousands of European Jews fleeing Nazi persecution during World War II.[93] Until 1965, these types of national origin quotas remained in place.

The vestiges of this privileged legal status of whiteness are in evidence today. Many still recognize the unhyphenated term "American" as referring to whites, unless otherwise noted. Also, large numbers of immigrants choose to racially classify themselves as white, especially as they feel increasingly economically prosperous.[94] This legal history helps us understand the problematic nature of white racial identity; in some instances, the legal definitions do not directly correspond to the image accepted by society at large.

We are now at a point of summary. Multiple threads woven together form a provocative hypothesis concerning how and why the white race was created. Admittedly, the evidence is but a brief outline of one slice of our history, but its importance is that it points toward what for many is a blind spot. The totality of the perspectives presented reveal an argument favoring the view of the white race as a

1. social construction,
2. initiated for the sake of economic and political privileging of one group of people over another
3. in the service of social control and economic/political stability

4. that depended upon increased individualism and the devaluation of communalism,
5. which was made possible by the modern philosophical worldview
6. and the creation of a new American identity based on negative views of others
7. that was supported by prejudicial pseudoscience
8. and was reinforced by the U.S. court system that linked naturalized citizenship with membership in the white race until 1952.

The evidence presented here can be taken or left behind with little consequence if there is no acceptance that these factors have something to do with our current cultural matrix. Clearly, my argument is that the historical creation of the white race has *much* to do with our current lives as white Americans and raises complicated questions concerning the associated meanings of whiteness and how they enter our teaching practices, school systems, and cross-race collaborations.

There are also many questions the analysis raises. First and foremost, why do we not learn about this history? To this I can only respond that much of the information outlined here clearly is critical of the United States. From my experience, there has been a general effort among many to focus on the positive elements of our shared history as a way to promote pride and patriotism. There is also a strong push to stay focused on our similarities and successes, while putting aside our differences and past bad acts.

This fits squarely with our tendency to believe that race is in the past and to focus on this history only exacerbates negative feelings that no longer have a valid place in our national dialogue. Recent decades have brought much of this to light, however, and many high school and college students today do learn some elements of this history. However, there remains an active resistance to focusing on these elements, and a concentration on this material remains relatively rare.

I did not learn about any of this information during my high school or college years. Ultimately, the people of color I met during my elementary teaching years alerted me to certain texts that I then chose to read. A particularly important one in my own development was *A People's History of the United States* by Howard Zinn.[95] This book offers a look at history from the point of view of those who were decidedly not the winners of the battles. Ingesting a different historical view did prompt me to feel pangs of guilt; I will not lie about that. But the increased knowledge also prompted further interest. I became dedicated to delving more deeply into what felt hidden, and that is when I found the information offered within this chapter.

My doctoral studies also offered me an opportunity to look at the psychological and philosophical developments. But my own outrage led me to look at the legal history, which for me was the most shocking. As I am sure is also true for many people, this history had previously felt far removed from my life. Learning how recent this history is, as well as how clearly it seems to relate to contemporary issues, made a profound difference in the way I see myself in the world. Our present unbroken ties with our past then became easier to witness.

A LIVING HISTORY

If we believe that we have moved beyond our racial history, we remain ignorant of the ways this history of whiteness continues to affect our lives. Many of our twenty-first-century educational issues have racial implications related to the themes just discussed. If a small group of people were to sit and do a simple brainstorm, a myriad of ideas might flow forth. But for the sake of offering at least a few examples, what follows are some perhaps subtle and not-so-subtle connections between the past and the present.

One way we see this history reflected in our contemporary educational institutions is in the debate surrounding the consideration of race as a part of the college admissions process. The idea of consciously creating a diverse campus that proportionally reflects our society raises immediate ire in many. Never mind the long-standing history of "legacy" admissions that historically benefited whites with little outcry. Never mind that a disproportionate number of students of color strive to achieve within lesser-funded schools that offer less access to advanced courses. (Readers might consider looking at Jonathan Kozol's *Savage Inequalities* if any question remains that the educational playing field is far from level.[96])

When participating in debates regarding anything even remotely sounding like affirmative action, white folks regularly speak of people of color taking white people's places. Generally assumed is the idea that the person of color is less qualified and less deserving, although this is generally unproven. Within these issues, we see white folks protecting a historically created position of privilege, such that mandates for the creation of an overall level playing field are seen as personally injurious and unfair to white people. We focus on the individual instead of the collective. We see the enactment of imagined race neutrality in the present instead of witnessing how historical, systemic inequity continues to shape generations of people's lives.

Second, the history of whiteness exists just under the surface of every debate concerning American values, multiculturalism, and diversity. Very often, resistance against the language of "American values" is quickly deemed unpatriotic. But knowing the history as just presented helps us understand why the same person can value democracy and freedom and yet resist calling them "American values" at the same time.

Knowing this history helps us understand why, to many people, "American values" suggests support for individualistic, competitive consumers who privilege objectivity and science to the detriment of people who value a cooperative, communal lifestyle, a resistance to environmental degradation, and indigenous spiritual belief systems. In short, knowing this history complicates our use of the term "American values" as we recognize that many associate those very values with oppressive and degrading treatment of people considered not white, not Western, or not modern enough to fit within our capitalistic, consumer-driven society.

In light of this, we can see why this issue of what counts as essential "American" history underlies debates over history and social studies curriculums. Essential to admit is that the teaching of history is not politically neutral. All approaches fundamentally take a stand, even if that stand is to allow the status quo to rest as is. In the dialogue surrounding the teaching of the traditional, Eurocentric form of U.S. history versus adopting a multicultural approach, not infrequently the debate becomes characterized as a fight between racists on the right and guilty liberals and special interests on the left.

We read newspaper articles about politicians' wives who called for the destruction of informational booklets due to arguments over the inclusion of national standards seen as portraying the U.S. too negatively.[97] We read books that highlight the *Lies My Teacher Told Me*.[98] I am not naïve enough to believe that reading this short history is going to radically alter anyone's fundamental political orientation. I do hope, however, that this information allows us to see that our beliefs and values are shaped by our relationship to this history and that there are very good reasons for people to (1) push against a sanitized, feel-good version of our past and (2) find themselves uncomfortable relating to systems and ideals historically aligned with the development of white identity.

Looking more broadly, how many of us interact with students who have inculcated the belief that doing well in school is a *white* thing, that achieving middle-class status, delaying gratification, and being productive within the academic and business communities would involve assimilating into whiteness? Although this resistance does not characterize most students of color, there is a decently large and disaffected group of youth of color who reject traditional curricula. Of primary importance to me is what we do about this situation. If we cannot see the linkages between our past and present, we will do nothing.

But if we recognize our students' resistances as very understandable reactions to our country's racist foundations, we might approach our conversations and course material differently. Can we help our students access the information highlighting their forebears' important scholarly and scientific contributions? Do we understand the complexities of their resistance sufficiently to host an open and honest dialogue that can convince our students that success, productivity, and academic intelligence are *not* only for whites, helping them see the historically racist precursors for that way of thinking? Essential to understand is that we cannot effectively do this unless we, ourselves, know this history well and have fully developed understandings of the ways our own racial placement affects our view of the world.

Further, part of our development will have to involve considering how our approaches and procedures in our classrooms relates to this history. To name just one example, we might look at the issue of individuality versus communalism. Many elementary teachers focus on group work and collective processes in order to build social skills and expand learning opportunities. Yet how far does this extend? There was a time when the business sector cried out for workers with improved teamwork skills and high schools responded with increased cooperative grouping strategies. But we would do well to look deeper into our history to see the ramifications of our much longer-lived past wherein the success of the individual has been more highly prized than that of the collective.

It was not long ago that I witnessed a colleague speaking to a group of parents, many of them immigrants, letting them know in no uncertain terms that they were now in a competitive country and that their students would need to stop relying on each other for their success. How do you think this attitude might affect this teacher's delivery of instruction, her relationship with her diverse student body, and the parents' view of the school?

The fact that we have a competitive system is not the core of the problem upon which I hope to shine light. The essential problem is that when we are blind to how this system developed alongside a white identity, we cannot step outside of ourselves in order to evaluate when it is beneficial and when it causes problems. The unconscious nature of our acceptance of values termed "American" and our inability to witness how their adherence affects us as well as others is ultimately what requires focused attention.

A final example of how history is reflected in our contemporary educational system involves the way schools have, for a very long time, been where assimilation takes place and where the politics around immigration find grounding. Not so many years ago, schools were designed for certain groups specifically for assimilation purposes. These days, the most obvious and widespread manifestation of the politics surrounding assimilation is the English-only approach to instruction that many schools follow. This is not to say that English should not be learned, but it serves to highlight that we are in a political phase wherein many would like English to become the "official language" of the country.

This is reminiscent of our legal history that traditionally helped ensure that the United States remains a "white" country and that many white folks are loath to embrace the changing nature of our population. English learners are, sadly, increasingly considered a drain on resources, and some teachers even resist learning the types of sheltered instruction techniques necessary to make content comprehensible for their students. We fail our own students and our hopes to become a country free of racism if we cannot see the linkages between current debates over immigration reform and our history of legal exclusion based on race.

Each of the above examples clearly involves complex factors in addition to those outlined here. Yet if we wish to create more conscious teaching practices and deeper relationships with students, parents, and colleagues, our ability to recognize how the historical construction of whiteness continues to play out within our educational systems can be extremely useful. Only when we see the deeper issues underlying the overt debates will we have the capacity to see ourselves clearly, relate to others with a deeper respect, and approach our teaching practices with more insight.

UNCOVERING A HEALING HISTORY

If we stop our inquiry after uncovering the hidden history regarding the development of the white race and its cultural associations, we risk leaving ourselves with a frustrated sense of paralyzing guilt. For me, concentrating only on the history related to whites' enactments of injustice brought a tremendous sense of heaviness. I began to ask, what are we supposed to do with this information? We certainly were not born during the early formations of white racial identity. Yes, we might take seriously the various ways that we now see the associations with whiteness pervasive in our country's current debates. But each of them is also related to other issues, and figuring it all out can be quite confusing. What is the next step?

Fortunately, there is another aspect of our history that has been covered over, one that can offer us a way forward. We need to not only challenge ourselves to go more deeply into the guilt and shame-inducing history, but we must also seek out the examples of those who found ways to respond to the injustice. There is a long history of white antiracism that needs to be brought out from the shadows. Since the beginnings of our country, there have been white folks fighting against racism and the systems that privilege being white.

Whether or not we are ready to follow in activist footsteps, we can learn from the past antiracist history and investigate how that history informs current antiracist educational efforts, many of which also incorporate anti-imperialist, anti-oppressive movements. Becky Thompson's *A Promise and a Way of Life* is but one general reference.[99] This book charts the history of antiracism and offers a good look at the lives of those who reject associating with oppressive actions in the world. We can also look into the development of critical pedagogy and culturally responsive teaching practices and the effects they have had in diverse classrooms.

Witnessing this history is one of the first steps on the way toward doing *ally* work. The various avenues offered by antiracist educators can offer us models of what it can look like to become responsive to oppressive actions associated with whiteness and begin to act in accordance with new principles, principles that go beyond being "American," loving freedom and democracy, toward those that allow us to link those ideals with witnessing actions that truly build justice for all within our classrooms and institutions.

Enacting a search for models can be a liberating undertaking. We do not have to remain mired in the dis-ease that comes from either turning away from our whiteness, or facing it and then becoming guilt-ridden. Finding models that can offer us a better way to deal with racism existing today, racism that has its origins in our history, can offer us a sense of direction.

NOTES

1. A quick online search for racism in regards to any aspect of history is likely to be fruitful. A first step, however, would include reading Howard Zinn, *A People's History of the United States: 1492–Present* (New York: Harper, 1980).

2. A couple of good resources related to white racial identity, one contemporary and practical, the other historical, include Janet E. Helms, A Race Is a Nice Thing to Have: A Guide to Being a White Person or Understanding the White Persons in Your Life (Topeka, KS: Content Communications, 1992) and Noel Ignatiev, *How the Irish Became White* (New York: Routledge, 1995).

3. J. Hillman, *Healing Fiction* (Woodstock, CT: Spring, 1983).

4. W. D. Jordan, in J. Hillman, "Notes on White Supremacy: Essaying an Archetypal Account of Historical Events," *Spring* 46 (1986): 29–58.

5. W. D. Jordan, *White over Black* (Baltimore, MD: Penguin, 1969), 11.

6. Hillman, "Notes on White Supremacy."

7. G. Jay, "Who Invented White People? A Talk on the Occasion of Martin Luther King Jr. Day, 1998, http://www.uwm.edu/%7Egjay/Whiteness/White nesstalk.html

8. T. W. Allen, *The Invention of the White Race*, vol. 2 (New York: Verso,

1997). No doubt many can cite different authors in an attempt to discredit the line of thinking offered here. But before dismissing the ideas presented by Allen, I suggest looking at Allen's text in order to get a sense of its comprehensive detail and thorough analysis. Or you might consider reading a summary of the book's argument created by the author, available at http://clogic.eserver.org/1-2/allen2 .html

9. Allen, *The Invention of the White Race*, 249.

10. Allen, *The Invention of the White Race*, 20.

11. Allen, *The Invention of the White Race*, 21.

12. Allen, *The Invention of the White Race*, 186.

13. Allen, *The Invention of the White Race*, 185.

14. Allen, *The Invention of the White Race*, 147.

15. Zinn, Howard, "History Is a Weapon: Drawing the Color Line," http://www.historyisaweapon.com/defcon1/zinncolorline.html

16. T. W. Allen, "Summary of the Argument of *The Invention of the White Race*" (Part Two), http://clogic.eserver.org/1-2/allen2.html

17. Allen, *The Invention of the White Race*, 147.

18. Allen, *The Invention of the White Race*, 134.

19. Allen, *The Invention of the White Race*, 125.

20. Allen, *The Invention of the White Race*, 195.

21. Allen, *The Invention of the White Race*, 197.

22. Allen, *The Invention of the White Race*, 195.

23. Allen, *The Invention of the White Race*, 197.

24. Allen, *The Invention of the White Race*, 197.

25. Allen, *The Invention of the White Race*, 198.

26. Allen, *The Invention of the White Race*, 198–99.

27. Allen, *The Invention of the White Race*, 198.

28. Allen, *The Invention of the White Race*, 239.

29. Allen, *The Invention of the White Race*, 239.

30. Allen, *The Invention of the White Race*, 248.

31. Allen, *The Invention of the White Race*, 249.

32. Allen, *The Invention of the White Race*, 250.

33. Allen, *The Invention of the White Race*, 250.

34. Allen, *The Invention of the White Race*, 251.

35. Allen, *The Invention of the White Race*, 249, quote from Edmund S. Morgan, *American Slavery, American Freedom: The Ordeal of Colonial Virginia* (New York: Norton, 1975), 328.

36. Allen, *The Invention of the White Race*, 249, quote from Philip Alexander Bruce, *Social Life in Virginia in the Seventeenth Century: An Inquiry into the*

*Origins of the Higher Planting Class, Together with an Account of the Habits,
Customs, and Diversions of the People* (Richmond, VA: Printed for the author by
Whittet & Shepperson, 1902), 137–38.

37. Allen, *The Invention of the White Race*, 252, quote from T. J. Wertenbaker,
Patrician and Plebeian in Virginia (New York: Russell & Russell, 1959), 212.

38. Allen, *The Invention of the White Race*, 45.

39. Allen, *The Invention of the White Race*, 257.

40. Allen, *The Invention of the White Race*, 253.

41. Allen, *The Invention of the White Race*, 252.

42. For a thorough history of the Irish workers' struggles, please see D. R.
Roediger's, *Wages of Whiteness: Race and the Making of the American Working
Class* (New York: Verso, 1991). Some important issues considered include: Why
were the Irish not seen as white? The text suggests that

> There were good reasons—environmental and historical, not biological—for com-
> paring African-Americans and the Irish. The two groups often lived side by side in
> the teeming slums of American cities of the 1830s. They both did America's hard
> work, especially in domestic service and the transportation industry. Both groups
> were poor and often vilified. Many Northern free Blacks who lived alongside Irish-
> Americans not only knew that their families had been torn from Africa by the slave
> trade but had also themselves experienced the profound loneliness, mixed with joy
> that Frederick Douglass described as the result of escaping North from slavery, leav-
> ing loved ones behind. (134)

Another questions is, How did the Irish struggle to achieve white status? To
which the text answers, in part, Irish Americans "solidly voted for proslavery
Democrats and opposed abolition as 'nigerology.' . . . They also "became leaders
of anti-Chinese forces in California" (136). Additionally,

> the making of the Irish worker into a white worker was thus a two-sided process. On
> the one hand . . . Irish immigrants won acceptance as whites among the larger Ameri-
> can population. On the other hand . . . the Irish themselves came to insist on their
> own whiteness and on white supremacy. The success of the Irish in being recognized
> as white resulted largely from the political power of Irish and other immigrant vot-
> ers. The imperative to define themselves as white came but from the particular "pub-
> lic and psychological wages" whiteness offered to a desperate rural and often
> preindustrial Irish population coming to labor in industrializing American cities.
> (137)

"Politicians began to speak of Irish as part of the Caucasian race during 1830's
and it continued" (141–44). "Irish sought to rid their places of employment of

blacks (after having taken over their jobs) to escape the connection with blacks" (150). Another essential source is Ignatiev's, *How the Irish Became White*.

43. Allen, *The Invention of the White Race*, 253.

44. I have to admit my own struggle as I discuss this topic. The use of the term "American" offends many people. I understand why people take offense. I am a citizen of the United States, living on the North American continent. Quite logically, I am North American. Using the more general term "American" to describe those living within the United States excludes all those living in Central and South American countries, as though they are not Americans. To many, speaking as though we, in the United States, own the term "American" smacks of privilege, arrogance, and a dismissal of those south or north of our borders. My choice to use the general term American to describe the development of a white racial identity particular to the United States is not made lightly. I struggle with this language and would hope that we might find another way to relate to ourselves in the future. However, at this time, this is my most likely path to connect with the majority of white U.S. citizens, who consider themselves, simply, American.

45. P. Cushman, *Constructing the Self, Constructing America: A Cultural History of Psychotherapy* (New York: Addison-Wesley, 1995).

46. Cushman, *Constructing the Self*, 36.

47. Cushman, *Constructing the Self*, 39.

48. Cushman, *Constructing the Self*, 61, 346.

49. A. L. Morales, *Medicine Stories: History, Culture and the Politics of Integrity* (Cambridge, MA: South End Press, 1998).

50. Cushman, *Constructing the Self*, 43.

51. T. Morrison, *Playing in the Dark: Whiteness and the Literary Imagination* (New York: Vintage Books, 1992), 52.

52. Morrison, *Playing in the Dark*, 34.

53. Cushman, *Constructing the Self*, 41.

54. Cushman, *Constructing the Self*, 57.

55. Cushman, *Constructing the Self*, 61.

56. Cushman, *Constructing the Self*, 59.

57. Cushman, *Constructing the Self*, 51.

58. Cushman, *Constructing the Self*, 52.

59. Anne-Marie O'Connor, "Diverse Realities of Mysteries," *Los Angeles Times*, July 5, 2006.

60. R. Tarnas, *The Passion of the Western Mind: Understanding the Ideas That Have Shaped Our World View* (New York: Ballantine Books, 1991).

61. Tarnas, *The Passion of the Western Mind*, 319.

62. Tarnas, *The Passion of the Western Mind*, 400.

63. I. F. Haney Lopez, *White by Law: The Legal Construction of Race* (New York: New York University Press, 1996), 96.

64. DeGruy Leary, *Post-traumatic Slave Syndrome*.

65. DeGruy Leary, *Post-traumatic Slave Syndrome*, 59.

66. DeGruy Leary, *Post-traumatic Slave Syndrome*, 60.

67. DeGruy Leary, *Post-traumatic Slave Syndrome*, 61.

68. Haney Lopez, *White by Law*, 97.

69. Haney Lopez, *White by Law*, 43.

70. Haney Lopez, *White by Law*, 44.

71. Haney Lopez, *White by Law*, 41.

72. Haney Lopez, *White by Law*, 41.

73. I. F. Haney Lopez, "White by Law," in *Critical Race Theory: The Cutting Edge*, ed. R. Delgado (Philadelphia, PA: Temple University Press, 1995), 542.

74. Haney Lopez, *White by Law*, 63.

75. Haney Lopez, *White by Law*, 52.

76. Haney Lopez, *White by Law*, 28, 56.

77. Haney Lopez, *White by Law*, 544.

78. Haney Lopez, *White by Law*, 50.

79. Haney Lopez, *White by Law*, 27.

80. Haney Lopez, *White by Law*, 51.

81. Haney Lopez, *White by Law*, 67.

82. Haney Lopez, *White by Law*, 71.

83. Haney Lopez, *White by Law*, 72.

84. Haney Lopez, *White by Law*, 69.

85. Haney Lopez, *White by Law*, 80–86.

86. Haney Lopez, *White by Law*, 86–91.

87. Haney Lopez, *White by Law*, 91.

88. Haney Lopez, *White by Law*, 79.

89. Haney Lopez, *White by Law*, 44.

90. Haney Lopez, *White by Law*, 46.

91. Haney Lopez, *White by Law*, 37.

92. Haney Lopez, *White by Law*, 38.

93. HistoricalDocuments.com, "The Immigration Act of 1924," http://www.historicaldocuments.com/ImmigrationActof1924.htm

94. Moore and Fields, "The Great 'White' Influx."

95. Zinn, *A People's History of the United States*.

96. J. Kozol, *Savage Inequalities: Children in America's Schools* (New York: Harper Perennial, 1992).

97. R. Alonso-Zaldivar and J. Merl, "Booklet That Upset Mrs. Cheney Is History," *Los Angeles Times*, October 8, 2004, A1.

98. J. Loewen, *Lies My Teacher Told Me: Everything Your History Textbook Got Wrong* (New York: New Press, 1996).

99. B. Thompson, *A Promise and a Way of Life: White Antiracist Activism* (Minneapolis: University of Minnesota Press, 2001).

Part II

THE JOURNEY
INTO WITNESSING

Chapter Four

Fellow Travelers:
Engaging the Journey

The five years I spent at the elementary school in Inglewood, California, forced me to develop a more in-depth and complex understanding of race, class, community, and consciousness. Wanting to make use of this learning while pursuing an advanced degree, I left the elementary school with a dedication to inform and convince my home (white) community of the brilliance and potential residing within the youth of Inglewood and similarly gang-infested and violence-ridden cities throughout the United States. My early projects focused on the struggles of inner-city youth of color and the need for adults to stay open and observant in order to see the gifts lying within these strong, vibrant young people.

What became clear to me, however, was that the ability to truly *see* the youth of color and the search for life inherent in their pursuits has a lot to do with our ability to witness how our thoughts, attitudes, and behaviors are informed by our racial experiences. Making my need to become more skilled at this witnessing more pressing, I was rehired by my former school district to teach middle school while completing my doctoral degree. After years of receiving important mentorship from people of color, I felt the need to find other white people who had looked deeply within to identify how being white affected them, white people who could be models for me.

I looked for really particular people. They needed to be competent in maintaining close cross-race relationships and had to see race as playing a significant role in our society. This holds great import. There are plenty of people, both whites and people of color, who move through the world looking for Kum-ba-ya moments, skirting the shadows, and fighting to keep the peace at all costs. I really needed to talk with people dedicated to confronting race issues.

In other words, I needed to speak with people who also understand the magic of Hecate's transformative brew, who see the need to focus on the hidden, battered side of our psyche in order to find healing for our deepest wounds. Within this general search, I especially wanted to find white people who have sat in the fire, white folks who have withstood the heat of anger, resentment, and rejection from people of color, white folks who know the importance of bearing witness to the dis-eases bred from racial injustice.

Educators and professionals from various backgrounds across the nation received calls from me. I requested to speak with them about race, friendship, and whiteness. More times than not, I first contacted people of color whom I either knew or had heard of who then suggested that they had a white friend or colleague who fit my interest. Occasionally, connections occurred in the opposite direction.

In the end, I interviewed sixteen people, eight white folks and eight people of color. Sitting with them required me to travel north, east, and south. Starting in Los Angeles, I visited Berkeley, Seattle, Chicago, Washington, D.C., and New Orleans. I had known four of the sixteen previously, one through a family connection and three as distant mentors. Of the eight pairs of colleagues, six are highlighted in this text because their stories are most valuable for educators.

However, there are times when I include particularly relevant and revealing comments and dialogue from the other individuals. To be clear, in no way are these people superhero personages, and some might not even be exemplary models. Each of them continues to struggle and recognize needed areas of growth. In this way, they are perfect models because they are relatable human individuals who are out there struggling, perhaps a bit father down the path, but not yet fully arrived.

My learning process involved interviewing the white folks and their friends/colleagues of color for equal periods of time, both individually and as a pair. The formal research project that originally came from these dialogues offers a balance of their voices. However, based on this book's stated intention to help white people witness their whiteness, the white folks' voices here receive increased space in this introductory chapter.

Chapter 4, therefore, concentrates on how a subgroup of the white folks became conscious of their racial identity and what facilitated their ability to come to that perspective. In some instances, their colleagues of color enter the dialogue, offering us insight into how we might maneuver through this challenging territory ourselves.

Chapter 5 then considers the role that conflict plays within the relationships, chapter 6 explores the various meanings these folks associate with whiteness, and chapter 7 delves into the lingering racism they continue to face and how they deal with it. Collectively, the voices offered in these four chapters comprising part II of this text illustrate many of the essential issues white educators need to face when deciding to confront dis-ease regarding race, to construct a viable, healthy white racial identity, and to develop a teaching practice that subverts white dominance.

Structurally, the three men are introduced first, followed by three women. The order of appearance reflects no privileging of male voices, but actually serves a more specific purpose. Each of the three women not only describes her early experiences regarding developing her sense of what it means to be white, but she also identifies her friends/colleagues of color as essential facilitators in the developmental process. For that reason, their stories are a set of extended voices following the shorter men's introductions.

Questions to consider at the start:

- When did you first become aware of your racial identity?
- When was the first time you learned about racism?
- Has anyone been important in your learning regarding race issues?
- What does it mean for your life to be a member of your race?

THE MEN

Michael Meade is a 60-year-old community educator who lives on Vashon Island in Washington. He is a professional storyteller, mythologist, and author of *Men and the Water of Life.*[1] Michael produces and leads multicultural conferences through his nonprofit organization, Mosaic Multicultural Foundation, some of which I have attended and referred to in chapter 1. Luis Rodriguez, a Los Angeles–based community educator who is best known as a Chicano poet and the author of *Always Running: Gang Days in L.A.*, identified Michael as one of his closest white friends and partners.[2] I have known both of these men for many years, have regularly attended of their workshops, and consider them mentors. I find their contributions essential, as their wise counsel has taught me to keep one eye on our essential connectedness and humanity while keeping the other on social justice.

Currently, Michael's teaching practice involves moving people through social strata issues such as race and class in order to connect people through mythology and poetry. But he could not do this work without a real psychological shift that prompted him out of his youthful environment. Michael talked to me about his upbringing. He said, "I grew up in a blue-collar, Irish, bigoted, and racist community [in New York]. I mean, ridiculous, so racist that Italians were considered a different racial group. And anybody who wasn't fair-skinned, freckled, eating potatoes, or something was like an enemy group." And yet, Michael remembers, "in the midst of it feeling there's something wrong with this. . . . It feels stupid and forced." Michael's statements are reminiscent of the history of the creation of whiteness offered in chapter 3 wherein certain groups, specifically the Irish and Italians, were not originally considered white during early immigration phases. The divisions sparked through this process continue to mark people's consciousness regarding who is part of the white race, and therefore who is acceptable within some groups.

Michael talked about a moment when his perspective radically altered on a day when his "crew" left their neighborhood to go to the beach.

> Once, we went to the beach with our little crew of fourteen- and fifteen-year-olds and with the older crew from the neighborhood. They seemed much older, yet they were probably seventeen, eighteen, and nineteen. They'd been through this for years and were pretty hardened. We were at Jones Beach. It was unusual to leave the neighborhood and no one would admit it at the time, but there was a certain amount of fear present already because we were way outside our boundaries. And the way people from the neighborhood act when we're outside our boundaries is get defensive and ready to fight. Fear turns into defense on one hand, but with very little provocation, violence on the other. . . . Drinking beer, hanging out on the beach, . . . playing the role. There were a couple of guys, clearly friends, sitting near us on the beach. One was Black and the other white. I saw it right away

and thought, "Oh, I hope those guys move or else somebody's going to get hurt."

The older guys from our neighborhood tended to do harm before considering what the meaning of something unfamiliar might be. So, I size up the situation and figure unless the wind blows the right way, those two guys are going to get their asses kicked in a way that they've never seen before. I have my eye on it, I'm not in favor of it, but I don't know what to do about it. Finally someone said something and I know that words will lead to action real fast. So I said something to try and deflect it, which was dangerous because it could turn on you fast, especially with the older guys. That led them to say, "OK, you go over there and tell that Black asshole and his fucking fairy friend [it gets to racial phobia and to homophobia real fast] to get off the beach. And if they don't do it, you kick their ass right there." That's how the game goes. So I can't really say no, in terms of my understanding at the time. So I go over and say "Listen, don't even think about this situation. Get your stuff, get up, and just walk away. If anybody says anything, just keep walking."

They said, "What are you talking about?"

I said, "The people I'm with are gonna kick your ass real soon."

"Why?"

"I don't have to explain why. Just take me at my word. You will get hurt. Get up and get going."

So, the Black guy understands. He looks around and says, "Let's go."

The white guy says, "Well, that's not right."

And I said, "Aw, man. What a dummy." Where does this guy come from? Probably a nice neighborhood or something. "It's not about what's right. It's about saving your ass. Get out of here now."

Maybe ten minutes later, the white guy comes back. He walks up to the group. . . . I thought, oh no, this guy doesn't know how bad he could get hurt. . . .

He stood there with his voice cracking and said, "This is not right; not fair. This is inhuman." He didn't even curse. And no one did anything because he was telling the truth. But that didn't mean he was going to survive the experience.

Now, they all looked at me, 'cause it's now my job. So I got up and went over to him and said, "That was brilliant. Now get the fuck out of here." I think that was the right combination. He needed to somehow know that he was right, but that he wasn't so stupid as to want to lose all his teeth at this moment. So, he left and it was over. But, for me, I was like, wow. . . .

I realized that what he said was the absolute truth. I knew that how we acted was distorted. . . . That was a pivotal experience for me. And one thing that came out of it was feeling real scared afterwards . . . scared of the realization of how dangerous it is to be genuine, to have knowledge and act on it.

Coming to reject the racist ideology of his upbringing, Michael had to create his own sense of self. In some ways, his approach reflects aspects of what we saw in chapter 1 regarding replacing a white identity with ethnicity. Not feeling part of what he sees as the white group, Michael identifies with his Irish heritage, an identification that holds both literal and imaginative truth.

When I identify as Irish—I mean I'm not Irish, I've been to Ireland as a visitor and my mother was born here and my grandmother was born here. But when I was really looking around for a way to explain what was happening to me, I didn't feel part of the mainstream. Once I got into serious issues in my life, I didn't feel like a part of the white culture in the sense of the forced homogenization that white people go for. And I instinctively knew that it meant losing my sense of self. And I also noticed how quickly, if you go against it, you are out. You are not even second-rate. You are gone. And I realized that I don't want to be a part of something that just casts you out like that. That's why I think I've had some sympathy for people of color because I realized how a white person can be cast out of the white group for not having the white idea, even if you look like you should have that idea. So those things made me alert to it. I said, OK, what's legitimate here? I can't say I'm not white in the sense of not being of European ancestry. I mean I look like I am.

So what is there in the range of things, and I think I'm lucky because both sides of my family are from Irish roots. So I adopted Ireland on an imaginal level. I began to check my ideas and ways of looking at the world against James Joyce and Yeats. That's who I felt aligned with. Not just because I love the beauty of what they're doing, but because I think there's some internal resonance that I've inherited. I memorized Yeats' poems when I was driving in my car. I did it to find myself, to locate myself on the highways, you know, in the confusing chaos of the highways of life. And I would find things in the rhythms of the poems. I would feel like I come from this mostly unseen place.

In identifying with Ireland on an imaginal level, Michael finds a sense of grounding, something beyond being white.

Yet Michael does not turn away from whiteness. His attention toward his cultural heritage and personal rejection of mainstream whiteness is not an escape from the difficult history of oppression in this country. Michael reflects on his own family's past and the part they played within the larger history of whiteness:

> There's a point in American history where had the Irish and Scottish been more courageous and genuine they would have aligned with the Black and enslaved and indentured folks because the Irish and the Scots were also indentured. But they saw a way to slip out and I have to own that, too. It's part of my own heritage and one of the greatest mistakes in the history of this country. There they were, a white-appearing group who were escaping colonization in their own land and could have deepened that sense in this land as well. Being "white" became a way up and out and I know my own family went for that.

Michael holds the tension of multiple realities. First, he recognizes the value of reclaiming an ethnic identity that holds beauty and the promise of connection and a sense of place, albeit imaginal. Second, Michael sees the meanings of whiteness and seeks to react against the problems that come with adopting the values traditionally associated with being white. Yet, third, he rejects contemporary whiteness without denying his connection to its history and current manifestation.

In many ways, this combination allows Michael both to be more aware that issues of race require visibility and working through, and yet at the same time, his complex perspective does not always hold these realities of race at the forefront of his thinking. This tendency surfaces when he is in conference situations with his friend Luis Rodriguez, as we will read about in a later dialogue. For me, Michael's example is important. Through Michael we can see how a person can be highly perceptive about how race and class issues surface in many instances, while at the same time need to stay open to hearing about moments when this perception fails.

The second man spoken with was Bob Roberts, a 60-year-old white community educator I interviewed in pre-Katrina New Orleans, Louisiana. I learned of Bob through the documentary film *The Road to Return*,

which featured the work of Project Return. Bob was the executive director
of Project Return, a nonprofit dedicated to reducing recidivism in parolees
when we met.[3] He is also the author of *My Soul Said to Me*, a memoir
about his community-building work in a Louisiana prison.[4]

Meeting Bob, I was struck by his openness and complete engagement.
Talking to him in some ways was like sitting next to a starving man
receiving a plate of food after a long period of fasting. He dove into the
interviews, expressing his deepest concerns, pains, and hopes. His interview was one of the most emotional. It seemed that he longed to have
more conversations like the one we shared in his small office with the air
conditioning blasting and the buzz of a busy community center just
beyond the door. Bob's voice is invaluable because he highlights the challenges white folks face when moving outside of white social norms.

Bob talked about his early experiences. "I grew up in a tremendously
conservative society, Shreveport, Louisiana. My neighbor, who was Jewish, used to say it was so conservative that we even called our rabbi
Bubba." He also spoke of growing up poor: "Even though we were poor
and my mother had to work to support us, my mother and father both, . . .
we had a maid. As a white woman [my mother] could make more than a
Black woman . . . so she could take part of her pay and pay [the maid]."

Segregation marked his upbringing. He said, "I never went to school
with a Black person, all the way through high school, college, and even
dental school, until I went back to school for social work. It was the first
time." Bob also spoke of his first recognition that segregation was wrong:

> I grew up in the era of segregation. I never knew anything was wrong with
> segregation until I got on the trolley one time and my caretaker, my second
> mother, the woman who was our maid, sat in the back of the bus. She didn't
> belong back there. She was my mother. She took care of me. She scolded
> me. She spanked me. She held me.

Bob said that although "there was a time when I bought into the racial
stuff in my high school years," that he extended respect to adult African
Americans as a youth in a way that went against the norms of the time.
This respect emerged when interacting with his elders: "I carry this thing
of respect for elders. 'Yes sir, no sir.' I was a little Southern boy. I carried
that right over racial lines. I can remember going through the cafeteria

lines in junior high school and high school and the servers were all Black women and saying, 'Yes, ma'am, yes, ma'am.'"

His first close relationships with African Americans outside of his home formed the summer after his father's death when he worked in a warehouse. He writes that "the Black laborers in the warehouse" showed him kindness. He describes them as "men who had known and deeply respected my father. . . . Those men took me under their wings and taught me how to endure hard labor, how to shoulder the hundred-pound flour sacks with my small frame, and how to put up with the incessant insults that the boss threw at all of us."[5]

Bob currently questions much about our culture and said that "there's nothing like getting outside your own culture to learn about your own culture, to go learn about another. I lived in Germany for four years and that's what really started opening my eyes." He spoke about a time during that period when he began to study WWII. He had some books and conversations that made him question issues of sanitization and culpability within warfare. He said,

I was reading [a] book one night and [the author] talked about where after the beach had been secured and they moved inland from the beach, he said a crew would come on shore and this crew would pick up all the body pieces. He talked about finding a face in the sand. And he talked about leaving whole bodies lying there in the waves and then after they'd cleaned up all the pieces they would invite the journalists onshore to take pictures of whole bodies like you saw in the movies . . . sanitizing the true violence of war.

And by then I had a collection of WWII books and some with pictures. And I even had this Time Life book with a series of pictures and it was two in the morning and I furiously got up and threw down all the books on the South Pacific and went through all the pictures—these were Time Life and were full of pictures—to see if I could see anything but a whole body. And the lie about it all! And if there was ever a turning moment, a turning against our military and what it had done, and was doing in Vietnam, and is still doing it now. Boy, that was a moment. Realizing I had been lied to. All those movies with John Wayne and all the glorification and sanitization of violence and warfare. . . . God, by the time Steven Spielberg came out with *Saving Private Ryan*. . . . There was an opening scene where the first 30 minutes are the D-Day invasion . . . that opening scene was full of body

parts and not whole bodies . . . and people complained about all of the violence. . . . But it was the first movie that depicted the truth. And I wept. I
was so angry that it took so long. I was 55 years old before anybody told
the truth.

Emotion emerged as we talked and I asked Bob what that experience
opened up for him. He answered that he found himself "looking at myself
in the mirror thinking . . . how else have we been lied to? What else is
being held back?" Bob finds this learning essential in terms of his ability
to relate to people who come from different backgrounds in the United
States. Realizing that he needed to question cultural assumptions and the
media's portrayals prompted him to delve deeper, under the surface, in
order to understand other ways of seeing, locating hidden truths by listening to different versions of history and people's experiences.

This last realization is what characterized my whole experience with
Bob. He is a man dedicated to facing shadows. Sitting with him over the
course of a weekend, I learned a lot. He taught me about owning up to
lingering forms of racism as part of a dedication to truthfulness. He also
taught me about the loneliness and isolation that can come when big
moves are made to confront our personal relationship with race issues
without community support.

The third man interviewed was Spencer Brewer. Spencer is a white man
in his late 40s who lives in the predominantly white city of Yucaipa, California. He is a composer, musician, and founder of a high-tech business.
Spencer does not consider himself an educator. He is far too modest, and
his efforts at educating his community are generally subversive and
unrecognized. Yet I include him here so that the reader can get to know
his story. You see, Spencer played a significant role in aiding the production of one of the most widely used antiracist teaching tools in the country, *The Color of Fear*.[6] Lee Mun Wah, the producer and director of this
and other educational films, spoke of Spencer as his longest-term white
friend and colleague.

I knew neither of these men prior to the interview process. Since the
connection came through Lee Mun Wah, my first contact with Spencer
occurred when he breezed through Lee Mun Wah's home in Berkeley and
into the backyard where I sat. He entered with a confident stride and a
slightly off-kilter demeanor, presumably due to his hurried trip on the

road. He had driven several hours to be a part of the process, and we began the formal interview almost as soon as he arrived due to the late start time.

We had little opportunity to share in the niceties that might normally precede such a personal conversation. However, Spencer seemed to take a deep breath and, for the sake of his friend, open himself up to the process, trusting me with his personal tales without resistance. I find this significant because Spencer shared some really tormenting and personal stories, both about his own upbringing and his relationship with Lee Mun Wah. To be honest, I was stunned at the depth of his sharing, the way he sat at times at the edge of his seat, while at other moments he would think long before responding, giving me a chance to notice the breeze, the wind chimes, and the birds in the trees surrounding us. It was almost surreal, sitting in such a peaceful environment, speaking of such difficult experiences.

Spencer talked of being raised in Texas "in a family that believed . . . that Black people would never excel, and not to expect much from them because they are not intelligent. . . . My grandmother was a blatant racist. My father . . . is a racist. And I didn't agree." Spencer said that as he got older he rejected his family's way of thinking. He spoke of an early confrontation with his grandmother:

> There was a woman who helped raise me. She also raised my father. She was a Black woman and she went to work for my grandmother when my dad was two. She lived in the back house with her husband and she raised my father. She was also my grandmother's maid and did everything. That was the time when that was status quo back in the 20s and 30s and Leena went on to take care of and raise us boys. She rode the bus six different connections through Dallas to get out there and did her thing and put up with all that stuff and wore her white shift, whatever you called those things, and rode the bus again after work, all six places to get back home. When I became a teenager I began to question my parents on all of this. Why doesn't Leena eat with us? Why is it Thanksgiving and she's sitting in the kitchen? Why is it Christmas and she's wearing this white shift and sitting in the kitchen? It got kind of rough with us until one time my grandmother just told me what's so. And I said, "I don't agree. This is not the way it is. This is not the way it is supposed to be."

Spencer continued to reject his family's messages about race but knew that racist messages were ingrained in him to a significant degree. He also mentioned the way that the socialization process in his home community demanded certain behaviors: "You know in Texas, I'd actually have to act a certain way, even as a white male, to walk past [some] guys . . . you have to go even further than being white in Texas. You've got to be the good ole boy."

The big shift for Spencer occurred while watching the film *The Color of Fear*, produced by his friend Lee Mun Wah.

Now, understand, I still had this underlying face that I was brought up to believe that Black people are scary and don't expect too much out of them. When I began to walk, this is what I was told. You have blue shoes on and you are going to wear blue shoes. I never questioned it, until I started questioning it. I still couldn't get rid of the voices, the conversations that just came out immediately. Oh, there's clouds outside, is it going to rain? There's a Black person, should I cross the street? It was just a gut instant reaction.

But, as I got older and did a whole lot more work on myself I started questioning all this stuff. Oh, . . . I'm having this reaction; I'm going to stay where I am on the sidewalk. I was challenging all these things that were coming up inside me constantly. This is bullshit. I don't believe this. Where is this coming from?

But when I saw the film, what changed for me is I started listening to each one of these gentleman's truths that were in the film and they were saying it from the most vulnerable place they could. I had never been witness to that conversation before. I think that is what has been most powerful to so many people. They have never witnessed that conversation before, not said like that. I hadn't. So when I heard what they had to say, especially Victor—what an eloquent speaker Victor was, how incredibly scary looking he was just as a Black man—and so here's a guy who looks scary, and is incredibly intelligent and articulate and speaks very directly to the point and has an enormous amount of pain and anger inside him about his life going this way. I really, really got that. I mean I really heard it. Each of them, I heard each one in their own ways. When I walked away from that I was left with, I'm gonna change, I'm gonna do it differently.

This new perspective completely altered Spencer's sense of self and of what he needed to do in the world. Yet before Spencer saw the film, not having had the recognition regarding how racism and whiteness play out in his interactions with others, a situation arose that caused Spencer's relationship with Lee Mun Wah to become unsustainable for years.

The next chapter discusses both how Spencer's lack of perception posed problems and also how his current perspective helps the relationship continue. For me, Spencer is a prime example of someone who did not begin to see the importance of racial identity until well into his adulthood. He has struggled to understand its effects and now witnesses how his white identity plays out on a regular basis. Hearing about his approach to witnessing has been really helpful for me. Although orienting this text toward educators, I find that I must say openly that there remain too few white educators involved in this work. For this reason, hearing from people outside the general field and figuring out how to apply his wisdom to our experience has been revealing for me. Ultimately, Spencer reinforced for me that there are many ways to educate for justice.

THE WOMEN

Through close cross-race relationships, white people come to under-stand race experientially (not just abstractly) and to realize they cannot afford to distance themselves from the realities of racism.

—Becky Thompson

This section begins with this quote from Becky Thompson because each of the three white women interviewed mentioned the important role their colleague of color played in their racial identity development. The first woman interviewed was Karen Teel. She is an affluent white woman in her mid-50s. She is an assistant professor of education at Holy Names University in Oakland and currently lives in the predominantly white, Northern California city of Lafayette. I learned about Karen through Jennifer Obidah, her African American colleague, who was then a researcher and full professor at UCLA. Jennifer and Karen coauthored the book *Because of the Kids*[7], a text that documents Karen's efforts to become a better teacher for African American students with Jennifer's help.[8]

Karen was the first person interviewed for the project. We met on a cool February day in a hotel room on a weekend when Karen and her husband had come to Southern California to attend a family function. I was nervous. Karen was gracious and warm. I began formally. Karen told stories. She moved back and forth through time, reaching for the moments where emotions ran deepest. Like Bob, she showed me her deepest pains and offered up her most heart-wrenching challenges for full view.

I was impressed at Karen's ability to admit continuing struggles with racism. At the same time, I struggled to make clear what I meant about perceiving the effects of being white. With her heart touched and my nerves frazzled, I started to understand why Jennifer was interested in their pair being a part of the project. Karen is an important voice in this book. She allows us to see someone who is on the path toward witnessing but who still has a goodly distance to go.

Karen grew up in Fresno, California, in the 1950s, an all-white, middle-class community. She described her upbringing as "idyllic."[8] About her family life, Karen said that she "wasn't raised in a family that [was] activist. My mother was very concerned about the so-called downtrodden . . . she was always ranting and raving about injustice. But she never did anything about it. Neither did my father." Yet Karen spoke of a time in college when she studied abroad and fell in love with a dark-skinned man from Tunisia. She said, "My mother immediately flew over and led me away to England."

Karen never had any cross-race friends growing up. In fact, she "felt like it would probably be impossible to get to know somebody really well from that culture, from that background, because I felt very guilty about my history and legacy as a white person." Karen said that this guilt erupted in graduate school as she recognized the oppression that African Americans face:

I started reading a lot of literature about that experience and a lot of new theories . . . about why African American students were not succeeding in our schools and a lot of it was associated with racism. . . . I started to become more and more outraged by what I was reading. . . . I became more reflective and angry and confused about everything I was reading and hearing. I was also visiting classrooms in the inner city and seeing the elementary schools and seeing these incredibly bright and enthusiastic African American children. And then I'm reading this literature about how they are falling through the cracks in middle school and high school and about the achievement gap and all the issues that African American educators were writing about.

And I was becoming very anxious. I felt like I wanted to do something to make a difference, to work on myself as a teacher and to prove through different teaching strategies and a different grading system that would be more supportive academically and culturally of African American students. I wanted to prove that they were indeed just as capable as any of the other kids. But at one point I questioned, why did I care? Why do I even care? Socioeconomically, I don't even need to work. My husband was a banker and there was no need for me to do anything. But I loved teaching. I had mostly taught all white students until I went to graduate school. So why was I drawn to this whole African American scene and allowing myself to go through all of this pain and concern?

Karen felt a sense of historic sadness and regret and says that she "was worried about this guilt driving my interest in working with African American students because I didn't want that to be the reason."

Working with these feelings of guilt is something white educators need to be able to do, hopefully with other colleagues who can support each other. Karen's story intersects with my own and exemplifies white educators' need to both (1) acknowledge how we benefit from past injustices and (2) help each other be part of a movement toward increased equity within our schools, allowing our guilt to subside enough to stop us from becoming immobilized.

Ultimately, Karen did stop teaching her predominantly white classes and dedicated herself to teaching African American students—not out of guilt but out of determination to improve their educational experience and success. Karen even sought out help to improve her teaching practice, inviting Jennifer in to her classroom as a part of Jennifer's dissertation project. Karen revealed, however, that she had secretly hoped that Jennifer would find no criticisms. Instead, Jennifer challenged Karen far more than she had anticipated. Karen talked about why she valued the often tumultuous and painful process.

I just saw the power of it, the strength, and how enriching it was. . . . I just saw when people got together and problem solved, got together and made decisions, that it was just so amazing when you had more than one mind trying to work it out. . . . And I've seen things that I didn't like about myself, and I wanted to change it, and I didn't know what to do about that. That, I think, is a gift . . . that I blame myself and see myself as partly responsible. I don't know if you would call it a gift, but it's something you have to have in order to change, in order to believe that you need to change, how you are relating to people or doing this or doing that. You have to believe somehow that you are not perfect, that you are at fault, you have some weaknesses, or you don't quite have it all figured out, and you need help.

Karen opened herself to hear about her weaknesses, taking up the challenge to make modifications.

Karen now recognizes the profound transformation her relationship with Jennifer inspired, far beyond her work in the classroom. She described how Jennifer has helped her completely alter her worldview:

> It has been an incredible journey, an incredible awakening for me as to what it is like to be African American in this country today and how much privilege I have as a white person.
>
> [Jennifer] has been an incredible gift as much as my mother, which is a weird thing to say. But, you know, when you think about who has really seen through you. I mean she sees through me. And she brings out what's good and brings out the truth in my soul, in who I am, and I know it's right and I know it's beautiful.

The learning Karen gains through this collegial relationship did not come easily for either of them.

I asked Karen how often racial challenges come up between them. She told of both the frequency and quality of these moments:

> When we are together? It comes up every time we are together because I will have a thought. I will say something. I will do something. And either I'll catch myself or she will point it out to me, that it is an example of being racist that is not conscious. And then we will get into this long conversation about it, analyzing it, and I will end up in tears because, again, I don't like it. It is ugly.
>
> It just gets deeper. It is like I am an onion and I'm being unpeeled and all the layers of conditioning and socialization and living in a racist society are there and she is trying to unravel all of that, help me unravel all of that, so that I see the truth, I see myself and who I am and what's molded me and what's really happening in the society.

When I asked Karen what makes her stay and sit through those tears she said that it is "because it is wrong and I want it to change." After many years of collaboration and learning, Karen feels more confident speaking about her own increasing awareness. She said,

> I am more aware of what African Americans experience. And what I have done because of what Jennifer has shown me, explained to me, shared with me. I have been much more aware of things that happen around me when I am in a mixed group, or when my friends talk about African Americans and education, for example, and what they think is going on. So I am seeing, hearing, denial whether white institutions could be racist and denial. I mean I had an experience with a group of white friends I meet with once a month. They are all teachers in education. [They] read our book and said, "We don't believe you are racist. We know you. You're not racist." And I just looked at them and said, "You don't know me. And I don't think you know yourselves."

Even with the countless conversations and realizations, Karen still feels a great deal of tenuousness when it comes to relating to people of different backgrounds. Her unresolved anxieties and unhealed sense of self cause her to question her own ability to form additional friendships across racial boundaries.

> I worry that they won't . . . this is where I get emotional, they will think I have some motive for wanting to be their friend, that there is something I am after. Why would I want to be their friend? And that's totally . . . Jennifer would say, you are trying to think for them. You're trying to lay stuff on them and that is so racist.

Karen acknowledges that there is still a lot that she does not see. She would like to engage others to help her increase her perception but says that she is not around enough people who can have that conversation with her on a regular basis, as she and Jennifer now live far apart.

In Jennifer and Karen's book, Jennifer writes about her exhaustion from the need for African Americans to continually teach whites: "I got tired of wondering why Karen couldn't just acknowledge certain things. . . . Why does Karen have to be taught how to relate to African Americans? . . . Why do African Americans have to keep teaching White people how to relate?[9]

Just like Karen, I depended upon one of my Black friends to help me see the effects of race and racism on relationships. Recognizing this is precisely what has led me to believe that white people really need to help each other develop the capacity to witness our own white identity. We so often depend on people of color to help us with this work, and when this guidance becomes expected we further enact the privilege of assuming that another person, usually a person of color, will come and help us fix our own problems.

Part of Karen's challenge is that although she has spent years facing issues of race, the idea of focusing on what it means for her to be white is still a very new concept. Although she is able to dialogue extensively regarding the privileges that come with white skin in our society and the racism people of color have faced, she still has difficulty naming what it means for *her* to be white. Here is what Karen had to say when I asked her what being white meant to her at our first interview:

> You know, to tell you the honest truth, I very rarely think about it. I think about Blackness. I'm trying to understand Blackness. Maybe until I figure out blackness I won't be able to really understand whiteness. I don't know. But what it means to me is that I am very lucky in terms of this society and this world—well, this society, let's say—that I was born white and with all the—because it's the dominant group in power—with the wealth, wanting to sustain itself, wanting to support itself, I had every opportunity. Now I was not rich. It wasn't a socioeconomic thing or a class thing. But I never was discriminated against because I was Black. So everywhere I went, I was never followed around. Everywhere I went there were white people. We were all white and nobody ever looked at me funny.

Although Karen makes significant efforts to grapple with issues of race and see how whiteness involves privilege, her lack of focus on her own whiteness and what that means for her in terms of relating to others is unclear.

Karen's lack of insight into her own racial identity helps set the stage for conflict between the friends. We will learn more about how they move through their conflict in the next chapter. When I first contacted Jennifer about being a part of my project, she told me about Karen, their conflict, and her interest in seeing how the interview process might actually help them move forward. She also noted that she was not sure that Karen was the best example of someone who sees what it means to be white clearly. Although this proved to be true, Karen is a wonderful model for those of us who are at the beginning of our journeys and we can appreciate learning from both Karen's successes and failures.

The second woman interviewed was Katie Gottfred. She is a white woman in her mid 50s who lives in an exclusive, predominantly white suburb north of Chicago, Illinois. She is the founder of LEAP Learning Systems, a nonprofit organization specializing in language development. I met Katie through a family connection several years prior to the interview process. I asked her to participate in the project because I was impressed by her 20-year commitment to people of color in Chicago's Cabrini Green housing project, helping parents to code switch, preschoolers to increase their language skills, and adolescents of color to move into top college preparatory high schools. I was also impressed by Katie's 30-year friendship with Lorraine Cole, who was then the president of the Black Women's Health Imperative in Washington, D.C., and who is now CEO of the YWCA USA.

Of all those participating in the project, I know Katie best. We enjoy both a professional and familial relationship. At the same time, Katie and I approach things from very different points of view. For example, whereas I have experienced a sufficient degree of personal torment over dealing with class disparity, Katie focuses her view of class as being primarily about manners and etiquette, seeing economic disparities as practically inescapable.

Yet Katie has also been working at understanding race dynamics for decades and therefore she is an elder to me in this regard. Perhaps because of all this, our interviews were less about me asking questions and more about us having deep, challenging conversations. Ultimately, my relationship with Katie has been instrumental in forming my views, sometimes with me following her lead, other times reacting against her stance. Either way, I have found the push and pull essential in forming the more solid base upon which I now stand.

All that said, conducting the conversational interview with Katie allowed me to learn more about her upbringing than I previously knew. Katie described her maternal family as "socialist" with an attitude that "we should take care of everybody," that there is "no differentiation," and that "all people are all in this together." Katie spoke at length of her mother's influence on her life:

> She felt absolutely obligated to volunteer her time in the summer, and whenever she could, to help others less fortunate. So she gave every summer . . . working for the Mexican migrant worker camps. . . . I was six years of age and she was a first-grade teacher and we went and she took me along to play. . . . And as time went on and the suburbs moved out [and] the Mexican migrant worker camps disappeared . . . she would turn around and we would go into the [inner] city . . . and work with African Americans.

Her first recognition of discrimination based upon skin color and race came when she visited her paternal grandmother along with her Japanese American half-sisters. One of these sisters was "crying one night and she said 'Why does Gramma love you but not me?' and [Katie] immediately knew it was because [the sister] was Japanese." Katie recounted the realization she had in that moment:

> But it hit me in the face that I immediately knew why our grandmother favored me so drastically and it was horrifying to me that your flesh and blood could discriminate against you . . . realizing that my grandmother was prejudiced against her own flesh and blood because of racial differences.

This early recognition did not translate into Katie creating an identity around her racial position, however. Katie said, "I feel very ethnic myself because of being raised by my [maternal] grandmother who was so Norwegian." This gives her "a cultural identity." She said,

> Well, one thing that I've always said is that I have a culture too. But it isn't white culture. It happens to be Norwegian. My hang-ups happen to be the politeness issue. I was also raised in a situation where I felt that people of Norwegian heritage were much different than people of Italian heritage and etc. So the different European cultures seem very different to me. Just like you won't get a Nigerian to say, "I'm African." He'll say, "I'm Nigerian." You don't define yourself as a continent, except if you are Australian, and it is a continent. . . . Asian Americans don't say, "I'm Asian." They say "I'm Japanese" or Korean or something like that or the other thing. So, and

they are different. There are different cultural values within those. So I think it's important to see things as not just Black culture or white culture, but the nuances.

Katie was raised to take pride in her cultural heritage. Her family instilled a sense of being Norwegian without Katie requiring an extensive search to resolve an identity crisis. And yet, just as Michael noted that he is not actually Irish in terms of current Irish culture, neither is Katie Norwegian. Katie is a white, American woman with a Norwegian heritage.

Katie's concentration on her ethnicity, as well as her recognition that there is a lot of diversity among different cultural groups lumped together within the white group, makes it hard for her to see herself "as part of a larger white group." In a seemingly contradictory way, Katie simultaneously can say that "I'm part of [an] upper-class, upper socioeconomic group, privileged white people. I see the diversity of the white world too, and I'm really not a part of it. Not that I don't want to be, but I'm not." There appears to be quite a good deal of resistance to identifying with a larger idea of whiteness, even though in later conversation she easily discusses what it means when people say someone is "acting white," "the assumption of white America is that the justice system is fair," or noting that as a woman she was not "equal to the white, male supremacy in America." In this way, Katie uses the broad strokes of the white group only when it does not necessarily include her.

However, when pushed to consider the meanings of being white, Katie admitted that she does consider herself a WASP, a white Anglo-Saxon Protestant. She named her stereotypical images of what that means as, "being reserved, having a lack of a sense of humor, being somewhat rigid." Although these meanings exactly match those presented in the previous chapter regarding the development of the white, American self, Katie quickly began to relate those images of being a WASP as perhaps being a reflection of what it means to be Norwegian.

Katie struggles against the larger frame of what whiteness can mean for the sake of appreciating small differences. Her perspective draws a lot from the replacing race with ethnicity approach that many whites use to avoid taking race issues seriously. The question for me became: To what degree is she able to face race issues? And what does it mean to be white at the same time that she seems to resist seeing herself as white? Talking with Katie along with her friend Lorraine helped answer this question.

Katie spoke of the way that her friendship with Lorraine offered her a radically different lens through which to view the world:

> But it was really Lorraine who was my [first] deep friend [of color], and we would talk about how it felt, what it felt like. "Gee, this feels like this to me and why does it feel different to me than you? And what does that mean?" . . . I don't think I would have been here without a deep close friendship where I could talk about this. It's not something that I could read a book about. . . . Understanding my own perspective and realizing that my own perspective was from my . . . not having to deal with being of color in America.

The altered perspective gained within the friendship has had a profound affect on Katie, her work, the success within it, and how she sees the world.

In fact, Lorraine believes that her influence inspired Katie's work in some way:

> You know, we talked about our different experiences constantly. And interestingly enough, my doctoral dissertation was all about language acquisition in African American children and because we talked constantly about everything, including our research, I often credit her interest now based on her living with me all those years, working in those areas. And it's ironic that that's where I thought my career would take me.

For Katie's part, she also knows that her mother was a strong influence in her decision to do the work she does. And yet, Katie readily admits that Lorraine is a main contributor to her ability to do the work well: "I don't think I would have been as successful because I wouldn't have been able to see things from the other side as much. So I would not have been as successful because I would have still been coming from my view as a white woman." Here, we see that although Katie resists locating herself as part of a white group, she can readily admit that being white shaped her worldview. Only through the years of dialogue and listening did Katie develop the skills she would need to be able to "see things from the other side," the side not marked by whiteness.

Another profound change for Katie is the degree to which she now thinks about race. Prior to meeting Lorraine, she did not consider the racial divide with seriousness. Yet the learning she received through her friendship with Lorraine is evident as we discuss how often Katie now sees issues of race. Prompted by a discussion with Lorraine concerning how often Black women think about race, Katie spoke about how much race is now a consideration for her: "Daily at least, if not more. I mean . . . for me, I've made it a mission. And maybe I've made it a mission to some degree because of Lorraine making me conscious that part of the problem of class warfare—at least in Chicago it's warfare—is racial." This view clearly separates Katie from those who use a concentration on ethnicity in order to avoid issues of race in our society.

Lorraine believes that Katie's response is unusual and that Katie is a "different sort of white person." Lorraine speaks of a conference she recently organized to illustrate:

> The focus of the conference was on outreach to African Americans and the participants were all white representatives of predominantly white organizations . . . who wanted to know how to outreach to African Americans. . . . And just listening to the conversations [of] these people from all over the country and how they thought about race, it was apparent they were coming to this scenario naïve. This was like truly the first time they were confronted with questions of race or the questions of interactions with African Americans. If you asked them this question—and I'm considering these typical white folks, as opposed to "different kind of white people"—I would say they think about it very, very rarely, certainly never sat to contemplate it, because in the one-day conference it was a life-transforming experience for many of them, again because they were hearing things they had never heard before. They heard the "r" word discussed, racism, and discussed it. . . . I mean they never had to think about racism before. You know. Their daily existence did not give them a reason to think about it. The conference provided the special immersion experience on race.

In Lorraine's mind, part of that special situation is that Katie lives in Chicago, a city they both consider one in which you cannot escape race. Yet I imagine that part of Katie's special situation is simultaneously the effects of Katie's long-standing friendship with Lorraine and the work Katie does in the world.

Recognizing the complexity of identity formation, it appears that Lorraine's view of Katie as a "different sort of white person" might support

Katie's view that she is not associated with the larger white community, even as she recognizes the ways whiteness marked her earlier perspective on the world. Somewhat similarly to Karen, Katie also has dedicated herself to keeping issues of race and racism in focus but without clear insight into how she personally relates to how being white marks her world.

As we will see in a later chapter, Katie continues to struggle in terms of creating a positive sense of self as regards her racial identity. A continuing part of her journey consists of her feeling comfortable in her own skin in certain situations. Chapter 6 also reveals how Katie's ability to talk about whiteness as a particular perspective benefits and supports her relationship with Lorraine. Similarly to some of the other white folks interviewed, Katie offers an amazing example of what witnessing can mean while simultaneously exemplifying areas where struggles continue.

The final white woman interviewed was Cayce Calloway. Cayce is a white woman in her early 40s who lived in Laurel Canyon, the hills above Los Angeles, at the time of the interview. I consider Cayce a community educator. Although her primary job is as a photographer, she also taught radio production for youth programs serving students with gang-affiliated backgrounds. Cayce's colleague and friend Amanda, a Latina, referred me to her. For all of Cayce's affluence, Amanda continues to struggle to survive economically. Amanda is a former prisoner who now uses her earlier experience to teach life skills to parolees through her organization, Adelante. Amanda befriended Cayce when they worked together on a project to get youth who were working toward life enhancement removed from the Los Angeles police's gang database.

Cayce and I met for the first time at her home. We sat in her small kitchen overlooking a steep, tree-lined street. She appeared younger than her 40 years, very energetic, lively, and humble in regards to her life. Yet for all of her dynamism, we began slowly, with Cayce carefully choosing her words. Her manner betrayed her recognition of the importance of these topics and she moved through the interview very thoughtfully.

Cayce told me that she grew up in a small southern town in Georgia and she refers to her upbringing as "idyllic" in a lot of ways, having "parents still together, two brothers, the dog." Although she never had a close African American friend growing up, there were several African Americans who came over to the house as family friends. She reported proudly that her father, who was once in local politics, was also known as a bridge builder in the community. Cayce attended "some of the earliest integrated schools in the South" and recalled her experience:

> There had been so much going on in the Civil Rights movement that people were kind of like walking on eggs and so as a kid we didn't really notice that there was anything awry. There was a Black part of town, like there is here, and most of the Black kids lived in the Black part of town. But it wasn't like we couldn't go there. It wasn't a scary place.

She did not recall any racial tension at school, but she imagined that might have something to do with her being in a small town. Yet, she noted, "I certainly grew up hearing racial jokes. That had not gone away."

In sum, Cayce said that, "I would have thought growing up that I didn't have a lot of prejudices." But since then her perception has changed: "I probably grew up in the kind of 'Yeah this race thing is behind us.' . . . That was probably more my feeling. . . . We need to just be colorblind and just look at each other as people. And it wasn't until the last ten years when I realized, no, it's really not that way." Cayce's perspective shifted in response to the events surrounding two key events, the Rodney King beating and the O. J. Simpson trial. These events made her aware that she "didn't live in the city that I thought I lived in." She says that they were "real wake up calls for me" and that she had not realized that "everyone was so unhappy." Cayce said that, "At first I was just kind of blown away with how could this possibly be happening? And then what I decided I was going to do is figure out what city I did live in."

Cayce sought out experiences that both confronted her with the segregated nature of Los Angeles as well as her own unrecognized prejudices. Cayce talked about what she learned.

> So just an understanding of holy shit, if you just look at a map of Los Angeles and you look at how much of it is occupied by places you've never been and how small, actually, the ruling, privileged, elite of Los Angeles live in a very small portion of the city. And that was really eye opening to me. It was like "wow." Then I have done a couple different projects that have had me in a lot of different areas and in a lot of different people's homes. And this is one of those prejudices that I didn't realize that I had where I assumed that people who were poor were also sloppy, or whatever. I don't know if I'm saying this right. But I was kind of blown away when I

started going into people's houses. I was doing a project called Community Voices Project for a while where I worked with kids. . . . So I would go and people would write these little blurbs about themselves and I would go and record them and put them on the radio.

Interacting with progressive white folks also taught her about how even in the attempt to be sensitive, white folks who are as-yet unresolved about their own whiteness can operate out of racial prejudices in offensive ways.

That was another thing actually. People said to me, when I started this project, "You just need to go interview them and then edit together. You can't ask them to write anything. That's a white person's way of thinking." And what I found out, no, that's a white person's way of thinking, the assumption that these people can't write their story, because sometimes they were really good. Even some people who were not terribly literate, when asked to focus their thoughts in a couple of paragraphs, wrote amazing things. So I decided that instead of having people come to me, or the station, or doing it over the phone, that anybody that I worked with on Community Voices that I would go to them. So I just went to a lot of different places in LA and I would go into these houses that I had seen from the street, these little tiny houses, and they were immaculate. And they were decorated and they might have three sons in prison, but they've got family pictures everywhere. And everything is in place and that was a big one for me, realizing that poverty and . . . sort of a lower level of living physically were not one and the same. And it wasn't like people had the most expensive furniture, but it was everybody had put-together houses, in some cases, more put together than some of my friends who were kind of transient, college-graduate-school types.

Cayce's newfound recognition regarding the flawed nature of the color-blindness approach led her to see that the movement forward is "about redressing some serious, deep prejudices and wrongs." She said that

It fucked me up for a couple of years, actually. It was really hard because I had just come out of Warner Bros. making this film and I'd been there for four years, actually it was before that that this all happened, but it was still being there in that environment and learning all this other stuff at the same time, it was hard. At that point, I went through that thing of questioning how come I've got so much and these people have nothing and feeling bad about who I was and trying to downplay who I was . . . so I had a hard time

living in my own skin for a couple of years. And interestingly, I can probably bring it back around to Amanda in it. She was probably one of the people who helped me realize I am who I am. The best that I can do is live
consciously and not try to kind of pretend that the world is not [as it is] . . .
to see truth. But she was probably really helpful in that. . . . To me, I've
come to terms, I think, with that, that that is the point of who I was born. I
think I've moved beyond the feeling guilty about it.

Cayce's sense that the point of her being born as a white person is to come
to terms with race issues is reminiscent of my own belief that the work I
am meant to do in the world as a white person is to become as aware of
these race issues as possible so that I can do something about them. Cayce
went on to describe how Amanda helped her move out of her sense of
anxiety over her whiteness.

She did it simply by accepting me, and everything about me. It's like she
knew who I was and where I came from and she wanted to be my friend
anyway. She's the one who kept pushing the friendship. . . . She helped me
understand that we are who we are and we can work at being the best version of who we are, but that we don't need to denounce ourselves.

Amanda's acceptance of Cayce, an affluent white person, as a worthy
human being in the world prompted Cayce to develop a positive sense of
self.

Yet even though this resulted in a reduction of guilt, Cayce went on to
discuss how her learning also prompts her to continue immersing herself
in social justice issues. In other words, she uses her positive sense of self
in order to become more responsive to race issues, a stronger witness, not
to turn away from the work.

In some ways, Cayce's experience is not unusual. White folks struggling with guilt often find personal validation within relationships with
people of color, just like I did with those working in Watts. What is different, however, is that Amanda's unconditional acceptance of Cayce does
not depend on Cayce seeing herself as a "different sort of white person."
Cayce sees her whiteness and its relationship to social justice, yet she does
not separate herself from other whites in order to accept herself. Instead,
she works toward being the best version of who she is by continuing to

challenge herself to become more aware of her own deep prejudices and
how they play out in the world.

Further, Cayce sees that her entire relationship with the world has
changed both in how she sees others and how she sees herself. Cayce
spoke about how Amanda helped shift her worldview:

> Hearing Amanda tell her story and seeing what a struggle it's been for her
> to try to reconnect with her children and I'm way more compassionate. I
> have a lot of compassion for people. Not just not making a snap judgment
> but being more compassionate, knowing that you never know what drives
> people to do what they do and really intense pain drives people to do some
> really horrible things. And it doesn't mean they're bad. It doesn't mean
> they're evil. It just means they've made some really bad decisions. . . .
>
> A lot of the social justice movement allows people . . . [to] only meet
> other activists for the most part. Amanda was one of the people who intro-
> duced me to all the people that all this stuff was all about and showed me
> that they were real people. That's been really important for my own
> growth. . . .
>
> I just look at people differently. I look at the world differently. I read
> newspaper articles differently. It was a matter of the "Don't judge a book
> by its cover" thing. I don't think most of us realize how often we do and
> she really showed me, "You don't do that. And this is why you don't do
> that." And she introduced me to a lot of different people whom I might
> have judged based on what I knew about them. And she really sees people
> as people, on both sides. Her interest and willingness to be friends with me
> is also because she sees me as a person. She doesn't see me as a stereotype.

Not only does Cayce credit Amanda with helping her become a better
version of herself, but she also extrapolates from her experience to generalize about the benefits of being in cross-race collaborations with people
who can accept each other's full humanity. Cayce said,

> I think we both also understand that we each have something to teach the
> other. Or maybe what we understand is that we each have something to
> learn from the other. It's probably more that even, and so we really respect
> each other's point of view. . . .
>
> I think it is true that we see things in different ways because our back-
> grounds are so vastly different and our cultures are different and all that
> sort of thing. We do see life differently and I can say something, have a

quandary about something, and she will come up with something that will be just, "Huh, I hadn't thought about it that way." And that's where I really feel like multicultural relationships can really help each other if we understood that there are strengths and weaknesses and that we can fill in each other's gaps.

As beautiful as this image is, Cayce does not necessarily realize that Amanda's initial interest in befriending Cayce had a lot to do with Cayce's dedication to social justice issues and the good reputation that preceded her as someone who does not operate out of unconsciousness regarding race issues. Amanda told me,

> I think what was important about Cayce in particular is that I had already heard her name out there. And it was good things. You know, usually people say, "Hey, watch out." Or there's always a "but." I never heard that. So I had already known about her, not a lot, but you know, people bounced her name.

Cayce's journey, albeit only begun within the last decade, allows her to see deeply into her own whiteness in a way that many others I spoke with cannot. We will see in later chapters how this insight allows her to offer ideas that might support us as we move forward.

THE LONG ROAD

The six white men and women introduced in this chapter have all begun their journeys into witnessing. Some, such as Michael Meade, have already spent years challenging people to face race issues during workshops and conferences. Others, such as Karen and Katie, have dedicated years of their lives to educational equity within classroom settings, teacher development workshops, or community literacy projects but still struggle to talk about the whiteness in their own lives.

Some aspects of whiteness, such as the dominant, privileged position that whiteness holds within U.S. society, becomes visible relatively early on. On the other hand, a clear vision of how whiteness operates in our individual lives and teaching practices can remain hidden from consciousness when we face race only by paying attention to others, as opposed to our own sense of racial identity. Chapter 6 will more fully inquire into what these individuals do see once they begin to focus on what it means to be white.

Overall, we saw the distinctiveness of each individual's journey. For some, coming to see the meaning of race occurs during their youth, whereas for others perceiving the effects of whiteness emerges during later adulthood. Even though white folks need to take up the burden of opening each other's eyes to begin witnessing our own whiteness, we also have to acknowledge how many whites have long benefited from people of color who do this consciousness-raising work through relationships with white folks. I could have never begun the journey toward writing this book without the guidance of a Black friend who helped open me to understanding myself from a racial point of view. Not surprisingly, several of those interviewed also experienced this type of learning process wherein the ability to see the effects of race develops within a friendship with a person of color.

We also can see that just because we engage the journey toward witnessing does not mean that we will have an easy time moving along the path. Becoming more aware of our racial identity can spark increased sensitivity in ways that can stop us from approaching people naturally. Being open to race consciousness without a sufficiently strong sense of self can often lead to troubled moments and conflict. We might find ourselves even more confused about how to talk with our students and colleagues for quite some time. We likely will experience some moments worrying about saying or doing the right thing so as not to offend others with our questions and concerns.

Eventually, if we follow this path, we likely will end up at a crossroads where we are called to make significant breakthroughs if our collaborations with people of color are to continue to progress and our understanding of self is to be enhanced. The next chapter explores conflict and the challenges faced when we are confronted with blind spots.

Questions to consider at the close:

- In what ways can you identify with the stories of those introduced in this chapter?
- Have you experienced any radical shifts in your thinking about race during your life?

- Did being a part of your race affect your educational experience? In what ways?
- How does your racial socialization affect the way you relate to others today?
- How does your racial socialization affect how you approach your professional practice?

NOTES

1. M. Meade, *Men and the Water of Life* (New York: HarperCollins, 1993).

2. L. Rodriguez, *Always Running: Gang Days in L.A.* (Willimantic, CT: Curbstone Press, 1993).

3. *Road to Return*, directed by L. Neale, documentary film produced in 1998.

4. R. Roberts, *My Soul Said to Me* (Deerfield Beach, FL: Health Communications, 2003).

5. Roberts, *My Soul Said to Me*, 10.

6. *The Color of Fear*, directed by Lee Mun Wah, Stir Fry Seminars, 1994, http://www.stirfryseminars.com/pages/coloroffear.htm

7. Obidah and Teel, *Because of the Kids*.

8. Obidah and Teel, *Because of the Kids*.

9. Obidah and Teel, *Because of the Kids*, 90.

Chapter Five

Blindness at the Crossroads:
Leaps of Faith

On a warm day toward the close of my first semester of teaching, after hurriedly leaving my classroom, I waited. I sat in my car at the top of the hill and waited. We were to have met at 3 o'clock that afternoon, and at 4 o'clock I continued to wait. My friend's phone went unanswered and, for reasons too complicated to describe, I was unable to approach the door and search for him. I moved between worry and anger, yet knew intuitively that his tardiness was not due to any physical emergency. At one point I almost left, my annoyance having reached its breaking point. This was my first year teaching, and the way I spent each hour of each day was carefully allotted. I bemoaned having left textbooks and to-be-graded papers at school, believing the day would be too filled for the completion of that work. I was therefore unable to use that waiting time to prepare for the following week's activities and plans.

Righteous anger over my friend's rudeness filled me as I saw him slowly saunter down the path from his house and approach my car, and especially as he sat down in the passenger seat, offered a nonchalant greeting, and waited for us to move. I was incensed. For a while I stewed in my own boiling juices. Not too long later, my critique emerged and along with it came my insistence that I was owed an apology and that nothing could excuse what he had put me through.

This was my colleague, my mentor, and my friend. I was invested in this relationship in important ways. We supported each other's efforts at the school site, shared important insights regarding staff, brainstormed strategies to move forward, and he helped me understand the students and parents. Through what had often been difficult exchanges, I had learned a lot about myself. I valued him immensely and genuinely tried to understand our differences. But this went beyond acceptable treatment.

We fought. Even after an hour of painful arguing, neither of us was ready to let go of our positions. Frustrated to tears, I could hardly contain myself when he linked my felt sense of injury with my being white. After all of this time, after all the work I had done, how in the world could my whiteness have anything to do with this? His critique appeared nonsensical. He was rude, plain and simple. He was late. I was on time. Then he started questioning me about my experience of the situation, what meaning I had made of having to wait, and how that influenced my emotions. All the while, I was seething with the knowledge that at least to some degree he had acted unjustly.

However, once I made the choice to put my need for an apology to the side and dedicate myself to figuring out what merit his perspective held, things began to shift. Slowly, I started to see that maybe he had a point. The truth is that I had taken the lateness as a personal affront. I had privileged the schedule we were to keep over the relationship he was preserving as he kept me waiting. It took some time for it to become clear. But, in the end, I finally came to realize that my cultural upbringing did, in fact, have at least something to do with my reaction.

The importance my culture placed on time, my anxiety over productiveness, and my prioritized values were issues for me. Although I never gave up my sense that at least some apology was in order, letting it go for a time allowed me to see deeper into myself in a valuable way. Now, even though I avoid being late as much as possible and remain as productive as possible, I have a completely different experience when having to wait. There is an internal shift that I can make in order to operate from a different perspective, one that I have come to value. Looking back on that experience, and many others like it, I recall how hard it was to stay in the situation, wanting so badly to escape with my righteous justification. And yet, there is wisdom gained from having stayed to work through the difficulty.

Courageously choosing to engage the journey toward witnessing whiteness entails continually bumping into our blind spots. What do we still not see about ourselves? How are we supposed to respond to critique? Just as with our literal eyesight, there are gradations to our capacity to see ourselves clearly. This can pose serious problems for us in our workplace. As educators, we operate amidst a sea of relationships. Everything we do requires an ability to communicate and consider the needs of those with whom we work. Whether we are talking about relationships with students, parents, staff, or other faculty, the effectiveness of our collective work depends upon collaboration and appropriately respectful mutual regard. However, within this chapter, we concentrate our efforts to consider our relationships with fellow colleagues, those with whom we share a more peer-oriented working relationship.

When colleagues are dedicated to similar goals, we often find that a sense of mutual care and interest arises through the enactment of our work. The division between work colleague and friend can blur; deep, connected relationships can form. The formation of these ties is important because this depth of collegial relationship can be a hallmark of success-ful, ongoing change efforts (and thus the money and time dedicated to trust-building workshops and team-building efforts within many corpora-tions and institutions).

For this reason, for people wishing to become more able to sustain cross-race relationships in order to help improve the viability of mutually agreed-upon reform efforts in our schools, attention paid to certain pre-dictable racial dynamics that often play out is warranted. Let me be clear, this chapter focuses on the more subtle side of relationship maintenance. (At least, I think it is perceived as subtle for most white people.) Particu-larly, how does an individual's inability to witness his or her own white-ness affect the health of a cross-race relationship?

We must first remind ourselves of the general experience of dis-ease that white folks often have about race and what happens once we have begun to take up work to come to terms with that discomfort. Oftentimes, white teachers taking this journey can become haughty with satisfaction, as though there is nothing left to learn. We consciously eschew racism and even act against it, so what is the problem now?

Our classrooms may be filled with multicultural, multiracial artifacts, and our curriculum offers multiple perspectives and opportunities for crit-ical evaluation. We might even be able to express ourselves regarding the negative effects of racism, its history, and our determination to build a more equitable future that creates a level playing field and ends our coun-try's systemic white dominance. When we are at this stage of consciousness, we might become resistant to the idea that we continue to enact problematic behaviors that come from our experience as white people.

The conflicts that then erupt can indicate that we hit a blind spot. We might get challenged within a staff meeting or in a one-on-one situation with a fellow colleague. At times, we might find out through the grapevine that someone has taken offense to something we said or did. The commentary may appear unfair, characterizing our entire being as problematic. At those moments, we are at a crossroads. How do we take the criticism? What do we do with the information? Do we excuse our need to listen to the critique if we decide that the person challenging us is speaking from his or her own unresolved issues? Do we criticize the approach to avoid the content?

One of the difficulties we face is that our history has left each racial group in a general, but varying, state of distress. If white educators expect their colleagues of color to offer perfect explanations absent of emotion in order to pay attention, we continue to make excuses to escape from painful, yet potentially revealing, dialogue. The eruption of conflict is the heat and fire we must learn to withstand. Sometimes the message might come with the clean precision of a welder's tool that can cut through our blindness. More often than not, however, we might find ourselves awash in a firestorm.

The folks presented in this chapter have been in that fire. One has been burned, one only relatively tinged—but each finds a way to either stay in, or reengage, the dialogue. The intent of this chapter is twofold. First, the two stories illustrate why our ability to remain in deep connection cross-racially depends upon us witnessing ourselves. Second, they highlight the need for white folks to humbly sit in the discomfort of conflict over our whiteness, however it manifests, in order to find the learning we require for our own healing, the continuation of our relationships, and the improved effectiveness of our educational diversity and reform efforts. These moments of conflict require not only courage but also leaps of faith.

Moving through these relationship crossroads can bring us incredible learning. Yet this work of developing and maintaining cross-race relationships often requires working through issues such as anger, conflict management, feelings of guilt and shame, and personal racism if they are to thrive.[1] Karen and Jennifer and Spencer and Lee Mun Wah courageously allow us to peer into their moments of challenge. For Karen and Jennifer, the conflict is at its height through the interview process, the narrative capturing the turmoil and eventual healing gestures. For Spencer and Lee Mun Wah, conflict over issues of race resulted in years of separation, resolution coming only after significant learning and healing took place in each other's absence.

There is something else to keep in mind as we read these stories. The individuals involved in these conflicts have spent years working against racism. Some of them are well-respected and well-known figures in anti-bias training and regularly teach other educators how to better relate with their colleagues and students. Yet their own cross-race collaborative relationships continue to involve conflicts based in race. Their stories illustrate beautifully some of the most common issues we might face regardless of where we are on the path toward witnessing our whiteness. Whether reinforcing conclusions we have already drawn or prompting new insights, their stories let us know that the road is long and complex, and that conflict is part of the territory we must navigate.

I would like to say at the outset that sitting with these pairs was not always easy. Empathy grew within me as I listened to them present their truth, their take on the issues, and sometimes their deep pains surrounding it. Sitting with them together in pair interviews sometimes evoked anxiety within me concerning how to navigate this complex territory that might include anger, resentment, or misunderstanding. As I pieced together their stories, I took note that taking sides is not the purpose. Neither is offering a cold analysis that ignores the tugs of the heart, the inevitable compassion evoked when the human heart bears witness to another.

The intention here is to be generously honest about what I witnessed and the sense it makes to me. Understandably, some of my suggestions will differ from the felt experience of each individual. But the intent is to offer the essential bits and pieces of their lengthy stories along with some ideas about how these conflicts involve racial identity, the understanding of whiteness, and the struggle we face to emerge out from under the shadow of racism.

"WHY DO I ALWAYS HAVE TO BE THE ONE?"

When I invited Karen (white) and Jennifer (African American), both professors of education, to talk with me, they were in the midst of conflict.

At the time, this surprised me. I had anticipated discussions of past conflict but imagined that Karen and Jennifer's history of collaboration and
friendship would mean race issues were long resolved. After all, they had
coauthored a book several years earlier and facilitated workshops together
on issues of racism within education.

But, from the beginning, Jennifer stated her hope that moving through
the process with me might offer the pair an opportunity to work more
consciously through their conflict. At the same time, as an educator herself, Jennifer vocalized her hope that we might learn from them and avoid
some of the problems they face. When I invited Karen to participate, she
readily agreed and appeared to see the same value in the process as Jennifer. I met with Karen first. She spoke of the conflict this way:

> Recently Jennifer and I had this huge, probably the most intense experience
> in our relationship so far, and that is why I flew down [to Los Angeles], to
> see if we could keep this thing going. And she said, "You know, you don't
> have any other Black friends and we've been working together for 10 years
> and that makes me very uncomfortable." And that's probably the first time
> she's confronted me about being white and being in this little entourage of
> white friends and family.

Karen is like many white people who have ventured outside of a segregated, white world, but she does not yet feel comfortable enough with
herself to be able to consistently develop cross-race relationships with
people in her vicinity.

I remember when I was in this position. I worked with mostly people
of color, but the majority of my social world was white. As will become
clear later, part of Jennifer's discomfort with Karen's lifestyle has to do
with what isolation means for white people. Generally, being in a white
world means not thinking about race. This translates into white people not
doing any work to explore lingering racism when people of color are not
present.

When I met with Jennifer, she also spoke extensively about the situation leading to her recent confrontation and blowup with Karen. Jennifer
mentioned that although she likes spending time with Karen, she sometimes moves too far into Karen's way of life. Jennifer spoke of changes
she was making in response:

What I have realized since this episode with Karen is that I need to maintain balance in my life and stay connected with Black people. . . . Since the episode with [Karen], I am listening more to Black stations. I am seeking out dates with Black women a lot more than I have in the past eight years because I was consumed with living the easy life with Karen. I really liked going with her to places that I wouldn't normally go and spending money that I wouldn't normally spend and feeling class-wise like I had arrived. But part of that is leaving behind the reality of life for many people. And then I start to be afraid I'm feeling sorry for them because I am no longer in it. So I've started to reeducate myself. I'm going back into the immersion phase that Beverly Daniel Tatum talks about.

This immersion phase Jennifer mentioned involves an interest in surrounding herself with symbols of her racial identity and actively avoiding things associated with whiteness.[2]

But I also saw that Jennifer took on this "reeduation" process in a balanced way. She did not completely shun all things white. For example, Jennifer retained her dedication to working with people of all races toward common goals, like her interest in engaging in this interview process with me, a white woman. I see Jennifer's evaluation of white people on an individual basis as evidence that she drew from multiple racial identity "phases" at the same time.[3]

When Jennifer spoke specifically about her conflict with Karen, a primary concern was Jennifer's overall and seemingly long-standing sense that Karen had not moved forward sufficiently with her learning and intentions regarding race relations. Jennifer complained of Karen's continued hesitancy saying,

Karen doesn't do the work with the teachers in her class. She says she does, but, for example, over the years, if Karen has an issue with a Black student in her class, she'll call me instead. She won't duke it out with the Black student. I'll say, "Why don't you talk to the Black student?" and she says, "I will." And she never does. But she thinks by talking to me she's fixed it, which isn't true. Ok, the person hasn't changed. You haven't changed because you haven't gone to them. You know. That's doing the work. Not talking to me. She gets herself in places she thinks she's doing things, but she's really not. The moment you take the conflict out from where it happens, you are not doing the work. That's my opinion. So the universe is opening up all these opportunities for you to duke it out and you keep being polite and keep backing up. So I've become a safety net.

Jennifer explained that she felt Karen depended on her to tell her what to do with her African American graduate students and resisted having conflicts with those involved directly. Additionally, Jennifer also mentioned that for a great while Karen discussed connections she was thinking of making with other African American colleagues but that Karen never followed up with these. Karen's struggles are not unusual. As discussed in chapter 2, when white folks decide to face issues of race we can become extremely sensitive and nervous, not knowing quite how to act. Karen spoke about her fears:

Karen: I think I have other potential friends. They are people I really love being with that are African American. It seems like it is reciprocal and I am going to pursue that. But, I have these worries . . . still.
Shelly: You still have the feeling of tenuousness over the racial divide?
Karen: I do. And I worry that they won't . . . this is where I get emotional. They will think I have some motive for wanting to be their friend, that there is something I am after. Why would I want to be their friend? And that's totally. . . . Jennifer would say, you are trying to think for them. You're trying to lay stuff on them, and that is so racist.

Part of Karen's struggle involved Jennifer's stated opinion that Karen should develop more friendships with African Americans. In this way, Karen recognized that there was something self-serving underlying her effort to befriend the individuals she spoke of earlier. She knew that she was hoping to understand more by seeking out people of color. Karen also knew that plenty of people of color reject whites out of suspicion regarding their motives.

Even more discomforting for Karen was her recognition that at this point in her development she still makes plenty of offensive mistakes. Rejection, therefore, was not altogether unlikely. However, that does not take away from Jennifer's complaint that when white folks imagine how a person of color will respond and alter our behavior accordingly, we are not treating the person fairly. Chapter 8 will delve into this topic more specifically and will offer suggestions for how white people can move through this difficult phase of our development.

This period of increased awareness and effort, without all the requisite skills, is really challenging for white people. We want to break out and experience the world differently, but our new sensitivities often make us fearful of making errors. We also do not want to use people, and yet we cannot escape that there is something targeted about our approach at this point. I faced these same challenges myself.

Revealing for me was when I was first beginning to conduct this research with Karen and Jennifer and get feedback from my own teacher-friends of color, one of my best friends reminded me of a time about eight years earlier when I approached her and let her know, quite directly, that I was concerned about my only having men of color in my life and was interested in exploring what was going on with my ability to build relationships with women of color. She then admitted to me how, at that time years earlier, she had thought, "Ok, I guess I can help out this white girl. She seems well meaning."

We then began talking more frequently, found areas of commonality, and are now instrumental features in each other's lives. Beyond this friendship, however, our work collaboration now involves teacher education courses, racial justice, and community-building projects. But there was no vision for this at the outset. I had simply decided to confront my own anxiety and, regardless of my newness to these issues and the rejection that might have come, I took the risk to say it out loud to another teacher at my school site.

I also had not realized at that time what important insights I would gain by having a close relationship with a Black woman, far different than those from my friendships with men. This additional level of consciousness-raising has been really important for me. In some ways similar, all good intentions aside, Karen also knew that she still depended upon African Americans to act as a mirror and make her conscious of her own actions:

Karen: Jennifer was losing patience with me and I didn't understand that. But, I do now. . . . I wasn't looking at myself the way she was. "Well, if you want to do these things, why aren't you doing them? What is taking you so long? Maybe you don't really want to do them." But I think I'm just very cautious . . . and I don't want to lose what I have. And I think I am afraid of losing what I have, I think, replacing it maybe with something better. But I don't know that. But she's my conscience in a way. And I feel like African Americans who are my friends, if I have more African American friends, my conscience will be more. . . . I'll be more aware of it.

Shelly: Do you think eventually you can become your own conscience?

Karen: Yeah, yeah, that would be, yeah, right, where I wouldn't need anybody else to guide me down my path. Is that what you mean?

Shelly: Where you've learned enough to say I am ready to go and . . .

Karen: Yeah. It just happens.

Shelly: And maybe it's not 100 percent.

Karen: And I wouldn't be afraid anymore. I mean I used to be afraid of everything having to do with this.

Shelly: The race stuff?

Karen: I was afraid of the kids. So I believe I have made amazing progress. And that was another thing with Jennifer. She was making some comments that made it sound to me like she didn't think I had made any progress and that really hurt me deeply because I feel like I'm not the same person that I was. But again, these things, it is such a gradual change.

There are two important pieces here. First, Karen's progress stagnated because her white world rarely offered her feedback about the lingering racism she carried. Jennifer was the sole mirror in this regard. This was part of Jennifer's frustration. Second, Jennifer encouraged Karen's belief that increased involvement with African Americans was a primary way to break through her unconscious racism and speed up her learning process. Jennifer was not only trying to help Karen learn more rapidly, she was also trying to spread the burden around. Most people of color do not know white people who are aware enough to help mentor other whites into witnessing.

This unfortunate reality underlies my suggestion that we need to create communities of whites who can become our own mirrors. Only by doing this can we stop making friends with people of color for the purpose of seeing ourselves more clearly. Only then can we build cross-race relationships that do not carry the sense that we are using people. Then, we likely will also be able to build the type of alliance cross-race relationship necessary to support the real change efforts we seek in our educational institutions.

With tension mounting between Karen and Jennifer, the catalyst sparking their conflict's eruption was a weekend where the pair facilitated a professional development workshop for a group of teachers. During that weekend, Jennifer realized that within these work settings she was experiencing increasing amounts of frustration. Jennifer described the revelation she had during one particular weekend:

> I was getting so exhausted because Karen, it was getting so vividly clear, she was always on the other side. She and I were never fighting together in any of these spaces. In these spaces she was always over there and whoever I was with was always over here. What I realized, what she said at BayCES [Bay Area Coalition for Equitable Schools] when we were together was that every time I did that, tried to bring up issues, she felt that she had to protect her friends from me.

This prompted Jennifer to question why Karen was not worried about protecting her instead of protecting other white people who might feel threatened or challenged by what she offered. That questioning led to a significant degree of fallout, hurt feelings, difficult dialogues, and a fear on Karen's part that the friendship was all but over.

The conflict also called into question the level of trust Jennifer could enjoy within the friendship. Jennifer said, "I never trusted the relationship. I never trusted that it could care for me because when we met she was so on the other side of truth." This statement made me ask how much this friendship was based on their mutual work versus seeing Karen as a real friend. In answering, Jennifer suggested that a factor was their differing expectations concerning friendship:

> I was starting to see her as 90 percent friend, 10 percent [work colleague]. But, to me, all of the hard, honest conversation I was having was because of the friendship that I was starting to trust. But friendship to her, I think, means Kum-ba-ya. It means we are all good. We have no more problems. I love you, you love me, the Barney song. Friendship to me means we are now at the space where we can talk about the hard, sad, any difficult issue, and we can overcome it because we are friends.

This cultural difference in terms of how we host conflict is essential, and we pick this idea up again in chapter 6.

Yet the long-standing difficulty this pair had in terms of trust also contributed significantly to this conflict. Although not fully able to express it during our initial conversation, Jennifer later offered a follow-up explanation of how trust and caring was a part of this conflict for her:

> I had another epiphany about what happened that week and it was that I left [Los Angeles] looking forward to that week, feeling like we have 10 years. We have grown so much. I can truly be myself, myself in all its colors. Because even though Karen perceived me as being myself, there is a consciousness in me that I have always tempered over the years how much of myself I give to her. And I was giving all my full self, my good, bad, and ugly. And I got slapped. And she wasn't even conscious that she was doing it. I'm not assigning blame to her. There wasn't even a consciousness that I was allowing myself to be that open until I felt myself start to close up because I was getting more and more scared. But that week I would say that's the first and only time that I tried to open up that much with her. And I don't know that I'll, I think it'll take me a long time to allow myself to be that deeply open again. So I'd become very protective of myself that week. But it was an awareness that as much as I love her, that love doesn't protect me from her world. And her world is still the world that I have problems with. . . . And I used to think that our love was strong enough to sustain me even in her world. But I don't think so anymore. I think I still have to sustain myself. I had never put our love, our friendship to the test except for that week.

Jennifer further reflected that part of this conflict surrounded how hurt she was when she expressed her full self in Karen's world that she was met with resistance and anger on Karen's part. This prompted Jennifer to relate again to Karen's world with a sense of defensiveness.

Part of the hurt for Jennifer also included the fact that her recent gesture of openness had not been met with wounding in other environments. In fact, Jennifer noted that over the last year the more she revealed her true interests and ideas in the workplace, the more professional success she experienced. This helps explain the full context for their conflict. Underlying Jennifer's disappointment with Karen's racially isolated world, the sense of fighting on opposite sides, and the question of whether or not she could express herself fully within Karen's world, was the fact that Jennifer felt a sense of stagnation in her professional relationship with Karen. Toward the end of Jennifer's individual interview she shared this idea: "I think there is a lot of love there. I think if I go to the Bay Area for another reason, there's no way I wouldn't call her and say 'Can we hang out?' . . . I think what she's going to have to come to terms with, though, is professionally we might be at an end." With their friendship forming in direct response to their mutual work, Jennifer's attention to Karen's progress felt inextricably tied to her professional career.

From my early conversations with them both, it was clear that this needed to change. Ultimately, this highlights that relationships formed expressly to inspire racial identity development can be problematic if they are one-sided. Although elements of mentorship may be required for an honest relationships to begin, as I think it did with my friend and myself, she and I both found ways to contribute to each other's lives in valuable ways. Some might read of Jennifer and Karen's continuing struggles and wonder why in the world they would continue to work at this. If every exchange they have has difficult racial overtones, why keep trying to make things work? The answer became clear to me when I met with them together.

It took several months before I could sit down with Jennifer and Karen together. Within that time, significant resolution occurred between them. Karen reported on what allowed this to develop:

> When we got together . . . [Jennifer] came up with this great idea of each of us, for an hour, sitting and talking about how we see our life in the next five to ten years and how we see ourselves separate from each other and with each other. And that was an incredible process because it was just so clear where we crossed paths and where we didn't and how we felt. And I think that neither one of us really knew for sure what the other one was thinking. So to get all of that out in the open, out on the table to look at, was very, very helpful.

This process that Jennifer suggested helped Karen crystallize her thoughts about their future together and her work independent from Jennifer. Karen spoke of how things shifted:

> I know now kind of where my path's going to go and who else I can work with and that's underway. So as far as professionally and the relationship we had around racial and cultural differences, I feel that I am diversifying or whatever. I have other outlets. So now it's now more just feeling like

we're friends and we'll just get together on that basis. . . . The conflict is so hard, but it really helps to clarify and crystallize priorities.

This diversification of Karen's seemed an incredible advancement over her earlier dependence upon Jennifer. This prompted me to ask Karen about what she did during the months between our conversations. Karen credited her reading of Tatum's book *Why Are All the Black Kids Sitting Together in the Cafeteria?* as partly responsible: "That [book] shed a lot of light on what we'd been experiencing and also what I had been, how my thinking had been evolving and shifting and so I feel like, now, I don't need to depend on Jennifer as much."

It was obvious how much that weight had been lifted for Jennifer. Having mutually decided to create a more significant separation between their work as colleagues and their friendship, Jennifer felt more freedom to resist being a mentor within the friendship. Jennifer now can see herself acting simply as a friend to Karen:

I've looked at it and can say our friendship will last unless she says to me one day, "I don't want to be your friend." But my professional journey is *my* professional journey. It's not *our* professional journey. And having come to that conclusion is just so liberating for me because then, for incidents that come up, say it's me going up to Lafayette and we go to dinner and somebody says something, I'll just treat it like I treat a lot of the shit I hear just walking the streets hearing white people talk. If I don't want to say anything, I won't. And if somebody brings something up and asks a question, I can say, "I don't feel like talking about that right now" and feel very comfortable because it's not my profession. I'm in a friendship situation.

But this freedom was not the only thing that satisfied Jennifer. Jennifer continued to feel gratified that even without her guidance, Karen remains committed to working on issues of race on her own. Jennifer told of how important that was to her:

There are things that she's getting a lot of satisfaction [from] and dealing with the race issue head on. So she could have had the choice to say, "You know what, OK, I did this stuff with Jennifer. I'm going back to Lafayette and I'll say hi to a Black person when I see them. But I don't need this work." And she's continuing to seek it out for her own self, nothing to do with me, and that I appreciate a lot.

It is likely, however, that this shift will take some time to manifest fully.

Although Karen continued to commit to her work and spoke of groups that can help her on her journey, she still felt a sense of trepidation. Karen shared her continuing fears:

> Now when I'm with this group at Holy Names, there's two Black women and two white women. I'm finding that I feel very strange. And I think it's because I feel like on the continuum they are so far ahead of me. And I'm the new kid on the block. I'm putting it out there, but it makes me nervous because, and I'm hoping they'll jump all over me like Kitty [one of the white women] does. But the other two are not quite ready to do that with me yet.

Positively, Karen invites direct challenge, wants to purge herself from the racism she still feels within her, and now includes whites within this mirroring process.

Yet it is likely that Karen will continue to feel overwhelmed by the sheer vastness of what there is to learn if she continues to see the primary work as learning about the experiences of "others." When I first sat with Karen several months earlier, I noticed that she only spoke of African Americans. I had asked if her increasing awareness transferred to more appreciation for what other people of color go through. Karen responded,

> I just don't believe that I have the energy or the time to really at this point, to really learn as much about the Latino experience. . . . I don't have the time because I am spending so much time learning about, reading about, African American history and current experiences and so on. I just can't do it right now.

Months later, it appeared that Karen saw that her whiteness deserves focus.

Karen noted that the first time she read Peggy McIntosh's material, specifically the article "Unpacking the Invisible Knapsack," she felt that it did not pertain to herself: "It didn't apply to me necessarily. I don't know why, but I think that's what happens all the time. Things are intellectualized, but you don't really see yourself in it or think about it that much." At this point, Karen sees that part of her difficulty seeing her own whiteness involves the life she leads in which there is little opportunity for her to be confronted with her lingering racism or enactments of privilege.

For Jennifer's part, she always recognized that their conflict had a lot to do with Karen's lack of a regular mirror:

> For me, Karen's life doesn't really include racial conflict. Like she has a life with her husband and family and where she lives, that she could, like many white people in America, avoid dealing with race forever. And so it creates blind spots. And so when she's with me and I find that something she says or does emanates from that blind spot, whether or not she's conscious of it, I'm just compelled to react and call it. And because she may not be aware of it as a blind spot, her first response is defense, like "Damn, where did that come from?" Because it's like a mirror that she's not accustomed to seeing and feeling and looking into. I represent that. So that, to me, is fundamentally where the issues I have with her still come.

Karen intellectually agrees with this, and although it is difficult, continues to commit to increasing her awareness of white privilege and how it affects her. Karen said,

> The conflict we had really had racial implications. It had to do a lot with the white privilege idea and phenomenon. And that [conflict] just doesn't exist [between] my white friends [and me]. . . . And I guess I'm learning all the time about myself, about being white and what that means in a multiracial society. And when conflicts come up they are painful, but they are painful in that they are teaching me that I've got issues that I've got to address and to explore and so they're kind of . . . it's not like I have to decide whether I can stay friends. It makes me want to be friends more because I want to change. I want to be different. And [Jennifer] can't be the only one who helps me with that, but she's a very important part of that. And that's very valuable to me in addition to other aspects of our relationship.

If fully embraced, as Karen becomes more aware of herself, she may also find an increased ability to relate to all people of color within our society when she is able to operate from an antiracist perspective more consistently.

In terms of the conflict within their friendship, although Karen now intends to learn more about white privilege, to the extent that Karen continues to focus primarily on Jennifer's Blackness, she may continue to be blind to the role that her whiteness plays within the friendship. To help support the needed shift in focus, Karen might turn to an article written by Andrea Ayvazian and Beverly Daniel Tatum for support.[4] Within the paper, Ayvazian, a white woman, shares what she has learned through her experience of friendship with Tatum. She writes,

> In the end, I believe the issue for me is how I have come to understand social, political, and economic power and my unearned advantage and privilege as a white woman in a racist society. I believe the strongest things that I bring to our friendship, our relationship, and our connection is an understanding of the significance of my own Whiteness. I come at long last to our relationship with an understanding of my Whiteness, something that for several decades, I was helped to not see or to not recognize its significance. It is my understanding of my own Whiteness, not my response to her Blackness, that allows me to interact with Beverly in a way that continues to foster mutuality, connection, and trust.

I know this move has been essential in maintaining my relationships with at least one of the Black teacher-friends I made during my years at the elementary school. In fact, one of them openly states that I am her only white friend and that she believes the reason she trusts me is because of the work I do surrounding white racial identity with the AWARE-LA group discussed in chapter 1. As a Black nationalist, she feels that she is "coming out" to some of her Black sisters when she admits my role in her life and our closeness. This sense of trust, that I am doing the work I need to do to understand the role whiteness plays in my own life, facilitates our ability to collaborate on many projects, including training teachers to work with diverse populations in Los Angeles.

Returning to Karen and Jennifer, even if this understanding of how whiteness plays its role takes time to fully develop for Karen, the love these two women share, combined with the decreased focus on Karen's progress as part of Jennifer's professional work, will likely support their relationship as it continues. Interestingly, as this text is now being written two years after the initial interviews, one update on this pair is that they are currently collaborating on a new book that will build upon their previous work. From my experience with them, I surmise that it is quite likely

that the careful way this pair moved through their conflict, and the resulting shift in Karen's dedication to take up her own learning about her
whiteness, aided in the continuation of their professional relationship.
Their example offers current educators much to consider, such as:

- How often does your life ask you to see yourself through a racial
  lens?
- To what degree do you depend on people of color to help you see
  how being part of your race affects you?
- Do you value the idea of developing relationships that you know will
  be growth inducing, but challenging?

Beyond all the particular lessons this story offers, Karen and Jennifer's
experience illustrates how living a segregated social life can inhibit our
ability to see white privilege and highlights that conflict and disconnection is likely if we are not aware of how being white affects our interactions. That disconnection can prove disastrous when considering how that
can lead to the failure of change efforts on school campuses.

"I NEED YOU TO LISTEN!"

We now shift to a story of what can happen when a colleague of color
turns to a white friend for support and the white colleague does not have
the basis and background to witness the way race plays a role in the situation. Also important, though, is that this story highlights what can occur
when both members of a cross-race collaboration are simultaneously
stretched in new ways.

Essential to make clear is that although this text focuses on whiteness,
and particularly the need for white educators to witness their own behaviors, we cannot lose sight of the fact that people of color also move
through their own phases of growth. Ensuring the health of our collaborative relationships, and therefore their productive value in school reform
efforts, involves all of us being attentive to the ways that our partners
might be moving through discomfort around race issues. We read now
about the deep divide that can result when collaborators are not suffi-

ciently skilled at witnessing whiteness and in giving voice to the racial dynamics present in a situation.

Lee Mun Wah, a Chinese American, and Spencer, his white friend, experienced conflict to such a degree that they went years without communicating. Sitting separately with both Lee Mun Wah and Spencer on the same day, meeting each for the first time, I approached the conversations knowing almost nothing of the course of their friendship. After speaking with both individuals, I noticed that their experience of a mutual conflict years ago, one that led to a fallout lasting several years, was neither clarified nor fully resolved. Their stories about the same event were so divergent that I almost felt as though I were hearing about two completely different situations.

For Lee Mun Wah, the conflict between the two had much to do with him finally speaking out about the racism he experienced after many years of staying silent. With an upbringing teaching him to be sensitive to others' feelings, he had little experience directly confronting offensive behavior, such as racist jokes. Lee Mun Wah explained that, "It happened so many times, people joking about it, that I was probably more used to joking with it than fighting until later in my life." Yet this changed during his friendship with Spencer.

Lee Mun Wah's experience with an Asian men's group, as well as other situations that brought racism to the foreground, propelled him out of whatever remained of his learning regarding conforming to white standards. He recalled his first confrontation with Spencer about the racism he experienced within their friendship. He linked this moment with the period surrounding the production and distribution of his documentary film, *The Color of Fear*. Lee Mun Wah explained, "It was *The Color of Fear*, when it finally came out. Because I knew him way long before the film came out. He did ask me, 'Is there anything that I do that you ever find that's racist?' And that's when I told him and his wife, 'Yeah.' I knew they both were shocked." After years of friendship, Lee Mun Wah finally spoke about racism and how it related to white privilege. As he attempted to integrate what he learned filming the documentary, he approached Spencer about an incident that occurred during the editing of the music for the film.

Spencer, a music composer, helped an African American friend of Lee Mun Wah's edit the song the man wrote for the film. A few days after the work, the friend returned to Lee Mun Wah and complained about the treatment he received from Spencer. Some of the issues included the quality of the final product, an offer of a meal, and a request to spend the night at Spencer's home studio. Lee Mun Wah explained his understanding of the subsequent argument with Spencer and its relationship to his own newfound understanding of white privilege:

> And so I simply brought that up to Spencer and he got really upset with me, didn't think any of that was true, and I told him what it meant for me. It was the first really huge, humongous break we had. And I didn't realize at the time that it was occurring, I didn't realize how much anguish I had. And it wasn't necessarily towards Spencer as it was what he represented for me. . . . And it became very apparent to me that whatever I saw that he might be reminding me of, the similarities he might have, he did not want to identify with that. And so it became, and I think it escalated to a point where I got really angry and best as I can remember, I would say something and after he would respond I would just get so mad I'd interrupt him. So he felt very abused by me that I had shouted him down. . . . I mean it was so bad that we didn't talk for almost five years. He was really pained about it.

For Spencer, the conflict was not about racism as much as it was about his expectations regarding friendship. Spencer offered his side of the story:

> I said, "Mun Wah, we've been friends what—ten? fifteen?—years at that point? You of all people would know if I'm a racist. Have I ever done any of these things? Have you witnessed it?" and he goes, "It doesn't matter if I witnessed it or not. He experienced it, so that must be what happened." I said, "Well, where does my word come into any of this?" and he goes, "It doesn't matter. He's the one that experienced it. You need to deal with it." And we couldn't get past this because I said "Mun Wah, I need you to back me up as a friend. . . . You've got to see where the line is drawn that if you have a different experience of who I am in the world, and somebody that you want me to work with, then I feel like, as a friend you have to at least hear both sides. In fact, it's best to bring us all three together to work this out. But I hear that you are backing him up just because he is Black and I am not and where are we going to talk about this?" I didn't get anywhere. And it just got worse from there until finally, I said "I'm sorry, if this is where you're at and you see all these things and are not willing to at least

meet me halfway, then something here needs to shift. You are not willing to come to the table." He got really angry. He started screaming at me. I mean screaming, that I owed it to him, that it was my fault that it was all collapsing. No responsibility, zero. So it just dwindled and went out of the picture. That was what actually happened.

This event and fallout occurred during the postproduction phase of the documentary. During that time, the two had no further contact and Spencer did not see how racism or white privilege were part of either the initial difficulty with the musician or the fallout with Lee Mun Wah. At least he did not see it until he viewed the documentary.

Sometime later, Spencer attended the premiere for the documentary and described it as a life-changing experience:

> The minute I saw the film I turned around to the people I was with and said, "I never knew I was such a damn racist." I had no idea. . . . That fast. Instant. I mean, I got it. And understand, I brought David into this film and I helped Mun Wah put the whole damn thing together and I thought I was doing my part. I didn't come close. When I saw the film and I saw David, when Mun Wah turned to him and said, "Now, what would it really be like if everything they said was true, if it really was true?" . . . David broke. He completely broke. You know, I broke with him. If it is really that way. . . . With this knowledge, I could never turn back to turning a blind eye ever again.

Not only did the film show Spencer how he might enact racism, it helped him understand why Lee Mun Wah was so insistent about Spencer hearing the musician's complaints. Spencer recalled the revelation:

> When I finally saw the film, I really got that it was important for me to hear [the musician's] pain about feeling discriminated against that day. I had no model for understanding what that meant prior to that. I needed to hear that. Now whether I agreed with it or not doesn't matter. I needed to hear it. And it still doesn't take away the fact that I needed [Lee Mun Wah] to walk in the door side by side with me when we did this. Not taking sides. But, in one phone call I was erased from his friendship. Not by my choice, but by his.

This issue of simply listening, even though you might disagree, is an important one that surfaces regularly within cross-race dialogues among colleagues working within education. As described in the introduction to this chapter, the ability to set our personal belief system aside for a moment and open up to a completely different way of perceiving an issue or event is a skill.

But, as Spencer's story illustrates, we often do not know how important this really is until we have done it and experienced the results. Spencer spoke of his immediate reaction to the documentary and how it changed his life:

> That film changed my life. Even though I'd been his friend all these years, it wasn't until I saw the film. It just changed the way I viewed my life. . . .
>
> I would still tell off-color jokes pre-film. I won't now. I would think that I wasn't a racist pre-film. Now I know I was 'cause there's no way I could not be with all the training and all the stuff. Yeah, it's just impossible for me not to have been a racist.

Although Lee Mun Wah's film had an impact on Spencer and helped him to better understand their conflict, this did not offset the pain Spencer felt. This is also a theme that runs throughout many difficult interactions across race. Just because we understand something from another's point of view does not mean that the pain we feel if we are misunderstood or injured automatically diminishes.

Spencer spoke of his experience that night at the premiere of the film saying, "I wanted to congratulate him and hug him and do all of those things, but I filed out of there and didn't talk to him for another two years." This is another issue white educators must face head-on. What do we do when we feel stepped on? Even if we come to see that our racial socialization helped create a problem, how able are we to confront the situation and work through the difficult feelings? Do we avoid our colleagues and ignore the issues? If we can witness how white folks very regularly distance ourselves from conflict and then choose instead to stay engaged with our fellow faculty members, we can help salvage many a work-related alliance for the sake of our students.

Several years after the film premiere of *The Color of Fear*, with Spencer profoundly affected and Lee Mun Wah recognizing his loss, Lee Mun

Wah contacted Spencer in an attempt to repair the friendship. At first, Lee Mun Wah met with significant resistance and trepidation from Spencer. Spencer explained his reticence:

> Well, he called and said, "I really want to heal this. I realize that I have burned an enormous amount of bridges over these last few years and you guys are truly my closest friends that I got. Are you willing to meet with me?" and I said, "I'm scared to death to meet with you because I think you're going to do this all over again. I can't trust you. I don't know where you begin and where you end. You became an egomaniac monster around this film. You are not the person I worked with to help try and make the film, or supported you by helping raise the money, putting all the paperwork together, giving you the farm to record . . . a huge amount of support." This was not the person I knew. I said, "I don't want any part of that person. I don't trust you coming up here because I can see you blowing up and I definitely don't want to go to your house. So I picked a house in the middle, a mutual friend. I was willing to because I really valued this relationship. I wanted to heal it.

Once Spencer had the opportunity to fully express the pain he felt, and have it accepted, the friendship resumed. Spencer described the reconciliation and healing that resulted:

> So when he called and we met, he was very humble and very willing to listen. He'd been doing this for a few other people before he got to me . . . build up I guess [laughs]. I cried. I yelled. I was furious at him. And once I got rid of the anger, then what was left behind that was the pain and the sadness for being taken advantage of in our friendship. Once I said my piece, then he said his piece. And at that point, I felt like we could go to the next step because we had both said what we needed to say and where we had hurt each other.

Hearing from Spencer, I realized that although the pair had moved past this event and the resulting fallout, their interpretations of the core issues leading to the exchange had not been fully shared and resolved.

As my individual conversation with Spencer concluded, I had the sense that for Spencer, although he recognized that it would have been good for him to have listened to the musician tell of his experience, the key issue

remained his trauma of being taken advantage of and abused by his friend.
Yet Lee Mun Wah's description focused on his own anguish and Spencer's inability to self-identify with racism.

Sitting alone for a few moments, out in the garden, again with a surreal
breeze and birds chirping, I prepared for a conversation with both men
that was to immediately follow. I knew I needed to ask about this conflict.
I felt my own anxiety rise, not sure how sensitive the wounds remained.
It seemed clear that there was room for exploration, yet I questioned the
degree to which the two men would go willingly into that conversation.
Both men returned, sat down, and I asked my standard interview questions regarding the development of their friendships together. They did
not speak of their fallout.

My own nervousness caused me to leave my questions about their conflict until the end. As it happened, just at the moment when I announced
the issue as a final topic, we had to take a break for a few minutes due to
an interruption. We all stood and disengaged awkwardly. I felt the mounting tension during that five-minute lag. Later, Lee Mun Wah and Spencer
admitted feeling the same. We then resituated ourselves indoors to continue.

When we finally resumed the conversation, Lee Mun Wah began. What
follows is only a small fraction of the dialogue spoken within that conversation. The text offers the most essential points so that you might notice
the way the two men find resolution and understanding. It is likely that
their current, more advanced understanding of racial identity partly facilitates this:

Lee Mun Wah: I can't speak for Spencer, but I didn't think it was ego for
    me. I think it was more what Spencer represented for me in the situation
    and also how much I had never really been able to express my own
    anguish. . . . And also it was the time when I was becoming more able to
    put words to what I felt. The film gave me words to what I was really
    feeling that I had no words for. . . . But it wasn't as much that I believed
    [the musician] as much as I wanted him to try and understand why a per-
    son of color would feel that. . . .

    But I remember there were things that he said that would just, whoosh,
    I was so furious with, which I also owned up to, that that was an anger
    phase for me because, which I often think is really needed because as an
    Asian man, but that it was a phase that I had eaten for so many years.

And I don't think he deserved that intensity. But it was there. . . . And all of my life I'd been used to not talking about it. You know, and in some ways, that's probably a good practice. But it was at a high cost. And when I look back on it, I realize it was going from hardly ever talking about to suddenly "bam," being called a liar, and there's nothing in between in our relationship to compare to that moment. . . .

Spencer: Remember what I told you about whiplash?

Shelly: That's what I had a question about . . . to come fully into a new conversation we don't always enter it terribly gracefully. In the beginning, it's all the raw emotions.

Lee Mun Wah: I think all painful experiences are like that if you don't talk. I don't think there's any preparation for it, and particularly because I'm one of the key people who revolutionized the field to ask questions and go through the whole thing. So there was nothing before me to model it. And then it had to be a hard way to reckon it. But it was very traumatizing because we didn't know how to come out of it. And also there were lots of ghosts in the room, because for me it was ghosts of my family, things we never resolved.

Spencer: Any time we get impassioned with our stance or our beliefs, our phases in our life, our job is to give ourselves fully to it, everything we've got. And with all the new revelations and realizations you were having, finding your voice and how to say it, there's this thing, and I've done it myself a few times, when you become so impassioned with it that we believe that we do have the answer and everybody should listen to what we have to say, without compassion. It's just this is a new way of seeing. It's the new way of being. This is the way the truth is. I think in our case one thing that you stated later on the phone was that you wanted to hold myself and our relationship as this model for all these new things you were seeing and learning from doing the film. And as much as I felt honored by that, I had nothing to relate, to talk this way. I didn't know what it was to just witness what [the musician] had to say. . . . I could not be the person you needed me to be. I think that's where I think you felt even more anger because you wanted to show me as an example. . . .

Lee Mun Wah: There's one thing I want to say that hurt me when you just said something. It is that I'm real clear about one thing, even to this day, even when I was talking to you. It is not that I felt like I only had one way I wanted it to be done. The reason why it was so important for me to have you meet him was because I thought, and I remembered when I told that I thought how easy it was for white people to choose not to have to deal with this . . . just to have the choice to just walk out of it. . . . It was also around that period of time that I got ostracized because I was bringing up this issue.

Spencer: Yes, you were.

Lee Mun Wah: So I was watching how everyone could just avoid me and then how I got ostracized from the group.

Spencer: First of all, I have to preface a lot of this with this is pre-film. . . . I had no context for any of this. None. And I shared it openly post-film how much that I got out of this thing. This is all pre-film.

Lee Mun Wah: Now the reason he doesn't have pre-film is because I sat in the room. So when I sat in the room and started hearing these things, it started putting words to my whole life experience. And I don't think he sat in the [filming].

Spencer: No, I wasn't even there.

Lee Mun Wah: He wasn't even there when we did the filming. So I left with all of these things that, some of these things that weren't even in the film. So it was like carrying this energy.

Spencer: So, my point here is that this is pre-film. Post-film . . . I could totally see how I needed to witness for him, totally got that. That made perfect sense. Pre-this, there was no context. And there were several things that happened within this whole time, the first reason this really bothered me was, once again, no context of how to be hearing his point. We've got to keep that in mind. I'm coming from this innocent place in my mind, or so I thought.

At this point, Spencer described the various issues the man complained of, refuting their validity, and how Lee Mun Wah wanted him to accept that they were true without hearing his side:

Spencer: And what I needed from my friend was to stand up for me walking into the room with him. . . . Now my context, once again, was not about racial stuff. I didn't know I had anything to deal with. . . . I wish I'd gone to the table with him and done it differently. But I wasn't aware enough to do that at the time. The thing that bothered me though was the amount of adamancy, mashed with rage, mashed with not willing to listen to anything. . . . Whether I should have made the meeting or not, literally it was so fucked up. You were so hard on me that I got off the phone and I was hysterically crying. I just couldn't deal with it because you were so seething in those phone calls. . . . And now I understand that whether it's real or not, I was the one guy you really needed to come to the table that day. Of all the people around in your life, I was your model for how maybe it could work. . . . You really needed to go through this experience, to go through this thing you'd just learned. You had just learned it. But I didn't know that then. I wish I had. I would have gone open-heartedly. But I had no way of knowing.

Lee Mun Wah: Yeah, you know. I think you're probably really accurate. I think the part that, I don't remember, the adamant, but the feeling that I had the truth. I think that's what it was when I look back on it. But given what I know now and what probably happened was my escalation was probably identical to my family.

Spencer: Yeah.

Lee Mun Wah: I noticed with whites, but it was also probably true of my family, was that . . . when someone said something, was never relating back to what someone said, not acknowledging what someone had said. . . . So it was kind of like, in defense . . . his was the only truth, 'cause when I remember a little of the work I was doing at that time [it] was around, just hear him out.

Spencer: Yeah, you wanted me to hear him out.

Lee Mun Wah: Just hear him out. And I remember making that a real big point. And I remember that that was real hard for you. You were saying, "But it didn't happen. That's not true."

Spencer: And the same aspect where you wanted me to hear him out, I needed you to hear me out.

Lee Mun Wah: Exactly. And I didn't realize that what I was wanting, and what you represented for me was a white man . . .

Spencer: . . . who could take this leap . . .

Lee Mun Wah: . . . to not see himself as an individual, but to see himself as what he represented and to acknowledge himself as a [white] man. I wanted you to understand what he was talking about on the racial issue of here was a white man. But you insisted on staying on the level of just Spencer, and "This is just you and me, Mun Wah." . . . And I was trying to get you to understand what you represented for him.

Spencer: And there was no way that I could've. What context could I have come to the table at that point in your, our, history? I was not in the film. You were barely talking about it. I had not seen the film or gone through a workshop. No context to hold it the way you wanted me to.

Lee Mun Wah: You didn't. So that was part of the rising for me, was putting the words to "this is what I've gone through most of my life." And I

realize now that that was such a huge disconnect. But I had no previous
experience with it because it was coming out raw for me.
Spencer: Right.
Lee Mun Wah: And I had not begun my work around this. In other words,
all my work prior had been with people of color. I had not begun my work
with white people too with people of color. So I didn't have that experience of being in-between. . . .
Spencer: It was just incredibly raw, very caustic, very raw because it was
something that you really believed in and you finally experienced it. And
like I said, you were getting your words under your belt for the first time.

Years later, with both men able to negotiate the territory of white privilege and racism within the conversation, they worked through the old
wounds in order to develop new understandings of the conflict. Although
Lee Mun Wah began somewhat defensively, by the end he took responsibility for the intensity of his anger. Additionally, he saw that his approach,
his sense that he held the truth, posed part of the problem. Spencer, for his
part, recognized that their prior experience did not equip either of them to
maneuver through this difficult territory at the time of the conflict and that
a great deal of the trauma lay in their mutual inexperience confronting
issues of race.

A profound lesson we can learn from Spencer and Lee Mun Wah concerns our need to be witnesses even when the messages we receive do not
come in calm, friendly tones. Both of these men had a lot to resolve internally during the height of their conflict. Had Spencer understood his need
to witness and recognize what he represented in the situation, he might
have been better able to withstand the fire that came from Lee Mun Wah's
as-yet undigested experience of filming the documentary, an experience
that left him raw and searching for the right language to express his new
understandings.

Essential, however, is that we recognize this step as a true leap of faith.
Choosing to stay within a heated, conflict-filled dialogue regarding race
that at times might appear to be overly harsh or incorrectly managed is
something that white folks generally avoid. Our sense of ourselves as individuals, not marked by a race identity, preempts our ability to really listen
to someone who challenges us regarding issues of racism, especially our
own. Deciding that there is something hidden within the perhaps hurtful
challenge that is of immense value to us must come at first through a sense
of faithfulness.

Without prior experience, we have no evidence that staying through the dialogue will be productive. Yet if we can resist the urge to flee, if we can dedicate ourselves to listening deeply in order to find the kernel of wisdom contained within the argument, then we can become the kind of witnesses that continue to learn and are present for those who need to be heard. Understanding that this is often a challenge, we can ask ourselves:

- Have you ever withstood the type of rage Spencer felt that he received from Lee Mun Wah?
- What does it take for someone to stay within that type of heated conflict with colleagues?
- What would it take for you to set aside your sense of the truth to hear someone else's experience?
- What do you think will happen if educators continue to avoid racially loaded conflict, in general?

As difficult as it might be to do the type of listening suggested here and stay within heated conflict, these skills are essential in order to build the type of trust necessary to create sustainable cross-race collaborations. For far too long, colleagues have allowed race to be the elephant in the room. For far too long, this pattern has come about when faculty members of color make statements reflecting their experience, only to be questioned or dismissed by the white faculty around them.

If we are serious about witnessing our whiteness, then we will need to learn from Spencer and Lee Mun Wah that yes, sometimes the messages will come through in fiery, emotionally raw ways that can injure. And yes, we also must withstand that heat because we recognize that we represent something larger than ourselves. Finally, yes, the burning that we might feel may be a requisite part of building alliances with some colleagues of color who continue to feel the effects of racism on a daily basis.

AFTER THE FIRE

When we see strong, mutually respectful relationships between people of color and Whites, we are usually looking at the tangible results of both people's identity processes.

—Beverly Daniel Tatum

Within both of the conflict situations illustrated we see that true resolution involves work on both sides. Although any individual can freely remove himself or herself from a conflict, white folks have far too often walked away from conflict involving race. Further, when we refuse to humbly enter the crossroad and take the leap of faith to hear a person challenging us, we allow blind spots to remain. Our lack of self-understanding can then impinge on our ability to make and keep deep cross-race connections with colleagues.

Questions to consider:

- Which of the two stories seems most meaningful for you?
- Have you experienced situations similar in nature? If not, why do you suppose you have not?
- What concerns do these pairs' experiences raise for you?

No doubt that sitting in the fire can burn. But let us remember that transformation comes from Hecate's brew. The cauldron containing our medicine boils, creating the needed energy for movement. Yes, the shadows and darkness surround, but the light from the fire might just liberate. I know it has for me. Sitting through the tough moments is what really helped me clarify my view of what whiteness is and how my racial self emerges, not abstractly, but personally.

I now recognize that being white affects me deeply. My relationship to my cultural history makes a difference in how I see others, what invokes a sense of anxiety in me, how I respond to my inner sensations, and what judgments I make regarding my experiences. I am more related to the associations with whiteness presented in chapter 3 than I had previously recognized. Yet instead of this knowing remaining a source of pain, these newfound recognitions actually help.

Seeing how being white affects me not only helped me come to a more resolved relationship with issues of guilt, creating a healthier sense of myself, but I also began to notice that my relationships with my colleagues of color dramatically improved. The quality of my conversations began to change and our sharing flowed more easily and went deeper. This does not mean that I still do not occasionally find myself under fire. I do. In fact, chapter 8 will discuss strategies for how to move through this type of witnessing moment using one of my recent experiences as an illustrative example. Before we can do that, however, we need to get more specific about how being white can affect our lives. To do this, we can look at how the individuals interviewed see whiteness.

NOTES

1. C. G. Coll, R. Cook-Nobles, and J. L. Surrey, "Building Connection through Diversity," in *Women's Growth in Diversity: More Writings from the Stone Center*, ed. J. V. Jordan (New York: Guilford Press, 1997).

2. The "phase" Jennifer mentions "is characterized by the simultaneous desire to surround oneself with visible symbols of one's racial identity and an active avoidance of symbols of Whiteness" from B. D. Tatum, "Talking about Race, Learning about Racism: An Application of Racial Identity Development Theory in the Classroom," Harvard Educational Review, v 62 n1 (pp. 1–24) Spring 1992, 11.

Yet Helms's update to the theory Tatum draws upon recognizes that the "phases" are better imagined as "statuses." The shift in terminology intentionally highlights that an individual might operate from multiple statuses at any given time and a person can offer evidence of more than one status in a single conversation. In this way, Jennifer recognizes aspects of her behavior and attitude related to the immersion status from J. E. Helms, "An Update of Helms's White and People of Color Racial Identity Models," in *Handbook of Multicultural Counseling*, ed. J. Ponterotto, J. Casas, L. Suzuki, and C. Alexander (Thousand Oaks, CA: Sage, 1995).

3. The internalization status is one wherein the person can "assess and respond objectively to members of the dominant group." See Helms, "An Update of Helms's White and People of Color Racial Identity Models," 186.

4. A. Ayvazian and B. D. Tatum, "Women, Race, and Racism: A Dialogue in Black and White," *Work in Progress*, no. 68 (Wellesley, MA: Wellesley College, Center for Research on Women), 13.

Chapter Six

Connecting Visions:
Whiteness in Sight

School and Society is a prerequisite course I teach in the Education Department at my college. Each semester, around the third session of the class, after attempting to establish a sense of comfort and community within the group, I take my students into the depths of despair and ask them to face some very uncomfortable truths. We discuss educational inequity and its relationship to our U.S. economic system. The lecture combines information from a primary text and an analysis gleaned from a workshop with Paul Kivel, a well-known antiracist author. There is no doubt that the content offers a bleak view. Fresh faces, new arrivals to the profession, are generally horrified. Experienced public school teachers often sit with sad recollection of realities already lived.

Toward the close of the session, students respond to the picture painted, the discomforting message delivered that (1) our economic, social, and educational institutions *systematically* support inequity, (2) being part of dismantling structural injustice *cannot* occur solely through their work within a teacher's four classroom walls, and (3) activism beyond pedagogy is required if there is any investment whatsoever in widespread change. Many of my students find the foundational ideas presented that underlie these conclusions as radical, overly pessimistic, and cynical. I understand this because I have struggled with the same sense myself.

My life experience has been marked by privilege, access, and aid. Unfortunately, this is hardly the reality for many, and especially not for people of color. For those of us whose lives have largely been eased by those in our surroundings, accepting that there are structures that regularly

177

and systematically negatively impact people of color is hard to accept. I therefore must coax and convince my students to consider a view of reality that they might find unreasonable and heart-achingly depressing, but one that many, many folks of color experience as absolutely operative and real.

Essentially, my students consider this question: Even if this perspective has not been borne out within your life's experience, can you see why some people might see the world this way? I empathize with many of my students who defensively suggest that it is just too hopeless to be believed. I understand the cognitive dissonance created. The just world some of us grew up to see does not align with the view presented. Yet the difficult view that Hecate's message unveils is important to recognize. In order to successfully navigate our diverse school sites and develop and sustain real, working collaborative relationships across race, we need to understand why many of our colleagues hold the views they do. In order to do that, however, educators need to understand how our own sense of the world has been shaped by our social placement, especially how whiteness might play a role. We must witness ourselves.

Like peeling back the layers of an onion, the meanings attached to being white continually reveal themselves if we repeatedly ask the question "What does it mean to be white in the United States?" Before we delve into this question, however, let us first recall that everyone's experience of what it means to be white differs. Our experience of our racial identity is interconnected with our other multiple social identities, such as our gender, socioeconomic class, family background, citizenship status, and sexual orientation. All of these things, and more, make up who we are and how we experience the world.

A white, college-educated, heterosexual woman experiences the world differently than does a white, homosexual male without a high school diploma. A white, working-class woman has a very different experience from a white, affluent man. However, just as there are some experiences that are shaped particularly by our gender or class position, for example, there are also ways that our racial position influences our lives.

Understandably, the opinions of the individuals highlighted in this text might not match those of some readers. And yet, my hope is that when we look at the diverse group of meanings associated with whiteness, we might become better able to create a visual of the whole. I want to create this rather elusive and uneven big picture because seeing the broad view has important implications for our effort to become both effective witnesses at our school sites and better collaborative partners. Sure, making a commitment to become more active battling the various ways racism and inequity play roles within our educational systems is a great step forward. But a surface understanding can leave us unable to notice and challenge the less obvious forms. If we are to truly witness whiteness, then we need to create some depth of knowledge around its subtleties.

Before we turn to how the people interviewed see whiteness, let us take a quick glance back to the terrain already covered. Recall that in chapter 1 we saw that some people view whiteness as a way of being, a culture. Some common meanings include being just normal, achieving middle-class status, and living a segregated life. Chapter 3 detailed particular aspects of the history of the white race and how various associations with whiteness developed. This included whiteness as meaning American, Christian, Western, modern, innocent, free, individualistic, ambitious, and rigid.

These are some general ideas, a foundation from which to start. Important to note is that this chapter does not offer an exhaustive list of what it means to be white. These educators' perspectives are a place from which to begin. So although we are looking for a composite picture, we must also see that there will be holes in our vision still to be filled in through continued inquiry—for the rest of our lives.

We also have to be honest about this. White folks have not generally had clear vision in regards to this subject. The insights of the colleagues of color are therefore essential. Their insights help us fill in some of the gaps left open by the white folks, as well as help us see what being white looks like from a different vantage point. As Bob noted about his experience living in Germany for several years, going outside of our culture helps us better understand the very place from whence we come.

The two main sections within this chapter ask educators to consider the following: What are the arguments around seeing whiteness as a cultural way of being? What are the various particular meanings associated with being white in the United States?

WHITE CULTURE?

Let us acknowledge from the start that the broad view that speaks of *white culture*, a white *way of being*, or *white thinking*, never fully encapsulates the fullness of anyone. But let us venture forth with a sense of curiosity and appreciation for challenging messages in order to learn what is meant when our students and colleagues use these terms, and be open to the possibility that we are related to their meanings.

Recall from chapter 3 that "Western culture" and "white" are often considered related terms. Speaking from this point of view is Lee Mun Wah, who admitted that he uses white and Western synonymously: "In our culture we refer to white people as Americans. And I think that white Americans refer to themselves as Americans and I'm the immigrant or the alien. And so I try to not do that, so that they will hear that they are Westerners to me and not the only American." When asked if this difference continues even if he tries to adapt to the dominant culture, he said,

> I don't think that we're ever seen as Westerners. I think that we can even still be born here and be here all of our lives and people would never be considered a Westerner, or white, or American per se. In fact, for European Americans it's very integrated and established in their Western ways so that they don't know it. They don't know what values they have that are very Western and imposed on the rest of the world. And I say that in a way because I think that quite oftentimes people of color are always adapting to white folks and accommodating to them and I don't think the white folks, until they have to travel, ever do that.

This single quote alludes to two important issues. First, we see how even in our contemporary society being white remains linked with being American. Lee Mun Wah's statements exemplify how exclusionary this can be for Chinese Americans as well as other groups that do not blend in to the white group and thus remain marked as "other." Exclusion occurs even if Lee Mun Wah takes on American, white cultural forms of dress and manner. Although born and raised in the United States, white folks continue to assume that he is an immigrant. This does not happen to white-appearing people.

Second, Lee Mun Wah highlights that there is a culture that most white folks fit into, *white culture*, and that this is a culture in which most people of color have to consciously try to fit in order to maneuver successfully in this society. White folks generally do not move about our lives constantly wondering how we might need to modify our behavior in order to move through our environment safely or successfully. A feature of white culture, therefore, is an expectation that people ought to shift as needed in order to fit within white norms of behavior, dress, speech, and manner.

But this is not the only way that people link white culture with a broad philosophical approach. Bob, the white man from New Orleans, spoke of white culture by identifying what appears lacking in the United States in comparison to traditional, tribal societies. Bob defined white culture as "European culture, a culture that is further away from the indigenous world than say African or Mayan or Native American cultures, a culture that quit initiating its children long before other cultures did and so are further away from what is today still understood by indigenous people." For Bob, whiteness involves the movement away from a worldview he respects and admires, a worldview historically considered developmentally inferior by Western society.

What links Lee Mun Wah and Bob's perspectives is their use of the broad stroke of the Western or nonindigenous in order to highlight what white, Western culture, in their minds, neglects and excludes. As mentioned regarding the building of a broad picture, if we shifted into the exact details separating Western from Eastern or indigenous, these distinctions would assuredly break down somewhere. Yet, taking a step back and looking at the overall, generalized meanings, this perspective allows us to delve more deeply into the ways that our experience of the world allows us to evaluate the correctness of policies, procedures, and approaches to curriculum in our schools.

White culture is not always seen from such a wide lens, however. Narrowing our vision just a bit, Dr. Shirley Better, an African American retired educator and author who participated in the pilot phase of the interview project, concentrates on the different cultures that have been bred in the United States. She said,

> Whiteness is a culture, just like African American is a culture. I don't have to think about it a lot because everybody is raised in white culture, whether you're white or not. Everybody is raised within American white culture because it's the dominant culture. So it is as much a part of me as it is a part of you in the sense that I know all of the nuances of what is American culture. American culture is white, European culture added with a mixture of what we have here. So I don't have to think about it as separate. I'm aware of it as a difference. Everything that we have operating in our society

is whiteness. All of that is white culture, the language that I speak. But everything in our culture is white culture in the sense of how we mean it. We mean it as European based.

Shirley sees the dominance of whiteness, especially in terms of our societal institutions. She is also deeply aware of how the contributions of people of color are often included without receiving credit, like when she said that American culture is white but mixed with "what we have here."

Linking Western with American and seeing them both reflecting white culture admittedly presents challenges. Luis Rodriguez, a Chicano man, described how Western culture is perceived as white even though it is truly a hybrid:

> My feeling is that Western culture isn't really just European or white. It also draws from all the world's cultures. We can prove that the trajectories of African, Native American, Mexican, Asian, and Jewish and many other cultures have made up our Western culture. But I think there is a sense that the rule of it is very white, European.
>
> I think that is why it is hard to separate those dominant, even racial things that come up in Western culture. Because then you have people like Pat Buchanan, who defends it. "Western culture is the best culture," he says. Western culture is the best because white people have framed it and set the basic parameters of it. Yes, other people have been involved in it, but they are not acknowledged.

In recognizing the influential contributions made by the diversity of groups, Luis does not have a problem seeing himself as a part of Western culture. And yet, Luis also says that "whiteness is a way of being in the world." Luis is not the only one who perceives whiteness as a way of being. Jennifer also spoke using these terms. Jennifer, an African American, also said, "There is a white way of doing things, whether or not they own it as that." But Jennifer also questioned the role that class plays: "Those . . . looking in see it as so radically uniform that it is defined as a white way of being, where it might be a white way that is significantly influenced by wealth versus a white way that is significantly influenced by being white." The class connection reminds us that being white is often associated with a middle-class life or higher. Katie exemplifies this understanding when she acknowledges that her sense of self is far different than another white person from a lower economic class.

These statements highlight for us why working-class white folks often reject the idea that they benefit from white privilege, feeling outside the loop of the benefits that whiteness bestows. The oft-used term "white trash" also starts to make sense. With this term, it is as though we are saying that there are those who fit into white culture and those we would rather not see as part of our group. The middle-class status of the large proportion of whites makes poor whites the ill-fitting "trash" of the white community. When speaking of people as "white trash," we essentially state that we would prefer to throw away those less "educated," "cultured," or "affluent" and cut them out of our group since they do not represent the meanings we hold for what it means to be white.

More than one fellow teacher used this terminology at my school site without recognizing the deeper impact and meaning of her speech. We must stop to consider how the use of the term "white trash" is exceedingly offensive to folks of color who recognize clearly that the use of this term not-so-subtly reinforces the view of "real" whiteness as related to a systematically sustained, higher social status.

The ramifications of the economic connections to these ideas are far reaching. Luis also spoke of how economics affects racial identity within the Mexican American community:

> It's really weird, huh? So, then you get "white" as transforming to mean, not really race anymore, but power and economics. So, if you hold an economically powerful place you could actually be white. . . . Another example is that there are Mexicans here who are doing well economically. They look down at all the other Mexicans.

Luis' statements align with a *Los Angeles Times* news article reporting that large numbers of immigrants who feel increasingly economically prosperous racially classify themselves as white.[1] Additionally, this reminds us of the legal history we saw in chapter 3 in which Mexicans were often legally considered white even though the classification does not resonate with the opinions of the general populace.[2]

This can help us to understand why people of color who achieve middle-class status often begin to be referred to as either becoming white or as selling-out by the people in their home communities who are quite often less economically well off. Taking these considerations even further, educators can begin to note the ways this plays out on our school campuses and in our classrooms.

Overall, Lee Mun Wah, Bob, Shirley, Luis, and Jennifer offer broad ways of seeing that bring being white to the level of culture. This is in contrast to those who resist defining white or whiteness in any sort of general way, favoring instead a view of the diversity within it.

Only a few of the people interviewed resisted naming whiteness as a broad idea. When speaking about white culture, Perry, an African American colleague of Bob's, quickly stated that "you have subcultures within subcultures" even within the white community. And Luis, while speaking about whiteness as "a way of being" above, also noted that he tries to avoid seeing white people as a "monolith" so that he can relate to people on an individual level.

More insistent, though, was Katie, who never made a generalization about the meaning of being white. As you might recall from her introduction in chapter 4, Katie attributed this resistance to define whiteness to her upbringing, wherein she saw differences between people of various European cultures: "Just like you won't get a Nigerian to say I'm African. He'll say I'm Nigerian. . . . There are different cultural values within those. So I think it's important to see things as not just Black culture or white culture, but the nuances." The only way Katie could speak of her belonging within white culture was to narrowly define herself as a White Anglo-Saxon Protestant (WASP). Only then could she discuss her experience of the WASP subculture generally.

The choice to generalize versus narrowly focus is a tension that pervades the academic work on whiteness as well as our common everyday speech. The message offered in John Hartigan's essay in *Displacing Whiteness: Essays in Social and Cultural Criticism* is particularly helpful. He speaks of the tension when he writes that no matter how much we are able to see whiteness from a large view, that when we try to trace whiteness down into something specific or consistent that we can never really arrive at defining a succinct white identity that is common to all white people.[3]

So as we shift into the particular meanings related to what it means to be white, we understand that as these large associations capture something essential, they also lack consistency and cannot be used to automatically brand any particular individual. In this way, this offering *does* generalize what it can mean to be white—yet the intention is *not* to create a stereotype. In reflecting on the generalized meanings, we each must look deeply within in order to determine to what degree our practice reflects what can be termed "white culture" and its particularities. To begin to do that, we can reflect on the following questions:

- With what culture do you most identify?
- To what degree are you influenced by, and participate within, white culture?
- How is white culture reflected in your teaching style and/or educational practice?
- To what degree does white culture dominate your school site or institution?

BEING WHITE MEANS WHAT EXACTLY?

Sifting through the various responses, categorizing, and cross-checking the interview narratives, several meanings repeated often enough, or related closely enough, to call them themes. Some were long ago overheard ideas, while others expanded my own vision. This offering just scratches the surface, but at least we have a place to start. Readers might consider brainstorming with fellow colleagues to name their own associations with whiteness in order to add to the meanings offered here. But, for now, we start with the most common association offered: *white privilege*.

Being White Means Unearned Privileges

For those who see race as continuing to make a meaningful difference in our lives, far and away the most common meaning associated with being white is privilege.

Lee Mun Wah: Probably Peggy McIntosh in "Unpacking the [Invisible] Backpack" probably best illustrates what whiteness is, and not just as a power paradigm, but just in everyday experience of what white means to me.

Bob: It's a given. It's true. Being white is having privileges. . . . No law can change that.

Shirley: Whiteness is unearned privilege.

Spencer: What whiteness is? Privilege. That's all I've got to say, privilege.

Jennifer: It means privilege, whether assumed or in reality. Poor white people have that privilege.

Cayce: It is an absolute point of privilege really. There's no other thing that you can be born, with the possible exception of if you add man to that, being born a white man. There is no other more privileged place to be born into, period. Even the poorest white person in most circles is given more consideration than certainly your everyday person of color.

Lorraine: The first thing that comes to my mind is privilege. I have a hard time answering that question outside of the context of my everyday world that I am totally immersed in because I'm dealing with, my professional life has been dedicated to, eliminating disparities and everything that I'm reading constantly just reinforces the gap that exists between white people and Black people and particularly when it comes to Black women. We are at the very bottom of every index compared not only to white women but in many cases to Black men. So, you know, when you ask me what that means, it means access, it means less stresses, it means a totally different existence.

Knowing that most whites do not automatically understand what the term "white privilege" includes, our fellow travelers expanded and clarified. They then offered a variety of particular contexts wherein white folks receive unearned benefits simply by being part of the dominant racial group in our society. Again, this is but a small snapshot, hardly inclusive, simply a place to start.

Being White Means More Opportunities

Being white can be seen as conferring privilege in terms of education, economics, housing options, and employment opportunities:

Jennifer: It means opportunity, because most of them I interact with have some power.

Spencer: It's the privilege for being hired, getting a better house, living in a better neighborhood, getting a better education, getting a better seat at a restaurant, getting a higher-paying job, that's privilege.

Karen: I have anything I want. I can have anything I want . . . all opportunities are open to me. I can choose to do whatever I want and know that I'm not going to have barriers put up because I'm white. I might have barriers because I'm a woman. But I'm not going to have barriers because I'm white.

Worth noting is that along with Karen, Spencer questions the role that gender plays. He mentioned to me his concern that male privilege be recognized in addition to the advantages bestowed by race. This recognition highlights the interweaving of the multiple social positions we occupy, calling to mind how they can complicate and sometimes be contradictory, overlapping, and shifting.[4] In this way, one can be simultaneously advantaged by one form of privilege while feel disadvantaged by another aspect of our social identity.

Two of the people of color within this group, however, voiced specific charges concerning the role that economics continues to play in terms of the systematic privileging related to being white. Luis spoke of what the economic divide allows in terms of spatial and relational experience:

The big divide is really economics . . . white people have economically removed themselves by moving away from the inner city, or whatever it might be—they moved away from some real issues about cities and poverty and pain. . . . So even if they don't carry a white racial consciousness, they don't find a meeting place with other people.

Luis raises an issue that rests at the heart of the population demographics we find in central-city schools across our nation. Minority students all too frequently inhabit underfunded and dysfunctional schools within urban areas, while white students predominantly attend well-funded and academically supportive suburban schools.

Shirley focused directly upon the economic advantages of whiteness, using language taken directly from a book by George Lipsitz, *The Possessive Investment in Whiteness*, to discuss the way white privilege remains institutionalized: "Until whites are willing to give up that economic advantage that comes from the possessive investment in whiteness, all the integration and individual friendships [are] not going to change the central nub of that."[5] Lipsitz' book chronicles the various ways that white folks economically benefit from their being white. Picking up that book for the first time, I only made it through the first fifteen pages before putting it back down, so strong was my dismay at my own ignorance and desire to escape from the facts outlined in the book. While true that plenty of white folks live in poverty, there are still a disproportionate number of whites who do not. This feature of whiteness, the systematic economic advantages, is one of the most concrete and measurable, although often unrecognized by whites, and it has a tremendous impact on our educational institutions.

Complicating many white folks' ability to sit with this information is the idea that whites have now become disadvantaged within our society. There are two important points to make in this regard. First, our country's entire racial past would have to have been completely different for people of color to ever be considered advantaged in our country. Our racist past has set the stage for present conditions, and its disastrous effects continue regardless of a few policies that attempt to move us toward equity. Affirmative action programs, while helpful in forcing people to hire qualified people of color regardless of either obvious or lingering racism, have done little to alter the overall advantages whites enjoy.

Second, white people tend to believe that people of color who benefit from affirmative action programs are unqualified for the positions they gain. Yet, when listening to white folks discussing their newfound "disadvantage," the evidence to support the idea that they have been passed over for unqualified applicants is generally lacking. What we tend to ignore is that many white folks are really responding to the *loss* of privileges that have been normal and expected for centuries. When we try to force the equalizing of the playing field, it *feels* unjust to white folks because the new rules no longer appear to benefit us. Simply, white folks feel entitled to the best jobs, entry to the best schools, and so forth because that has been our experience.

Being White Means Feeling Entitled

Katie, Spencer, Cayce, and Lee Mun Wah specifically identified how white privilege relates to a sense of entitlement. Understanding what it means to "act entitled" is often a difficult issue for white folks, especially in a culture where white people regularly receive messages that we should "be all that we can be," that we are worthwhile and deserve good treatment, and that we have no boundaries except the ones that we put up for ourselves. Children in my predominantly white neighborhood were raised to believe that the world was our oyster and we could "have it all" with enough effort. Nothing was to be considered out of reach and our voices were considered valuable.

While these attitudes benefit us in myriad ways, quite often, these messages are neither conveyed nor reinforced in the lives of many people of color, especially students of color in inner cities. In fact, the enactment of this boundaryless, entitled existence can actually cause white folks to act in ways that are infuriating to people of color. As educators, we might ask ourselves how we enter spaces where conversations are already occurring among faculty, the degree to which our opinions in collegial conversations are offered in ways that assume correctness, and how we expect quality treatment from all of those we encounter on our campuses.

Katie recognized how a sense of entitlement affects her as a white woman. Katie described a time when she was one of the only white faces at a conference primarily geared toward Black speech pathologists:

> I thought, now this is interesting, I could come in here and sit and I'm assuming you're going to accept me into this. I'm OK. I'm free. Whereas if I had been one Black in [an] all-white [place] I would have thought, "Well, how is that? Is this OK? How am I acting?" But I was just, "Hey, I am OK." . . . But that freedom and privilege and access allows me to say, "Oh, I can pretty much be who I want to be and assume that I will be accepted."

For Katie, the ability for whites to feel free to enter any space regardless of its makeup or intent symbolizes the entitlement bestowed by a racially dominant position. The problem is not that being at events populated with primarily people of color is wrong. The point is that the freedom to feel comfortable entering these spaces with nary a thought about our approach is a privilege that white folks receive but that people of color regularly go without.

Spencer spoke about a different type of entitlement. He described a way of interacting in the world that assumes a certain quality of treatment:

> I am highly aware all the time of the privilege of walking into a restaurant and feeling, really feeling like I deserve the best seat, and not having to

think twice about it. . . . If I go out for a job and I know I am the best person for the job and I don't get it, I feel totally justified to get in that guy's face. "Who the hell do you think you are?" Most people, I have found out from my friends of color, would hold back because then they would be the "ugly" person of color making waves.

When Spencer brought up the idea that people of color do not feel the freedom to lash out when their personal interests go unmet, he also spoke to the lack of fear among whites. Being conditioned to see ourselves only as individuals, we do not generally worry about being viewed as representatives of our race.

With few exceptions, white folks are entitled to behave very badly without adversely affecting other members of the white group by association. We can pretty much behave as criminally as we want and never hear anyone say, "Oh, those white people, there they go again." Further, when white people are the majority of perpetrators of a crime, we rarely hear race discussed as an issue. Take, for example, the vast number of serial killers, school shooters, and corporate swindlers who are white. White people have yet to jump up and start questioning what is going on with us as a racial group to make us susceptible to enacting these awful crimes. Unfortunately, many whites have regularly made use of examples of people of color to justify broad, sweeping generalizations.

Being White Means Being Normal

Our privilege to avoid being named as a representative of our race exists because of the way white identity remains invisible to most white folks. Since seeing whiteness as "normal" is an identified pattern within the white community, this project specifically included people who consider race to remain an important determiner within the United States.[6] Perhaps not surprisingly, those interviewed recognize, and are critical of, whites who see being white as normal or invisible. Shirley notes, "What I'm trying to move to is finding another term to get away from the term whiteness because white people don't call themselves white. You don't say, 'my white girlfriend.' It's normalized."

Karen and Katie recognized that sometimes they continue to operate from the point of view of white as "normal." Karen saw it in her own relationship with her home environment and Katie even identified a moment when it hit her, literally, in the face:

> Karen: I think I am so attuned to, conditioned, to my own environment and the way things work in my own environment that I just assume that it is happening everywhere else.
> Katie: I remember the other experience that day [at the Black speech pathologist's conference]. I was going into the bathroom and looking in the mirror as I washed my hands and thinking, "Oh my god, what happened to me? I look . . ." And I realized that I had gotten so used to looking at color that I looked sick. I thought, "Oh, I must be getting sick because I'm looking so pale today." I didn't look normal. And that was an interesting thought for me . . . because suddenly I saw myself as not looking healthy and that something was wrong with my face because the norm for those two days had become looking at all sorts of colors of darker faces.

This begs the question, what are we conditioned to see as normal? How might our perception change if our world asked us to interact meaningfully with a diverse crowd on a daily basis? Additionally, this normality is linked to white privilege and entitlement, as this dialogue between Karen and Jennifer makes clear:

> Jennifer: Having everything you want for white people in this society is such a taken-for-granted thing, to name it "white privilege" connotes something negative and they've never perceived it or lived it as negative.
> Karen: It's normal.
> Jennifer: It's normal. So it's a normalized sense of entitlement, if you will.

Essentially, this takes us back to the fishbowl analogy offered by Shirley in chapter 1. White people are so used to being part of a society that does not prompt thoughts of racial identification on a daily basis that we do not see that most people of color experience the world very differently than we do. This obliviousness is also a feature of our privileged position.

Being White Means Being Unaware

A significant feature of white privilege is that white folks tend not to be conscious of our privileges and how the dominance of whiteness affects other groups.

Lee Mun Wah: I think it's what I could say about most white men, from my experience, a lack of awareness.

Jennifer: Part of whiteness is the unconsciousness, the believing in meritocracy that you work really hard to get everything you have and so you are lucky and you deserve it. So when you say whiteness and privilege, it sounds like somebody gave it to you without you earning it. And for white people who had to work, that notion is so offensive, but they don't interrogate what happens.

Cayce: Being in that privileged place, being of that elite, often carries with it a lack of understanding . . . I think when somebody says, "Well, they don't act white" it means they're not totally unconscious of the fact that their race gives them and us a privilege that we wouldn't otherwise have and also an understanding that it also gives us an ignorance.

Shirley: I think the difference between whites and nonwhites is that all the nonwhites who have lived in this country are very aware of it and sensitive to it and relate to it. It is whites who don't see it. It's sort of like being right-handed, which is what I say in my book, it's there, you never even think about it, the privilege and that everything is based on being right-handed.

This privilege to be unaware also plays out in white folks' common ability to remain removed from difficult situations, whether mentally or physically. Spencer still grapples in some ways with the learning that took place during his friendship with Lee Mun Wah. Spencer now recognizes that his choices of what to pay attention to are part of his racial privilege: "With this knowledge I could never turn back to turning a blind eye ever again because I've got the privilege to do that. That alone is sad, that because of my color, I have the privilege to see or don't see. I choose to see." It is also clear that this topic is of utmost concern to both Luis and Michael, as this pair spoke extensively on the topic.

Luis: I mean the privilege that they can walk away from people, Mexicans or otherwise. You don't have to know them. There is a privilege that you can choose who you want to connect with. . . . But some people have the privilege to ignore what they want to. They can ignore a vital and large segment of the population. It's a privilege. I can't ignore white people. I can't ignore Black people. I may wish I could, but I can't.

Michael: It's a tremendous ignorance. And I mean ignorance exactly. Some of it is people do not know, like Luis said, they know some of the history of African American and Anglo Americans, of slavery. They don't know anything about Mexico. They don't know anything about the war. They don't know anything and they're all right with that. I don't have to know. I don't have to take it on. So ignorance is part of it. . . . That's privilege, I don't have to adjust myself to understand.

This is as specific as we got regarding the privileges that come with whiteness. If you are interested in investigating this aspect more fully, an Internet search for Peggy McIntosh's "Unpacking the Invisible Knapsack" offers immediate access to a list of over 40 additional unearned privileges white people receive in our society that people of color cannot claim.[7] Overall, though, white educators particularly would do well to ask themselves the degree to which they recognize the way white privilege is enacted systematically in their classrooms, on their campuses, and between faculty and administrators. Keeping our ears open when our colleagues of color speak likely adds additional insights as well.

Being White Means Dominant, Valued Images

What it means to be white also means readily seeing images of people who are of the same racial background. The people of color interviewed predominantly note the pervasiveness of white people within the cultural atmosphere, especially in terms of media representation. This includes movies, television, magazines, and advertisements. But this also includes other environments where people are portrayed, including churches, gift card stores, and book illustrations.

Jennifer put it succinctly. She said of whiteness, "It means magazine ads that look like them, a world we move through that reflects them." Lee Mun Wah spoke similarly: "What whiteness means to me is . . . to see images that look like you every day of your life . . . to be yourself and see varieties of yourself and not just one or two things that restrict you for the rest of your life." The earlier discussion of normality and lack of awareness also relates to this experience. Luis discussed his impressions of whites in terms of the media:

[My wife] and I were thinking about how white people love each other. And I know white people don't say this. But when you are looking from our end of it, they are always putting themselves up there. In the movies, it's them. They love to see themselves. I mean, it's not a bad thing, but when you're coming from our perspective it's too much. They aren't even aware they're doing this. They think they are telling universal, human stories. But all the characters have their faces, their ways of doing things.

Luis' last line is particularly important. Many of us are so accustomed to seeing media images that confirm and support our way of living in the world that we do not understand why people of color might feel disconnected from stories featuring whites.

Many whites respond that "Of course there are more whites represented in the media because there are more whites in the country. What's wrong with that?" Well, not only does this completely ignore the racism that continues to be systematically perpetuated, but we also completely miss that stories are told from a cultural point of view. White culture pervades all stories featuring predominantly white casts. The need to see people who reflect one's own cultural values has massive implications for the entertainment industry and links to critiques that white adults, for the most part, only watch shows featuring people of color if they are exemplifying white norms. This, then, might have an effect on the portrayal of characters of color as each show pursues the largest audience share it can muster.

As our students are increasingly doused with media images from the moment they awaken until they return to sleep, educators should consider the ways that these influences enter our classrooms and school spaces. As we ourselves also are barraged by media images, we cannot forget that we, too, are seriously impacted by the way we develop perceptions of what is normal, beautiful, and valued. This quite likely plays itself out in our choices and cross-race interactions on a daily basis in our educational institutions.

Being White Means Being Knowledgeable

There is a pervasive perception of white people as experts in our society, which goes hand in hand with a regular dismissal of people of color. Through firsthand experiences, Spencer realized that people often do not see people of color as valid holders of knowledge. Spencer spoke of his recent experience raising money for a high-tech venture he was working on and said, "I realize that if I went in there as a different person of color in that room . . . I would not be listened to as well." If this is true, what might it mean for educators who attend professional development meetings led by people of color, administrators or teachers working under the leadership of a person of color, or students interacting with their teachers/professors of color?

Actually, this pattern of privileging white voices is so well known that some people of color working with nonprofit organizations or service projects occasionally bring a "buffer" to meetings with institutional decision makers. The buffer is a white person who acts as the spokesperson for the group and appears as the leader, even if the person in the top position is actually the person of color sitting to the side. Many people of color know that no matter how good their ideas and plans, a white person with the same offering is very likely be seen as more trustworthy and more knowledgeable than the person of color. This can lead to the belief that the search for funding and cooperation might be more successful if a white person appears at the helm.

Sadly, several examples from my own experience are easily recalled where this played out during efforts to promote programs to offer counseling services within elementary schools, mentorship opportunities, and other after-school service programs. Although most people would claim that they would *never* see a person of color as essentially less knowledgeable than a white person, the messages given and received that this *does* occur cannot be ignored. Many, many educators subtly reinforce this pattern unconsciously on a regular basis. The trick is that we cannot do a thing to disrupt it if we cannot notice it and name it.

Being White Means Isolation and Emotional Superficiality

The meanings associated with being white previously discussed are the more evident and visible in my opinion. A number of major texts written on whiteness allude to them to one degree or another. This next piece, however, strikes at the core of the dis-ease that many white folks face. These next two meanings resonate with my own personal experience so deeply that I was struck at my own surprise that they emerged as a theme.

My academic work did not often speak of these ideas, and yet they sur-

face regularly when I am in cross-cultural dialogues with peers and colleagues. Looking closely, we find that the following associations with
being white in some ways mirror the meanings described in chapter 3
regarding the development of a new, white identity, specifically Cushman's work regarding white identity being characterized by emotional
restriction and the isolated, self-contained individual.[8]

Admittedly, these meanings are heavily loaded and may not resonate
with all white people. But we do ourselves a disservice if we dismiss them
too quickly. Let us keep in mind that checking in with ourselves regarding
these generalized patterns in no way suggests that only white people face
isolation and surface-oriented relationships. There are certainly many
people of color who face similar challenges. In fact, *Bowling Alone*, a
book by Robert Putnam, thoroughly investigates how American society
in general has moved through many phases in terms of our social engagement during the past hundred years. He acknowledges that during the past
few decades, all racial groups have lost what he calls "social capital,"
referring to social relationships and civic engagement.[9]

Here we have to recall that what people consider "American culture"
and "white culture" are so entangled and variable that it is hardly surpris-
ing if many people of color are swept up into the meanings and associations as we try to speak of our experiences. For this reason, we should not
be surprised that some of the educators interviewed speak of white culture
in ways that might rightly also describe lives led by many people of color.
That said, isolation and superficiality arise as identified patterns by many
in relation to being white, and my suggestion is that we concentrate on
ourselves as we move to identify how to improve our own practice.

This section offers these ideas as two aspects of one larger theme
because teasing them apart is difficult. Ultimately, the image of a cross is
a connecting visual that can allow us to see their actual distinctiveness
with clarity. Imagine a cross with one arm outstretched to the horizons
and the other reaching simultaneously upward to the sky and downward
toward the earth. Notice how the arms of the cross connect while representing different movements. This is true of the following meanings. The
horizontal arm of the cross extends the various meanings associated with
disconnection and isolation, the ways that we interact with others within
our world. By contrast, the vertical arm holds the image of depth and sur-

face, the *qualities* of those interactions. The meeting point resides in their mutual interest in relationship.

Disconnection and Isolation

The arm of this cross extends quite a distance, for this category encompasses much. For those interviewed, whiteness can be associated with isolation, dissections, and disconnections.

> Amanda: Well, my first husband was half-Irish and I lived with his family. . . . The father was all white and the mother was half Spanish, but more middle-class white. So I got to see how they raised their children and I've been in prison and was raised with white girls there too. So I got to see a lot of pictures from poor whites to affluent whites. So I've seen that there is a disconnection. I mean, feelings are covered.
>
> Michael: One of the ways of sustaining cultural whiteness is isolation, like old Descartes. It's not a plot, just the resonance of bad ideas. Isolate the individual rather than see the individual as the contributor back to the collective. And the carpool lane is empty and there are four lanes filled with one person in each car and that's white culture pouring down the road, each isolated inside and hearing the news that reinforces the ideas of isolation and whiteness.
>
> Cayce: And white people for the most part have kind of isolated themselves. Their families are small. They don't always live close to their extended families. I mean I've lived away from mine for nineteen years. It's not that my family is not close. We are actually pretty close. But . . . there is like a boundary around white people that a lot of times people of color drop when they are together and white people don't always drop when they are with other white people. There's not this sense of community.

I would love to say that the above characterizations do not reflect my life, family, white friends, and their families. Unfortunately, there is a lot of it that seems right on. True, on some level these descriptions might reflect the general trend toward decreased social engagement.[10] Yet over the past decade, I have spent a lot more time around people from different cultural and racial backgrounds. I am very sad to say that this sense of white folks as being less emotionally connected, more isolated, and more guarded *even when we are with other people* resonates.

The pain that comes with admitting this is all the more intense because this is something that I have known deep down for quite some time. The patterns are so ingrained that serious effort is required to break out of habits that keep me alone when in pain and nervous about sharing difficulty with family and friends. I wish that this did not characterize a broader struggle. Unfortunately, there are too many white folks who exemplify these characteristics. The significant numbers of white folks who seriously battle depression and a sense of aloneness in the midst of seemingly comfortable lives and intact, loving families are too great. It bears repeating that, of course, white people are not the only ones who face these issues. But that does not mean that it is not a pattern characteristic of white people worthy of honest investigation.

As educators, we need to consider how this pattern might play out within our relationships with colleagues on our school sites. What are the dynamics that stifle deep connections? To what degree do we hold ourselves back when forming collaborative partnerships? Do we seek out aid, or do we act individualistically out of a need to appear perfectly competent?

Moving into broader territory, for some folks interviewed, whiteness also brings to mind the dissection of Latin America, the raping of Mother Earth for resources, a sense of separation from nature, and a disconnection from prior generations, our ancestors, and the sacred. There is also a collective sense that being white means having a wall built up between people, having something killed off inside that is required for holding a false sense of superiority, and an unwillingness to cross-racial boundaries. Here are a couple of representative statements.

Amanda: When I think of countries like Latin America being dissected, I think of white. When I hear of Mother [Earth] being raped and resources being taken out of her, especially her resources, I think of white. So I know it's not only white, that power and money comes in many colors. Politicians, always all white. Honestly, that's what we see. That's the real world I lived through.

Lee Mun Wah: In the Western thought, it's almost always, well, you wound your environment but there's no connection to your environment. "It's useful this moment, and if it happens to break down we'll figure it out." Or like George Bush or Ronald Reagan. "Well, if we ruin all of the clouds so there is no more rain, we'll just pour tons of salt on the clouds to get it to rain. Or we'll plant lots of little trees to make up for all the forest we've destroyed." But it's never the sense of interconnectedness. It's always isolation, even if it takes 500 years for something to grow back. But there's a sense that I'm connected to the trees and to the person and to the words and to the actions and to the generations that come. There's a sense of evolution and continuity, whereas I don't feel that in the Western culture and so when you ask me about my race and my culture, I think to me a Western thought is that they are separated, and hence why, and I've never thought about this until you just posed it to me, but perhaps that is where Western thought falls short.

From a big-picture point of view, this characterization may be fair. Western, white culture is linked with the Industrial Revolution, technology that allowed for increased use of both natural and human resources, and the purposeful destruction of communal forms of living within indigenous populations. Our history is rife with movements that led us to become a highly individualistic society dependent upon the existence of exploitation.

Taking Lee Mun Wah's approach for a moment and using whiteness synonymously with Western culture, we find that most of these associations are also located within Tarnas' text, *The Passion of the Western Mind*, discussed in chapter 3.[11] After analyzing the development of Western consciousness over its two-thousand-year history, Tarnas argues that, ultimately, the deepest passion of the West's masculine consciousness is to reunite with the whole, with all that it has separated itself from, including nature and femininity, and to transcend human alienation. This is no small critique. What these associations suggest is that being white is fundamentally related to being disconnected on a number of levels.

Further, the entire project of our Western, white civilization cannot be completed until we heal from these various disconnections and make use of whatever this separation has taught us in order to become more conscious. In other words, to follow Tarnas' logic, educators raised within the Western cultural matrix likely require a sort of radical healing that reconnects us with spirit, soul, self, other, nature, the feminine, and so on if we are going to provide a more holistic education for our students that promotes a sense of widespread connectedness. We look more closely at what this might mean for the possible transformation of white culture in our last chapter. We also must consider the implications this has for our arguments surrounding school curriculum and the role of environmentalism, feminism, and multicultural education.

Emotional Superficiality

Half of those interviewed used language that linked whiteness with life on the surface of emotion. Stories regarding surface and superficiality came with images of ease, cleanliness, and sanitization. Conversely, descriptions of depth brought associations of difficulty, struggle, and conflict. Bob and Karen both recognize how the avoidance of depth within relationships plays out. In his memoir, Bob wrote: "To my friends and me, friendships mostly meant being polite. Getting angry with a friend would almost always mean an end to the relationship."[12] Karen commented on the conflict she and Jennifer had recently passed through: "Just because there are conflicts, then that means that it's not going to work out. And we were having a conflict that made me think that our friendship isn't going to work out." The fact that both Bob and Karen spoke of either the actual end or perceived ending of relationships when faced with conflict accentuates the serious nature of the desire to avoid discomfort.

Lee Mun Wah and Jennifer both see this avoidance of difficult emotion as being a particular feature of white culture. Lee Mun Wah spoke of a general avoidance of discussing feelings:

> I think a cocktail [party] is actually my same experience of most white people around the country. . . . I don't think that the white folks talk about how they feel. I don't think white males talk about how they feel up front. I don't think they deal with it too often. It's what they do or what they're thinking or sharing information. But it's not always how they're feeling.

Yet Jennifer went even farther. She said that whiteness "means Kum-ba-ya. Only poor white people or white people who have had a major struggle in their life are open to talking about conflict."

Certainly, then, there are plenty of whites that enjoy very open, deep relationships. That said, the tendency to avoid conflict on a large scale has some serious implications for collaborative relationships. What do we believe about conflict? Can we transform our understanding so that we imagine that conflict is beneficial and invites us to be more honestly present? Or will we continue to respond by shutting down and anticipating the breakdown of the work?

Jennifer discussed her own relationship to the emotional ease she experiences when visiting white spaces with her friend Karen. Jennifer said, "I love the life [Karen] leads because of the ease of it. But the ease of it is a trap as well." Jennifer went on to explain, in two particularly illustrative sections, how this avoidance of difficulty proves problematic.

> You don't discuss tough issues. You can talk about plays and dinner and the last meal and the last movie and good, good things that happen to you. But bad, bad things that happen to you, you don't get the impression that anyone would want to hear it and sit with it. So it's very esoteric, very sanitized. . . .
>
> It seems that white, middle-class to upper-class Americans have a persona, or a way of being, that does not include conflict or discomfort. So that means that language is censored. Behavior is censored. Ways of being are censored and censored sometimes to the detriment of those who enact these things, and because the investment in normalcy far outweighs the investment in the human condition in all its complexity, the human condition gets sacrificed.

This last part of Jennifer's statement is really striking because it asks us to acknowledge that this surface approach might injure more than the white folks involved.

It is one thing for me to reflect on the myriad ways that my family rests stoic in the face of challenge and withholds information to protect younger members from anxiety. I even remember my father telling me that I did not have to go to my grandfather's hospital bedside because he thought it might upset me. My grandfather died, and my father then questioned whether or not I should go to his funeral. I was sixteen at the time, and all too socialized to accept this caretaking, excuse-making allowance to be self-centered. But I had never thought about what it would be like to be involved in that type of "sanitized" and "protected" space for people who are used to really digging into the difficulties friends and families face. It makes sense that the same level of attention to discuss challenging topics would also arise in cross-race collaborations among school staff and faculty.

If our fellow educators push us to alter our patterns and really speak openly and honestly about difficult topics, we can see how we might scapegoat them as the problem in the situation, see them as the instigators of conflict, and minimize their concerns in order to support a false sense of emotional calm. If these educators are right, that white educators tend to avoid the hard conversations more often, this pattern is highly destructive to a school faculty. Folks of color can end up being demonized and shut down, and white folks can move ahead without even knowing that they played a role in damaging the relationships. Being able to witness moments when this occurs and naming it would be a very valuable skill, admittedly one that takes many years of conscious work to develop.

Cayce also questioned the relationship white culture has with conflict and difficulty. Her analysis of the situation relates to Jennifer's in that she sees how whites often avoid tackling tough emotional issues. Additionally, Cayce added her recognition that whites collectively struggle less than people of color within this country:

> I feel that among white culture and white friendships a lot of times there is not a depth, that you don't have the depth of emotion. People stop before they get to the part that is scary. And I do think it's linked to the fact that the struggle within the white community has been fairly limited. . . .
>
> So for me to be in the midst of Amanda's family, going just about as deep as I'd seen family members go with each other, not just feeling emotion, but being honest and really working with each other, that is something that, to my mind, white culture has to learn. . . . In Black and Brown culture . . . there's like this family and extended family and you take care of each other and you hold each other up when there's a lot of emotion around it. And I think it's one of the biggest problems in white culture, that we don't do that. We support each other, but tidy, clean.

Cayce's comments favor a racial analysis, avoiding a discussion of how class position relates to the experience of suffering and trauma. True, her comments draw upon her personal experience as they generalize and offer a common, stereotypical view of relatively large African American and Latino families.

The essential point in Cayce's comment is her perception of the quality of their interactions. Although still generalizing, Cayce critiques what she sees within her own family, a tidiness and lack of depth that inhibits honesty and a real working through of familial problems. I would love to say that I believe that this is isolated to Cayce's family. However, her description sounds a lot like the way my family handles difficulty, and my white friends and colleagues often admit the same. Of course this does not characterize *all* white families. But if we do find that this is a fair assessment of our individual and collective selves in some way, we really have to spend some time reflecting on what else this might mean in terms of our ability to form healthy relationships across race within our educational practice.

Cayce also links the ideas of being disconnected and superficial with the way white people deal with our U.S. history.

> My theory about why we're this way in America is, how can you possibly live in a country where for 200 years you're enslaving a huge portion of your population and not have some kind of emotion? You have to put a lid on it. Otherwise, you couldn't be human and stand it, right? So I think that in this country we've learned to cover the bad things with really pretty things and that we don't show it when we fall apart.

Cayce's analysis fits with my earlier study of psychology. If people in a society must renounce their perception of injustice in order to avoid danger to themselves, the effect is "percepticide," the killing off of one's own perceptions and knowledge.[13] Our society generally reacts harshly against those who offer damning critiques of our country. Some white folks choose percepticide in order to shut down the cognitive dissonance of living with contradictions that we simply cannot resolve.

When those in our surroundings cannot witness, cannot tolerate seeing the pervasive injustice around them, and cannot hear our testimony, our own perceptions become silenced and pushed into the shadows. Michael also spoke of this defensive position.

> Imagine the ignorance of a culture that can take pride in not knowing and not learning, the damage done inside the oppressing people and their families. Because in order to sustain these ultimately nonviable ideas, something has to be killed off in those who continue them. People can only hold a false sense of superiority by remaining undeveloped and unrealized inside themselves.

Cayce and Michael's comments raise two issues. First, has our collective
history left white folks less able to deal with our emotional pains openly?
Have we had to shut down our perceptions in order to live within a racist
environment for so long that we have become numb in general, habituated
to covering over the pain residing just under our surface?

This would have serious implications for our ability to witness and
name the way racism and white privilege are enacted on our school campuses and within our interactions with colleagues. Second, might this
emotional disconnection affect our ability to face our own history? This
connects to questions surrounding teachers and their likelihood to employ
forms of multicultural education that do not shy away from the travesties
infused throughout our country's past.

As we have already discussed in previous chapters, the United States
continues to experience a splitting polarization regarding how we
approach our history. This emerges in educational politics regularly. How
should textbooks treat U.S. history? Which versions shall be told? Are we
in the business of inducing patriotism or creating a critical citizenry who
thoroughly vets the past for all of its injustices? Do we really have to
choose between them? Ultimately, while the debate rages on, one thing
appears clear to me. The idea of acknowledging the fullness of past traumas sparks fears that our country might not survive the process intact. No
wonder, then, that white society generally avoids looking at the past. It
also starts to make sense why being white is associated with an orientation that privileges a view toward the future.

Lee Mun Wah notes, "And that Western thought doesn't think of the
past. It only thinks of the past if it is relevant or useful for the future;
otherwise, it is of no use to them."

Michael sums up how the consistent striving of whiteness, the avoidance of anything that might get in the way, complicate, or delay progres-
sion, results in an inability to value difficult, conflict-ridden, and deep
emotional understandings:

> In trying to speed ahead, it attempts to distance from the past, which is
> imagined as primitive, rather than primal, ancient, resourceful, and deep.
> Thus, "white culture" remains surface oriented, superficial, obvious, lack-
> ing shading and soulful nuance. In avoiding the natural drops into the pri-
> mal, it become primitive and brutal just when meaningful change might
> occur.

This consistent movement forward also plays a role in what is sometimes called historical amnesia. This is related to the contemporary approach to our own legacy that seeks to deny the continuing effects of historical and contemporary racism.

These aspects of whiteness, both the isolation and superficiality, figure prominently in the minds of many of those interviewed. Clearly, this is a tremendous critique, a painful one at that. These deeper, more personal meanings are important. We cannot simply attend to them for the sake of our relationships with people of color. In order for our vision of how being white affects us to become consistent and penetrating, we have to honestly ask ourselves, to what degree is our teaching practice characterized by feelings of isolation and disconnection and an effort to avoid difficult dialogues?

Symbolic Meanings of Whiteness

Recall that a foundational base for the creation of the white race was the mistaken association between skin tone and symbolism. Two of those people spoken with reflected on how our racial whiteness interacts with the original misattribution of characteristic to skin color. Bob and Michael both referenced James Hillman's work on the fallacy of white supremacy.[14]

The writings and teachings of James Hillman heavily influence Bob's meanings of whiteness. In fact, a lecture by Hillman opened Bob to pay attention to the symbolism around whiteness. Bob understands the history concerning the connection between ancient color symbolism and its literal misattribution onto human beings as well as its resulting devaluation of dark-skinned peoples.[15] Once he learned of this, Bob began to reject much within our common vernacular that unconsciously builds upon symbolic imagery linking blackness with things our culture rejects and represses.

Bob talked about how he and a friend responded to this understanding:

> Because in all these cultures the color black was associated with evil and dullness and so on and the color white was purity and intelligence even in African cultures. But it was always, the colors were always cast upon archetypes of evil, not human beings. . . . And so all these archetypal images of black were suddenly projected onto a race of human beings. And if that

were true and all the images belonged to those human beings, then of course there could be racism and of course there could be invasions and colonizations.

It was very interesting. . . . We were in a conversation one time and I had just heard this at a lecture by Hillman. Malcolm [a Project Return cofounder] was still in prison. . . . And when I told him about this thing that Hillman said, he told me, "Yeah, I used to be called the black sheep in the family. I was the black sheep." So, we kind of agreed, we didn't use that term anymore just to discipline ourselves from that kind of thought. To get away from it, we didn't use black to describe anything.

Bob described that his conscious avoidance of using the word *black* to mean anything that might carry a negative connotation lasted for a significant period of time. He said that recently he found himself "beyond all of that" in certain areas. For example, he again uses the word *black* in a particular poem he likes to recite. For years, he replaced the original word *black* with *dark*. He believes that, to some degree, blackness has returned to the mythic, symbolic layer in his thinking, but not fully. This is something that continues to plague him.

Michael's discussion of the symbolic meanings of the term *white* also builds upon the work of James Hillman, and Malcolm X as well. Michael's speech highlights the way that religious images and symbols involve the mistaken use of the color white as a descriptor for a human being.

Well, I remember Malcolm X writing of when he was in jail and started to study the meaning of words like *white* and *black*. White means pure. White tends to mean clean. It can mean high and bright, up where the light shines. . . . He started working at racial ideas from there.

James Hillman has a good essay on that, the fallacies of white supremacy, the danger of identifying with whiteness as a natural indication of supremacy. The angels are depicted with white wings, so someone declares that their kind of white skin makes them an angel and the devils can be identified by their darkness, the incredible fallacy of taking things on the basis of appearances. White appearance is taken to mean being elevated and chosen by the light and Lord and heaven. Then, the most powerful person in the land lives in the White House. White is elevated, on top and in charge.

It's interesting, philosophically and in the history of symbols, that white often does have superior qualities attributed to it. In many parts of Africa, white means ancestors and the ancestors are the source of dreams and meaningful visions. But when they married the symbolic idea of white as elevated, pure, clean to the appearance of certain people, a historical literalism became the basis of opportunism and colonialism.

We live with the continuing complicated effects of those erroneous ideas. It's part of the disease of literalism and the people who have the worst case of it are those who believe in self-serving simplicities that make things "black and white." Claiming to "be white" makes them the elect, superior, chosen children of God.

Both Bob and Michael associate the misattribution of color symbolism onto humans with the historical legitimization of colonialism and exploitation. These understandings are in line with some of the historical texts described in chapter 3, such as Allen's work charting the invention of the white race.

Before we move forward to consider how these meanings can become so embedded in us that they emerge without conscious intent, though, let us stop and reflect on this last section detailing the particular associations made with being white. How might we see these associations emerge in our personal teaching practice, relationships with parents and colleagues, and educational institutions? Consider the following:

- If a newcomer exceedingly adept at noticing white privilege arrived to observe on your school campus, wander its halls, and sit in on classes, what would the person notice about the role that whiteness plays?
- In what ways might the associations with whiteness described in this chapter emerge within the communication that occurs between students, parents, faculty, staff, and administration in your institution?

A CLEARER VISION, A DEEPER CONNECTION

White people in general are not known for asking the types of questions posed in this chapter and going deeply within to locate (1) how they enact white privilege in their daily lives and (2) how whiteness marks their environments. Teachers, although as a group relatively more highly educated than the nation's populace as a whole, still by and large do not regularly sit with these questions. For this reason, people of color are often rather surprised, if not shocked, when encountering white educators who are adept at (1) naming white privilege and other manifestations of whiteness and (2) speaking clearly about how and why it continues to play a role in their practices and institutions.

Let me restate clearly, the purpose of white educators becoming better witnesses of whiteness is not to ingratiate themselves with people of color. This is not about being redeemed or validated. Instead, white educators need to be clear that when we can witness the whiteness present in our surroundings, we let our colleagues of color know that we can be a part of conversations that other white folks generally avoid, defend against, or deny. We take a step forward in our individual and collective healing process by being more available for deep, honest dialogue.

Essentially, as we connect more deeply with exiled feelings, challenging whatever tendency we might have toward disconnection or superficiality, we increase our capacity to create more open relationships with people of color. In some ways, our ability to witness white privilege may offer validation for the experiences and work of the people of color in our lives. At other times, our increased vision may help to build trust, connection, and mutual sharing. In either case, when white privilege can be named and discussed as a real factor affecting people's lives, the doorway opens for an entirely new ability to relate. With our full selves on the table, we can then begin to talk about the ways that our country's legacy of racism conditions us and lingers within our psyche in distressing ways.

NOTES

1. Moore and Fields, "The Great 'White' Influx."
2. Haney Lopez, "White by Law," 542.
3. J. Hartigan Jr., "Locating White Detroit" in *Displacing Whiteness: Essays in Social and Cultural Criticism*, ed. R. Frankenberg (Durham, NC: Duke University Press, 1997), 204:

However whiteness may be regarded at the level of greatest expanse [ideology, for instance], no continuous motivating or informing impulse can be traced down through the various levels of increasing specificity with absolute consistency. Nor . . . can we compile a more or less thorough aggregate of whites, abstract out of them a common condition or an intrinsic set of connections, and have neatly defined by these efforts a succinct, abiding identity—whiteness.

4. H. A. Giroux, "Postcolonial Ruptures/Democratic Possibilities," in *Border Crossings: Cultural Workers and the Politics of Education*, ed. H. A. Giroux (New York: Routledge, 1992).

5. G. Lipsitz, *The Possessive Investment in Whiteness: How White People Profit from Identity Politics* (Philadelphia, PA: Temple University Press, 1998).

6. Vanderryn, *A Qualitative Analysis of the Meaning of Being White American.*

7. McIntosh, "White Privilege: Unpacking the Invisible Knapsack.*"

8. Cushman, *Constructing the Self, Constructing America*, 62, 77.

9. R. Putnam, *Bowling Alone: The Collapse and Revival of American Community* (New York: Simon & Schuster, 2000), 280.

10. Putnam, *Bowling Alone*, 359.

11. Tarnas, *The Passion of the Western Mind*, 443.

12. Roberts, *My Soul Said to Me*, 19.

13. Lorenz and Watkins, "Silenced Knowings, Forgotten Springs," 3; their use of the concept of "percepticide" is taken from Diana Taylor, *Disappearing Acts* (Durham, NC: Duke University Press, 1997).

14. Hillman, "Notes on White Supremacy."

15. Jordan, *White over Black*.

Chapter Seven

Interior Shadows: Lingering Racism

Part of why I hate part of myself is simple: I can feel the lingering traces of racism in my own body. . . . It's easy to test. Put my white body next to a black body. What do I feel? What reactions kick in, immediately, before I have a chance to think? What facts about race can I feel in my body in that moment? How honest can I be about that? The fact is, I feel something different—a certain kind of fear—next to a black body than I feel next to another white body. The difference matters, still, after years of actively trying to overcome that learned reaction.

—Robert Jensen (2005)

Hopeful, optimistic, determined, and committed: From my experience, this is how most educators approach their work. My sense of hopefulness, optimism, determination, and commitment has been essential in my educational practice and in my work on race issues. The benefits of maintaining this stance should not be minimized. However, single-minded hopefulness and optimism around issues of race can lead to trouble when used to deny the lifelong challenges we face to end both the obvious *and* subtle forms of racism that emerge in our collaborative relationships and educational institutions. Unfortunately, there remains too much historical trauma, internal psychic conditioning, and continued exposure to overt *and* covert racism, and each will continue to affect our educational settings as long as they affect us personally.

Additionally, if we believe that working through the embedded whiteness and lingering racism within ourselves is temporary work, our determination and commitment suffer. Especially for white educators, the "American, can-do spirit" can unwittingly cause us to *over*estimate our ability to completely (1) excise racism from our psyche and (2) eliminate thoughts and actions that serve the maintenance of dominating whiteness. Admittedly, it can be depressing and overwhelming to accept that we will *not* completely erase the vestiges of racial trauma in our lifetime and that this journey we embark upon is never ending. Thankfully, it is also true that we can learn to witness how white privilege plays out in our collaborations with colleagues, classrooms, and schools, as discussed in chapter 6. We can then use that recognition to take action and disrupt its enactment, as we explore in chapter 8.

But we also need to acknowledge that beginning to notice overt enactments of racism and privilege and creating a witnessing practice are not the totality of what is needed. Witnessing *also* depends on our ability to reflect on and notice our inner psychic areas needing continued work. Basically, what it comes down to is that as we move forward and concentrate on developing an antiracist practice to disrupt the racism and white privilege we notice, we each also have to ask ourselves two very intentional questions.

We need to do a gut check because, when it comes down to it, if we cannot answer the following questions in the affirmative, we are unlikely to create an effective antiracist witnessing practice. We need to ask ourselves: As an educator, (1) Am I willing to accept that struggling against *enactments* of racism and white privilege will be a lifelong effort? (2) Can I dedicate myself to *ongoing internal work* against lingering racism within myself for the rest of my life?

The importance of those two questions became clear to me after several years of trying to disentangle how racism plays out within my life and teaching practice. I began to wonder to what degree educators who have grappled extensively with race issues still find themselves adversely affected. So, I asked: In what ways do the effects of lingering racism remain a challenge? Do any of these people feel that they have eliminated the effects of racism and/or dominating whiteness from their psyche? If not, how do they deal with the effects? Not one of the interviewees felt fully resolved over the issues. All of them courageously identified areas where they still struggle. The work that they have already done allows them to see the work that remains, and because of this their messages are both inspirational and helpful.

As it turns out, our chances of reducing racism in our educational institutions and practices depend on us knowing more about how lingering racism lives within us. We turn again to both the white folks and the people of color because this stuff is hard to figure out on our own. We are all affected by our social context, which is undeniably built upon a system of white racial domination. Because of this, we need to hear how white educators continue to face lingering racism within. We also need to hear how people of color experience the continued effects of living within a society built on systems intended to maintain white supremacy.

Gaining clearer insight into the wide breadth of trauma and confusion can help us stay connected to both ourselves and those around us when racially loaded situations arise within our collaborative meetings and in our classroom settings. I imagine Hecate's voice when proposing that we will be able to sit in the fire of confusion and distress with fewer burns if we build a relationship with that confusion and distress in advance.

"IT'S STILL THERE, ALIVE AND WELL" (JENNIFER AND KAREN)

As teacher-educators and college professors, both Jennifer Obidah (African American) and Karen Teel (white) have each spent many years focusing on issues of race and white privilege and their manifestations in school settings. One might think that this would place them above and beyond others who continue to struggle with racial issues. Yet, talking with these two, I found that they continue to confront internal difficulties regularly. Recall their recent conflict highlighted in chapter 5.

Karen spoke of the lingering racism she continues to face in herself. She is so accustomed to confrontation over her unconscious racist actions that she easily applies the term *racist* to herself: "I've heard so many stories of African American men walking down the street and white women moving to the other side of the street, so much that I am very, very aware of that. And I am aware when I do it. You know, I so believe that I am racist that I expect it. I actually expect it." Yet there are some areas that remain more difficult for her to recognize. She told of her first time learning about her lingering racism. Recall that years ago Karen had invited Jennifer into her classroom in order for Karen to improve her teaching practice. Jennifer formalized this process as part of her dissertation with

Karen's permission. At the end of the study, Jennifer approached Karen with her intention to publish the dissertation as a book. Karen then threatened a legal battle that she assumed she could win.

Karen described this experience as resulting in Jennifer making Karen see her internalized sense of superiority over African Americans:

> It must have been when we had the very emotional discussion about what had happened with the dissertation becoming a book. And [Jennifer] explained to me what I had done, did I understand what I had done? And I didn't think I'd done that. I just thought I was trying to protect what was mine. But the more she discussed that with me about how she felt, about what she saw me doing that she had seen so many white people doing in her life, and other friends' lives, that she just wanted to be sure that I understood what I was doing. And that's probably the first time that it occurred to me that I made a decision and acted on beliefs, taking action, based on some type of superiority complex.

Yet simply coming to see that this complex exists deep within does not immediately block continued eruptions or shed light on other past experiences where it emerges.

Within my conversation with both women, Jennifer responded to one of my questions concerning what prompts her to see Karen as more of a representation of whiteness as opposed to simply her good friend who happens to be white. Jennifer immediately recounted an experience when they were doctoral students at Berkeley wherein Jennifer asked Karen to read an article that Karen did not understand well. At that time, Karen confronted Jennifer in a copy room in front of a professor, asking her, "What the fuck is this?" Within our conversation, Jennifer, believing that Karen's behavior resulted from an unconscious aspect of white privilege, questioned Karen on what made her do that.

The dialogue that follows illustrates how resistant we can be to naming the feelings that arise when confronted with lingering racism. But the dialogue also shows the willingness Karen has to admit when she might be subject to their effects. Jennifer's difficulty is that Karen still needs Jennifer to show her when it occurs:

> Karen: I don't know. I think I was joking around in some way because what she had me read was so esoteric and removed from my students' reality

or my reality with them. And I was so shocked because of what I thought I knew about her and so on. And so I didn't like it. I really hate this esoteric, academic writing. I hate it, because a lot of it I don't understand. And I think, if I don't understand it, I mean, really, what are they trying to prove? What is the point of all of this? How is it going to improve education? So I think I was upset on that level. And then I really was incensed in a way, I guess. Also, I was probably nervous and conflicted because I didn't understand it very well and she was asking me to read it and get something out of it. And I wasn't getting anything out of it. But I also did respect her. So she must have gotten something out of it to ask me to read it.

Shelly: That is definitely not joking.

Karen: I guess not.

Shelly: So there was some actual serious anger in using that [language].

Karen: Yeah, and I really don't understand why I said it in front of [the professor] to her, because that was completely out of line.

Jennifer: And she knew how I felt about [the professor]. We had had months of conversations. I didn't like what he stood for and a lot of his work. So if you are you going to say this to me, it should be with me, you, and the copy machine. So it was a total disregard for my feelings.

Karen: Yeah. And so maybe it was kind of getting back at her for something.

Jennifer: Getting back at me for what? What did I do to you?

Karen: For having me read that and then I didn't understand it.

Shelly: You made her uncomfortable.

Karen: Yeah, you made me uncomfortable.

Shelly: Not that you intended to. But what you offered her made her feel uncomfortable and, forgive me, but she just got back at you. . . .

Karen: I'm not sure I get it either.

Jennifer: When somebody gives me something to read and I don't get it, the next time I see that person I say, "I don't get it." What would have been about that that you would feel uncomfortable enough that you needed to attack me unless you're like "Who the fuck does she think she is?" Then, why would I think I'm somebody? We were trying to get literature to support the presentation that we were preparing. So it was like an experiment. So what in that could be threatening? This isn't an "I'm your teacher, read this." This was like, "OK, I found this interesting. Read it." She could have easily said, "I don't think so." To me that's a big piece of white privilege right there. It's like, "How dare you make me feel uncomfortable?" Those are the times when I'm like, I don't need that.

Shelly: And that feels right to you that there might have been something in
that, still beginning the relationship and made to feel uncomfortable prey-
ing on your insecurities of understanding by this African American
woman?

Karen: Yep.

As discussed in chapter 1, there is something deeply ingrained in many of
us to identify with white people being challenged and attempt to locate
arguments to defend them. But before any of us goes down that path in
defense of Karen, let us remind ourselves that Karen did not flinch from
seeing how her behavior might be part of a superiority complex gained
from living in a society that historically privileges whiteness. She has
learned enough to know that this exists within her. But at the same time,
the sense of whiteness equaling something "better than" is so deeply
embedded that a frank dialogue is necessary to recognize each emergence.

So how does Karen respond to the knowledge that this "complex"
exists internally and emerges without conscious intent? Karen takes her
recognition of racism in stride, saying that she continues to work on it but
expects to mess up: She says, "I just say there's another example. It's not
over yet. It's still there, alive and well, and you need to keep working on
it."

But for Jennifer, relating with someone who is consistently unaware of
traces of racism takes its toll. In their book, Jennifer says that she feels
she is battling "the ghost of racism."[1] This is perhaps why Jennifer does
not often put herself in a position to deal intimately with people who
struggle in the same way. Jennifer shared how she sees potential friends:
"When I enjoy people I don't care what race they are. That is what holds
the potential. . . . [But] I don't seek out white people. That's another thing.
So any white person who wanted to be my friend had to seek me out
first."

And yet, Jennifer also said that moving through this experience with
Karen helps diminish the fears she recognizes she once had when interacting with whites. In fact, when asked about her openness to having me, a
white woman, come into her home for these interviews, she credited her
relationship with Karen: "That's one of the things I can see came out of
our friendship. I'm not afraid of white people. Not that I ever consciously
was, but I feel less threatened, like I've got to protect myself around them.
And that's all credit to her."

Jennifer and Karen both struggle with lingering effects of racism, dealing with fears and intimidation. They also engage together in a lot of work to bring it out from the shadows and dialogue openly. The continuation of their collaboration requires a commitment to go through these struggles together, even if struggling sometimes includes Jennifer taking a step away to immerse herself within Blackness for a time so that she can again appreciate Karen, her life, and what she offers to Jennifer's world.

Jennifer and Karen's reflections can help us see that when we accept that lingering racism is so deeply engrained that it emerges without conscious intent or awareness, we can witness ourselves without feeling like complete failures. Yes, we have more work to do. And we can see that continued openness to feedback is essential for our continued healing, since we likely will continue to have trouble noticing it on our own. At this point, let us ask ourselves the following:

- Has anyone ever suggested that your speech or behavior carries racist overtones? If so, how did you respond?
- How willing are you to invite colleagues to reflect and comment on how racism unconsciously emerges in your behavior or speech patterns?
- To what degree do you avoid cross-race conversations and collaborations due to fears about racial issues?

"IT'S ALL IN THE STORIES" (LUIS AND MICHAEL)

Luis Rodriguez (Chicano author of *Always Running*) and Michael Meade (white, mythologist) have been guiding voices in my life for over a decade. Many men have returned transformed from the men's retreats and conferences that they produce and facilitate. Participants in their events regularly come to understand issues of race, class, and community with a depth that allows them to create penetrating and lasting relationships across race and class barriers. Perhaps because of this, I was surprised when both of these men admitted that dominating whiteness and its privileges still penetrate their psyches.

Luis spoke of how living within a racist environment can breed feelings of inferiority. Yet Luis also discussed how he flips the script in some ways with a sense of superiority. Although there is a logical base for his feeling, Luis recognizes that any sense of superiority on either side is destructive, disempowering, and dehumanizing:

> Sometimes I feel superior to white people in general because I understand Western culture, but they do not understand me. I understand me. I understand African American, and the otherness. But I also understand them. I know that doesn't put me in a superior place. Maybe it just puts me in a strategically better position. Who knows what it does? But it does change my perception on dealing with whites because in many ways I think part of the struggle with white people is that, on the one hand, if you make them a monolith and hate them then you are almost making them superior to you. But if you tear them down and make them less than "human," you might think you are better than them, which is also not right. People do this all the time. Maybe they do this for their own survival, for their own defense. "I'm better than even this most privileged, powerful white guy. I'm still better than him even though I ain't got nothing."

As destructive as Luis knows this response may be, his response is a rather understandable defensive move, given that we live in a society dominated by images of whites as valuable and powerful.

Luis spoke specifically about how whiteness gets into his psyche:

> Oh yeah. It drives you crazy. You want to know why Blacks and Mexicans go nuts on people? It can drive you crazy. . . . Again, if it wasn't for the poetry, if it wasn't for the art, if it wasn't for the creative ritual space, it would be totally maddening. But those things help to address and alleviate things like this.

Here Luis spoke of his outlets, the ways he copes with living amidst penetrating whiteness. But this craziness also calls to mind an essay by Leonard Pitts Jr., *Crazy Sometimes*, in which he discusses how living with continuous racism while whites continually deny the experiences can cause one to begin to see it everywhere.[2]

Luis does not internalize the racist messages from the society to the degree that he consciously holds them as valid, but he still battles them regularly so that living within our society leaves him with intense anger.

Luis used a metaphor linked to his earlier work as a welder to explain his process of coping, his attempt to find balance, and the important role writing and poetry play:

> I have to temper my anger. I have to do two things with it. I have to temper it so it's not so fiery, burning everybody. But I also have to make it more precise. . . . I think the issue of being sharper is good, too. I envision this like a welder. You mix the oxygen and the acetylene gas until you get what's called the blue flame. This is the little blue flame in the middle of the larger white flame. When you get the mixture just right, this makes for the best cutting flame. Then you can cut through steel. That is what I think the Mosaic [Multicultural Foundation's men's conferences] events help me get to—to the blue flame. I'm still hot, I'm still angry, but I become more precise about how I deal with it. With story, with poetry, you really get to that cutting point. You don't obliterate the anger or the grief behind it, but you get more precise about how you handle it, and about what you're really getting angry at. . . . I hope maybe a guy like me can get to a place where we can't be angry like this. I don't think I'm going to get to that place. There is still a lot to be angry about. What I've learned, though, is to find a healing place for some of that. You know, the sweat lodge purifies and balances some of this. I'm learning more how to balance this anger. . . . I know the more I write, the more poetry I do, the more I am able, with all of my traumas and pathologies, to handle them better, to balance myself better in relation to these issues.

Luis' struggles with the effects of embedded whiteness continue, even after years of work and finding creative outlets for the intense anger the bombardment with whiteness inspires. Notice that although he hopes someday the anger can dissipate, he is not optimistic, as he sees little sign of an alleviation of the systematic continuation of white privilege.

There is no doubt that Luis' pessimism inspires a continuing recommitment to my work. In fact, it inspires additional resolve to proving that white educators *can* come together to heal ourselves so that we might demonstrate our capacity to match the dedication to healing Luis exemplifies. To paraphrase Shirley Better, we cannot dismantle systemic white privilege without white people working on the effort. We need more white folks to see what it means to be white, decide to actively do something to question the privileges bestowed, and organize each other in those efforts. White educators are uniquely situated to play a great role in this endeavor.

Michael, who rejected white culture early in life when he saw how it "forced homogenization" and "casts you out" if you go against it, depends upon his multicultural and multiracial network of friends and colleagues to help him avoid further internalizing whiteness as an adult. Yet Michael acknowledged that when left without these resources of perspective for a significant period of time, he finds himself subject to influence from the whiteness of the cultural surround, especially as regards media:

> Michael: TV is a great example. I need a break, but I'm always interested in stories. If I'm watching for a while I can start to think that the image of beauty is clean, thin, white, blonde. Then, if I suddenly see a woman who doesn't look like that I might not notice her distinct beauty. Or it could seem that the people in charge are white, that they should be because it looks that way. And there are assumed ideas. More of the people shown being arrested are nonwhite or all the rioting around the world looks to be Arabs or Africans or Mexicans. They don't show a bunch of white people doing some real damage as a group. They don't check in on the Ku Klux Klan. I don't think it's subtle really.
>
> Shelly: Now, what do you do when you are sitting alone, having watched TV for a few days, and catch yourself being infused with this emotionally, psychically? What starts happening to you?
>
> Michael: Oh, well, I usually start saying something to people and then I go, maybe I've been home too long. Aren't we supposed to go somewhere? Let's get an event going. Let's go get real people back together again. And it makes me realize that I've maybe isolated a bit. I haven't been on the phone talking with people or visiting with people. This stuff partially works on the basis of isolation.

Michael makes a conscious effort to reject dominating images of whiteness so as to guard against an unconscious embedding of them within him. And yet this does not mean that his conscious effort ensures the avoidance of all of the effects of living with the array of privileges whiteness offers in United States culture.

As we have already discussed, one of the results of living within our society is that most whites do not regularly examine issues of race. A result of this is that even people who spend years educating people on issues of social justice in terms of race and class miss moments where privilege emerges. Michael and Luis noted that, within their own conversations, Luis is the one who usually brings up issues of oppression:

Michael: One day we were talking and . . . you brought up something because it was on your mind or on your heart or both, and I was going, I gave a response, just what was occurring to me which had to do with the symbolic nature of it or something like that. And you said something about, "We've got to level the playing field. It's not even a level playing field." And I remember saying, "That's not the point. I'm not talking about a playing field. I'm talking about what's under the field." That's where I was at. And you kind of stuck with it . . . and I was anticipating getting into the conversation of the poetics and how the poetic images and you must have been coming out of, and I forget what the issue was but it had something to do with justice and having to do with oppression.

Luis: Which tends to be my thing.

Michael: Yeah. And the image you were carrying was leveling the social playing field so that everybody has a fair chance. And I wasn't alert to it. I was actually anticipating getting into the poetic conversation where nothing is level. It's all about movement and depth and height. And I mentioned it because, yeah, that's right, I didn't check in with Luis, you know, where he's coming from. I was just thinking about where I was going. And I think that would be, in your terms, a difference based on race and experience, and even privilege.

Luis: Perspective.

Michael: Because I realized that I wasn't worried about the playing field.

Shelly: Is that what you immediately go to?

Luis: I say it's my thing. The social justice issue is big with me. I bring it in some kind of way and I'm very much into that part of things. The funny thing about it is that when we talk about mythology and stories, sometimes you can be like, "Pay attention. What's that got to do social justice? What does that have to do with oppression?" Well, it has a lot to do with it and this is where you have to pay attention to that because he actually brings it in. It's all in the stories, right there.

Michael recognizes that his privileged position within this society can affect the direction of his conversation and thoughts in extremely subtle ways. Not feeling the need to continually raise the social and cultural issues to the foreground, Michael enters the mythic space more freely. This is contrasted by Luis' recognition that the stories Michael presents and works through within a mythic layer do, indeed, capture the social and cultural. Yet Luis also feels the need to speak about the issues more directly so that their participants do not to lose sight of them.

Taken together, Luis and Michael's experiences can help us understand the importance of being aware of how embedded whiteness not only affects us but also might live within our colleagues of color with whom we interact. Yes, we are trying to keep our eyes trained on ourselves. But there is also something important about understanding that living as a person of color in a white-dominated world has serious ramifications. Understanding how embedded whiteness emerges for all of us can help us better understand the dynamics playing out within racially loaded situations in our educational settings. After reading about Luis and Michael, we should stop to question:

- To what degree do you find yourself angry about how white privilege emerges in your life and educational settings? How do you respond to that emotion?
- In what ways might overexposure to media outlets affect your perception in racially prejudicial ways?
- How often do you raise social/racial justice concerns in conversations?

"I CAN'T GET PAST THE DYNAMICS" (KATIE AND LORRAINE)

Both Katie Gottfred (white founder of LEAP Learning Systems) and Lorraine Cole (African American CEO of YWCA USA) are used to working at the top levels of educational and health-related service organizations. Their decades of experience working across race in their professional worlds have also led them to management and administrative positions that require high levels of competency negotiating racially loaded situations. Striking is their ability and willingness to honestly admit the deep struggles and questioning they face as race continues to emerge in the foreground of their professional experiences.

As with Luis and Michael, the benefit of keeping issues of race close to consciousness emerges within conversations with both Katie and Lorraine. Recall that Katie has worked directly with African Americans for over 20 years in the Cabrini Green housing projects in Chicago. Crossing both race and class barriers on a regular basis, she has plenty of opportunity to grapple with these issues. Yet Katie recently found herself struggling to feel accepted at a benefit for Lorraine's former nonprofit, which was attended predominantly by African Americans:

> When I was at [Lorraine's] benefit last year, I found myself going around thinking . . . "How was I perceived there?" Maybe I'm more conscious of my whiteness now. I was conscious of "How are people looking at me?" "How are people perceiving why I'm there?" You know? "Do I belong?" And I was finding myself doing it, but at the same time I was asking myself, "Why are you?" But I kept telling everybody, "I'm Lorraine's good friend" so that I would be okay to be there. I was justifying my presence, like I'm really on the in. I'm not one of those do-gooders over there. I'm here because I'm Lorraine's good friend.

For Katie, a recently increased awareness of her whiteness makes her more anxious when interacting with a large group of people of color who do not already know her. She sees clearly the reasons for the rejection of white "do-gooders" and tries to distance herself from that image. The very real historical understanding of our past and continuing societal racism emerge for Katie in these moments to put her on notice that she too might experience rejection as part of that from which she prefers to feel distanced.

Another example of Katie's recent awakening to issues of whiteness and the unconscious, lingering racism she has residing within involved a situation in which Katie observed Lorraine go through an interview process:

> I saw [Lorraine] take total control of the situation, which at the time, I couldn't figure out what she was doing. Because, at the time, it seemed inappropriate for her to be doing that, and everybody, I could just feel the room reacting against how she was handling it. And I was surprised and didn't understand until later, after I read your proposal, that I said "Ah ha!" She was taking charge because she needed to. But if she had been a white woman who was taking charge . . . people wouldn't have made a judgment. It was the fact that this African American woman was taking charge of the situation even though they were very highly educated and saw themselves as very liberal. I saw them all reacting in fear of a Black woman taking charge.

Important to highlight here is not the charge that the rest of the group reacted against Lorraine taking control within the situation. Without their voices, that will always remain speculative.

But what we can see is that the basis for Katie's interpretation comes from *her experience* of the situation. Katie initially perceived Lorraine's approach as inappropriate. She felt the room reacting against Lorraine. She came to believe that it was the right approach and that Lorraine's race modified its acceptability only after more deeply considering whiteness and its unconscious effects while reading the proposal for my study. For Katie, this entire experience opened her eyes to how pernicious and subtle lingering racism can be, even within highly educated and socially liberal people, such as herself.

When given the opportunity to speak with both women together, we returned to this subject of the job interview to get Lorraine's perspective and to further question Katie about her initial response:

Shelly: What was your experience of what [Katie] had to say about all this? I haven't even talked to you about this.

Katie: It took me reading [the proposal] that I had this epiphany that this really was . . .

Lorraine: It was about race.

Katie: It was about race.

Lorraine: And first of all, let me go back, it was my fear going in, knowing the organization. I articulated more than once, am I going to be wasting my time throwing my hat in the ring?

Katie: Just to be a token.

Lorraine: I said I don't really have time just so they can check off on their affirmative action list that they interviewed one. So I only want to do that [interview] if this organization, if you think given your involvement with this organization, it has changed substantially enough that they are ready to truly consider me for the wonderful talent and all the things that I can bring to this organization. And then going through the process, and we can fast-forward to the final outcome and look at what they were looking for. Look at the qualifications. Look at what they said they wanted. They wanted someone who could take them to the next level. I was overqualified in terms of the specific qualifications that were required. I certainly had everything they wanted, plus.

Katie: Plus the imagination . . . and the fear factor was [there when] you took charge of the interview process.

Lorraine: I don't think that was it. I could have interviewed any damned way.

Katie: That's probably true.

Lorraine: And the outcome would have been the same.

Katie: They would have thought of a reason.

Lorraine: I know that. They would have made up reasons.

Shelly: Why did it take until my proposal to make you see what was going on?

Katie: Well, because I kept saying, "No, these people can't be. These are chairmen of their departments and whatever."

Lorraine: You know what other thing that was interesting was, that the concern later on that there was no white male interviewed. That says to me they were doing a little affirmative action checklist for the interview process, but they ended up hiring a person who represented the largest racial demographic group in the profession, who met none of the qualifications in the original job description, which is supposedly what they were looking for even in terms of experiences and direct management of budget size. So, based on qualifications alone, it was obviously not the person that they had originally said they wanted.

Katie: I wanted to talk about their unconscious fear.

Shelly: Did you think it was an unconscious thing, Lorraine?

Katie: That they weren't going to be able to control you?

Lorraine: Oh yeah.

Katie: I think some of it was unconscious at least.

Lorraine: And part of it too is that I could have played the game. I know I could have played the game.

Lorraine later noted that "playing the game" in that situation would have meant being "conciliatory."

What is perhaps most important about this exchange for the purposes of this text is the way that Katie was at first unable to recognize the subtle race dynamics, but then later learned how her perception was not quite sensitive enough. Her process illustrates that part of what can keep us blind is refusing to admit that educated people whom we respect might also have unconscious, lingering racism within their psyches too. This is an essential point for educators who are used to believing that we ourselves no longer carry any subtle racist tendencies. Of particular importance for our ability to witness is the admittance that we, too, have embedded and lingering racism locked within.

While discussing how unconscious the effects of race can be, Lorraine described an experience she had many years ago. This story illustrates how race can affect even the most basic decisions we make, such as how to maneuver around a city to go to a department store:

> Coming out of work one day with a white colleague, we were going to Marshall Fields, and instinctively I went left when we went out of the office building to State Street to take the L. She was going right to go up Michigan Avenue. My way, I wouldn't have seen any white people. Her way, which is the way I ended up going, she didn't see any Black people. So it's like even maneuvering around the city, it's strategic in terms of who you want to interact with. . . .
>
> And even the entrance to Marshall Fields that I went through with her seemed to be a predominantly white entrance. Now this just blew my mind that here this is the same store I've been going to for years, same city, same destination, going from point A to point B—but because I am a Black person, I typically go a certain way. If she went [that way], she wouldn't see any white people. I'm going her way, I didn't see [any Black people]. I thought 'this truly is segregation.' You can maneuver around the city from point A to point B and do it in a segregated manner . . . and not even realize it.

When considering the effects of white privilege and its embedded images, Lorraine offered a personal example of a time when the historic images of white women sitting on pedestals and Black women as Jezebel figures emerged for her so strongly that she left a meeting in tears. The experience occurred when Lorraine worked for a previous organization and a white, female board member publicly chided her instead of going through the usual channels of speaking privately with her boss and having him speak to her. However, it was not the criticism what was paramount for Lorraine. What was paramount was the intersection of racial and gender dynamics that were evident in the situation. The particular woman bringing the criticism was reputed as having highly questionable moral behavior. In stark contrast, Lorraine had grown up in a community and family in which the females strictly and consciously defied the negative stereotypes that have plagued Black women for centuries. So, the scenario of being a Black woman of high moral character who is being criticized by a white female Board member who had a reputation of being a "tramp" had stronger racial overtones than professional role relationships. Lorraine explained the trauma she experienced:

> Lorraine: To me . . . that was probably one of the most humiliating situations in life I can ever remember in life being in because, number one, I am sitting across the table from a tramp, a white tramp as far as I'm concerned, who is on the pedestal in the eyes of the world. Despite her reputation, she is the world's ideal. "Their ideal" is pointing her finger at me telling me that I'm flawed, telling me that I'm this and that and the other. She's putting me down. I just couldn't get past the dynamics to even deal with issues at hand that I considered all trumped up anyway. We volleyed back and forth and I felt that I refuted the issues. But that is not what bothered me about this scenario.
>
> Shelly: This historically gigantic issue.
>
> Lorraine: Yes. And I left that meeting . . . I mean, I was incapacitated after this meeting. I had to leave. Just reliving that, it was just incredibly horrible and I can say that I was just totally, totally wiped out after that.

Years later, what continues to make the experience so painful is not recalling the criticism. The pain is in the release of the historic and embedded images from their position under the conscious layers, the image of white women as pure innocents to be protected and Black women as promiscuous and readily critiqued. This is a poignant illustration of how deeply embedded the historic privileging of whiteness can be and how it can erupt without invitation, striking deeply regardless of one's consciousness of, or investment in, the ideas and images.

Lorraine's attentiveness to refuting these types of cultural stereotypes makes the eruptions of the images especially painful. Earlier in the interview, Lorraine mentioned her conscientious approach to work situations:

> Because Black women have had to endure negative stereotypes of being the Jezebels with low morals and all of that . . . that stereotype that only fast girls wore red fingernail polish. [I'm] constantly trying to refute those kinds of stereotypes about Black women, making sure that my dress isn't too short or anything like that. I just interviewed for a position not too long ago. I make sure that I have a long skirt when I interview so that when I sit down my skirt doesn't go up over my knees, wanting to make sure that I look even more than corporate. There are things you do with those stereotypes in mind.

From this account, we can see that embedded images of whiteness concerning gender issues continue to adversely affect Lorraine.

Some readers might wonder how these last two anecdotes, the meeting situation and Lorraine's approach to interviews, are related. After all, the woman criticizing Lorraine in the meeting was not pointing her out as being promiscuous or a Jezebel figure. The stated content of the situation was work related and, to some, this might make this association seem a stretch. But, the content of the speech is not the point. These issues are deep and affecting. If we dismiss the way historical images resurface and injure, we remain oblivious to what occurs as subtext within our dialogues and interactions in our work environments. Staying attentive to how embedded whiteness might play a role in our interactions can be helpful, but only if we can create environments safe enough to allow room for open discussion. Before moving forward, then, we should stop to ask ourselves:

- What are some ways that well-educated, white liberal people continue to act out racism and white privilege on your campus?
- How comfortable are you in environments where you are the minority? Do you ever want to distance yourself from liberal "do-gooders"? Why?
- How might images of historically significant racial stereotypes emerge within conflicts with colleagues in your educational settings?

"FILES THAT CANNOT BE DELETED" (BOB AND PERRY)

The image of white women linked with goodness has also affected Bob (white, cofounder of Project Return) and Perry (African American, coworker). One example included a time when Perry confronted a member of the management team at the nonprofit where they both participated in a community-building process. The conflict arose as Bob later challenged Perry on the appropriateness of his confrontation of the white woman:

Perry: But when he confronted me, I didn't say it then, but it came about. He's doing that because this was this white girl.

Bob: And my image of that is that there would be times when y'all would confront [her], but [she] was a lightning rod. But still, she was management. And I didn't think management—just in general, Black, white, take all that out of it—that management confronted like that. And what I did, I would hold back and hold back from protecting [these two women] because they were white.

Here we can see how easily our attempts to subvert racism can remain troubled. Bob tried to consciously subvert the historical privileging of white women within the community-building process by *not* saying anything.

Yet when Bob did raise the issue at a later time with Perry, Perry reacted to the situation as though Bob *were* privileging the white woman. In this way, although both men could discuss how their interpretations and interaction had to do with the effects of historical white supremacy during our conversation, their personal interaction at the time deteriorated when the underlying issues linking the situation to white supremacy remained unvoiced.

For Lorraine, Perry, and Bob, the emergence of the image of white women as holding a protected and honored place within the society affects their interactions. This is hardly new. bell hooks notes how white women are deemed protected and pure, while African American women are considered all things opposite when she writes, "devaluation of black womanhood is central to the maintenance of white supremacist capitalistic society."[3] This also links us to the discussion around the creation of the white self in chapter 3 where Toni Morrison links whiteness with the theme of innocence and newness within American literature.[4]

The consideration of whiteness as devoid of stain or corruption is a core feature of white privilege and clearly embeds itself within the psyche of many within our society. The testimony of Lorraine, Perry, and Bob demonstrate that simply rejecting this privileging consciously, and even acting to counteract its continuation, does not necessarily put an end to the painful way that it erupts, angering those whom the negative stereotypes have injured and frustrating those who would seek to end its hold. Without the capacity to be open and honest about these things, they fester.

Bob spoke extensively on what helps perpetuate the lingering racism within him. He spoke of "recordings": "We all get certain recordings when we're growing up. I believe this. Everybody has them doesn't matter where. From the ghetto there'll be different ones. . . . It's there and I think we've all got it. If you don't acknowledge it, you're denying it." He told of his experience coming to see racism as wrong and yet still not being able to turn off the voices that emerge from deep within: "I've always been able to hear the racist voices from being raised as a Southern Baptist and going to where I am now. . . . I can hear the old preachers saying, 'You heathen.'"

In response to a comment that it is difficult to find people who speak so candidly about being subject to these lingering effects of privilege and racism, Bob revealed that he himself is only just beginning to give voice to these issues:

> Bob: In all my years, I've only talked to people about it for the last three or four months and now that I'm, after 15 years of struggling with this, I'm realizing that it's not going to go away, and it's a discipline that I have to force upon myself and I think I'll always have to force it. I think I'll always have to force it. . . . Here's an example, and I've noticed this for years. If I'm watching the news, if a Black child has died, a Black teenager has been shot, there's a voice in me that tries to tell me that's not as important as if he were a white boy. And I have to say, "Oh, yes it is." I have to argue with that voice and say, "That mother loved her child just as much as if she were white." But I have to say that in order to, I have to make it as important. It's not automatic.
>
> Shelly: When did you realize that?
>
> Bob: Years ago. Years ago when I first started this work I would realize how much I cared about the people I was meeting, Malcolm, Perry, prisoners, Black criminals, and so on when I began to see who was really there and was making all these tremendous changes in myself. And all these changes were occurring. And yet these voices were still there. And I kept thinking, well eventually they will go away. But they never have. And it's just in the last few months that I've said, "They're just not ever going to. They're just not going to."

This admission reminds me of what might have occurred for whites while watching the fallout from Hurricane Katrina. How many white people unconsciously thought the situations were less dire because they were happening to a large number of Black people? How many white people were aware enough of their internal racism to consciously discipline themselves to stay focused on the trauma occurring?

Bob went on to describe what happens when he is not conscious of the "recording" that is playing in his mind:

> I sway from being oversensitive to, [during] times of stress, to being not sensitive at all, to reverting to my shadow, my worst side. So that's been my interracial struggle all along, to fight my way out of racism and turn off those voices and maybe, maybe it's going to help me to realize those voices are never gonna go away. They will always be my struggle. And that somebody else is just going to have a different kind of struggle.

According to Bob, these recordings and voices affect everyone, regardless of race. Yet he acknowledged that the script varies depending upon one's racial position and upbringing.

These voices affect Bob and Perry's work relationship. Bob began by attributing his sense of disconnection and mistrust between himself and Perry to these recordings:

Bob: There seemed to be a barrier I couldn't break down. There seemed to be something that was still there about, that was racist that was because I was white. And now, I start thinking, have begun to think, that it's the very thing that I possess myself. It's these old tapes that we've learned and that are just there. It's in the mental banks.

Perry: I said that yesterday.

Bob: It's on our hard drive and they cannot be deleted. They are files that cannot be deleted.

Shelly: Perry you're agreeing. What . . .

Perry: I said that yesterday, not in those same words, but I said that.

Bob: And I've said before, I will never ever get Perry's complete trust. There were times when I would say things and he would say something back to me and I would think, that's just that stuff. I didn't know what it was then. But I felt excluded because of my race.

Shelly: And the tapes that you're talking about, you have them, too? The tapes are that he's not trustworthy?

Perry: Yeah. Right.

Shelly: And he's got his own tapes that he was talking about?

Perry: And you know, it's not something that I run around on a daily basis with it up front in my head. But it's there. I mean, it just needs to be triggered. I don't know what the trigger is. Maybe he could say the wrong thing and there it comes. Just like I tell you, I walk in the courthouse. The minute I walk in there I see all these Black faces and I'm seeing Black and white then. It's there. It's just there.

Bob: Yeah, right, and I don't think it's ever going to go away.

And yet, while Bob sounds pessimistic here, in some moments he wondered aloud if there might be a way to break through the tapes of which they speak: "And I'm just wondering if finally bringing it out, and not hiding it anymore, the problem was that I was constantly hiding it. I was just battling it. . . . And I wonder if talking about it, like I have been for the last few months, is improving it, is having a possible effect."

From Perry's side, he did not use a label like "recordings," but Perry recognized that when he and Bob are in conflict, he is prone to imagine that Bob is thinking of him in racist terms. Perry noted that then he begins to see Bob in terms of his whiteness:

So Bob calls me in and talks about it. And he starts to get loud and he starts to turn into the white man. He starts to turn into the white man. And not 'cause he got loud, but I could see it coming that he's angry, that he's upset, and if I had to read his mind—'cause you can't hear what's on people's mind unless they say it—but if I had to read his mind, I would've said, "This Black motherfucker, this nigger, has done something I told him not to do." But that's what I would've said if I had to read his mind.

Clearly, with these inner scripts, these vestiges of racism erupting during moments of conflict, it begs the question, what allowed these men to continue their working relationship? As we continued our discussion, they offered a suggestion:

Perry: But you see what Bob has in the back, he says those seeds that were planted by his parents, his relatives, and me, that's gonna be there. That's always gonna be there. But you know what? I think that becoming conscious, knowing that it's there, and knowing that it's poison . . .

Bob: And talking about it.

Perry: And talking about it.

Bob: Acknowledging it.

Perry: And when you get into a situation that consciousness will make you better able to deal with it and work it out. You see?

While optimistic, this depends upon them being conscious in those moments. Yet these issues tend to arise during the moments when we are *not* conscious. This is all the more reason for us to develop a sense of humility so that we might be better able to receive critique and feedback from the colleagues on our school sites who challenge our behavior.

Overall, though, as stated in the introduction, optimism can play a tremendously important role in the success of educational work. Bob and Perry's honest, open, and thoroughly self-examined example of the type of frank dialogue that is possible offers hope about our future. The more that educators are able to name the dynamics they face and share them with each other, the stronger the likelihood that we will be able to create sustainable collaborative partnerships and make the changes we hope to implement in our schools. In the spirit of self-inquiry that Bob and Perry illustrate, let us ask ourselves:

- What racist "scripts" or "recordings" play out in your head?
- To what degree do you trust your cross-race work colleagues enough to share with them your struggles around your internal racial "scripts" or "recordings"?
- To what degree do you feel trusted by your cross-race work colleagues?

"I DIDN'T REALIZE I WAS HOLDING ON TO THAT" (AMANDA AND CAYCE)

Amanda Perez (Latina, founder of Adelante) and Cayce Calloway (white, photographer and youth worker) serve particularly challenging populations. Part of their work has involved negotiating with state agency officers, particularly law enforcement officials, in order to gain opportunities for youth who are learning life skills so that they can expand out of gang-affiliated social structures. Spending their time in the extremely diverse, and yet deeply divided, Los Angeles community has encouraged both Amanda and Cayce to witness their reactions to racially loaded encounters on a regular basis.

In some ways similar to Luis, Amanda spoke of the ongoing effects racism has on her self-confidence. The Eurocentric perspective that views

Western culture as (1) the epitome of evolution and (2) having unlimited possibilities and value, when looked at from the point of view of a person of color, is unforgivably false, demeaning, and dangerous. In a culture dominated by whiteness, those who are not treated as though they are white can internalize opposing messages of limited possibilities and devaluation.

Amanda recounts her difficult experience spending time with her first husband's family, a white family in a similar economic class position as herself:

> Amanda: When you're raised with racism it leaves, I don't know how to define it, but you feel intimidated, you feel less than and even though you meet them on the same plateau you still feel less than because of the way you came up.
>
> Shelly: So it wasn't even how they were acting toward you?
>
> Amanda: No. It was my stuff. But I couldn't be around them. I was not myself. I remember them telling me, why are you always so quiet? Why can't you? . . . But I couldn't feel it. It was like "I shouldn't be here." To tell you so much that my daughter came up blue eyed with blonde hair. My daughter. And when I saw her, I was like [gasps]. Talk about racism, my girl. People used to think I was the nanny.
>
> Shelly: Oh wow.
>
> Amanda: Yeah. And a lot of times it was good because I could get into places with her. A lot of times it was not.
>
> Shelly: Like she was the ticket to you getting in?
>
> Amanda: To certain places, yes ma'am. . . . I was like seventeen with a little blue-eyed, blonde-haired baby. It was crazy. So racism has always been a struggle for me and here we go again. I didn't know I was being racist with my child. She was my child. I love my child. You know what I'm saying? But there were issues there, not with her, but with the family, certain family, that I just couldn't identify it.

This sense of being intimidated around whites is not isolated to the family situation.

Amanda also discussed experiences passing through white spaces while traveling and how she coped with the emerging feelings:

> When I would leave town, even in the airport, and if you're like in Texas, in Houston, and you're catching a flight and it's all predominantly white, I

would feel a little bit intimidated and I would have to talk to myself. "You know you can get through this one. They are just like you. They are no different. Don't let them make you feel intimidated."

Although these experiences occurred in the past, Amanda recognizes that she still faces the same fear, intimidation, and self-critique when she goes on interviews today: "The only part I guess I struggle with when it comes to Caucasians is that when I try to get a job and it's a Caucasian person I have to fight that 'Oh, she's white so she's going to think she's better.'"

Recently, I spoke again with Amanda, shared with her some of the conclusions I have come to since our initial interviews, and she told me an additional story about one of her earlier jobs as an administrator at UCLA where she held a position equal to a group of white women. She recounted that her early experience watching her mother act as the maid for white people reemerged such that she began to act as a caretaker in her workplace and serve the other white women during meetings. We then discussed that as a white woman, had I been in those meetings, I might have interpreted Amanda's behavior as a culturally lovely way of being, as though she were simply being attentive to people's needs. I would have completely missed Amanda's discomfort and internal challenges existing within that space due to the differences of experience our lives offered.

The felt response in the face of whiteness that Amanda describes is not new. It relates to bell hooks' discussion of whiteness as terrorizing wherein she writes that "many of us pretend to be comfortable in the face of whiteness only to turn our backs and give expression to intense levels of discomfort."[5] For a white educator, this might be difficult to take. Yes, bell hooks can be understood as meaning that being around white teachers, professors, administrators, and staff can invoke internal feelings of terror in people of color holding whatever level of status or rank. We might defensively suggest that this is a reversed, negative prejudice that is essentially unfair.

Yet bell hooks effectively counters this argument when she says that this representation "emerges as a response to the traumatic pain and anguish that remains a consequence of white racist domination, a psychic state that informs and shapes the way black folks 'see' whiteness."[6] Although bell hooks speaks particularly of whiteness as terrorizing in the Black imagination, Amanda's experience is perhaps not fundamentally

different. bell hooks' analysis can extend to the experience of any person
of color still pained by living within a system dominated by whiteness. If
so, this also describes the ingrained intimidation felt by Amanda any time
she entered dominantly white spaces or when a white person appears in a
powerful position and can make a decision that affects her livelihood.

Amanda spent most of her youth within state systems wherein whites
held most of the powerful positions. With this in mind, it is no surprise
that Amanda describes her most serious difficulty with race these days as
when she deals with authority figures:

> My internal racism isn't so much color. My internal racism is against the
> cops, against authority. That's my second nature, I would say. So when I
> evolved in my own mind, I had to begin to work with them. I had to make
> myself talk to them. And I fight with that every time I'm in there and I have
> to talk to police officers. I have to be white because if I ever want to advance
> with what I'm saying I need to make friends.

For Amanda, whose primary work involves teaching former prisoners
skills to guard against future infractions and incarceration, interacting
with parole officers, police, etc. is a large part of her lived experience.
Notice also that for her, being able to speak with figures of authority
involves the need to "be white." She explains this as referring to her
speech patterns, dress, as well as other cultural cues that whites might
assume are normal, appropriate, or professional. But Amanda recognizes
that it is a way of being that helps her to "make friends" so that she can
accomplish her educational work.

While Amanda struggles against the eruption of an internalized sense
of inferiority in the face of whites in powerful positions, Cayce, like
Michael, recognizes the need to consciously refute the internalized
images of whites as symbols of authority. Cayce spoke of the effects of
embedded images of whiteness within her, even though she consciously
rejects them. Cayce shared how social conditioning results in her seeing
whites as authority figures and her struggle to move beyond this:

> Just the images of authority have white faces. Presidents, chairmen of the
> board, principals, teachers, they all have white faces. . . . I was raised so
> that Jesus looked kind of like my white husband, bearded and light-skinned,
> and God looked kind of like Willie Nelson. So I've tried to sort of rid

myself of an anthropomorphic God thing anyway. But it's still, that's in my head as well, this notion that the biblical images and the biblical stories. . . . Probably if we can really go back and look at . . . I'm sure there were no white people anywhere to be found.

Although this issue of authority is one that is very conscious for Cayce, there are moments where she continues to learn about her own lingering racism and the ways they affect her interactions with people:

> Cayce: I would have thought growing up that I didn't have a lot of preju-
> dices. And then I still will occasionally, something will happen and I'll
> be like "Ah, wow, I didn't realize that I was still holding on to that."
> Shelly: Could you name one?
> Cayce: When we were just on our honeymoon, we were in Amsterdam and
> there was a young Black guy who was the concierge in the hotel and I
> found him irritating. I thought he was insolent and was irritated by him
> because we'd ask him about something and he was not very helpful. And
> my husband and I talked about it later and he said, "You know, sometimes
> you're really hard on young Black men." You know, I was like "Really?"
> He said, "Yeah." I said, "OK." That was just one of those things that I
> had to think about and I said, "I can't stand that sort of angry, insolent
> thing that I see." And he said, "But you aren't that way with young
> Brown men." And so, I don't know, I think there's always been a fear
> factor there, not a fear that somebody was going to hurt me, but a fear
> that I wasn't going to be liked. You know, that fear that I could not ever
> leap over that wedge.

When asked if her negative reactions to Black men feel like some type of self-protective leap at being the first to reject, Cayce explained her sense of it this way:

> I'm just going to kind of be indifferent toward you before you can be indif-
> ferent toward me. So I think a lot of my issues around race come up in that
> way, in not putting myself out there. . . . I give Amanda full credit for the
> fact that we've been able to maintain a relationship because I would never
> have assumed that she would have wanted to. So when she did, then I totally
> opened up.

This comment is similar in some ways to Katie's fear of rejection at Lorraine's predominantly African American benefit last year. Katie's fears relate to her recognition of historical and current racism and how it affects some African Americans' interest in accepting whites. In the same way, Cayce did not imagine that Amanda would be interested in forming a friendship with her, a white woman. Yet Cayce's anxiety also involves generalizations about an "insolent" thing that bothers her in regards to young Black men. Perhaps important is that Cayce has had significant experience with Chicanos/as since moving to Los Angeles. However, she did not mention forming any close working relationships with African American men. This may have some bearing on her husband's observation concerning how she treats Black and Brown men differently.

Cayce also discussed how racial conditioning affects her perceptions of Mexican immigrants:

> The Hispanic people who choose to come to Los Angeles have this kind of deferential thing that goes on . . . this sense of an acknowledgment that there is a hierarchy. And when I went to Mexico City that wasn't there, obviously. . . . And I noticed it right away. I noticed it and it was so different and I was kind of surprised at the time that I didn't notice it here before . . . all these Hispanic people were walking around with the confidence that we walk around with here. And that was it. It was the very same attitude there that white people have here. It surprised me. I noticed it almost immediately.

Important to recognize is that Cayce was able to perceive that living within a system dominated by whiteness shapes the behavior of people of color only when she left the United States and visited a location where whiteness is not "normal." Then she saw that living within the whiteness of American society shapes her, too. This reminds us again that unless we are thoughtfully moving outside of our regular routines and boundaries that we are likely living with narrowed perceptions of our world and how we operate in it. This likely has serious consequences for our interactions at our school sites with staff, faculty, students, parents, and administrators that go unacknowledged.

Cayce also spoke of how she responds to her recognition that white privilege continues to affect everyone and that a conscious shift in behavior on her part is necessary:

> Given what I feel like is a regrettable hierarchy that we have, I try to make sure that when I am . . . in a situation with people of color that I don't in

any way try to act out that hierarchy. I don't like it. It's not . . . how I would like for the world to be and so I, a lot of times, will go into almost an area of deferring a little, particularly if I feel that I'm out of my own world. I am not the person who knows the most, and white people, a lot of times, don't allow for the fact that they don't know things, that there is this overall sense of "we could take care of these little Brown people if they would let us." It's bullshit. But it is a sense in the world . . . and I have a mask that sort of says, "I'm going to step back. I'm going to do what I'm supposed to do here. But I'm going to stand in the shadow a little bit because I need to in order for us to advance."

Amanda even suggested that Cayce's orientation helps their friendship:

Cayce: I try to find a real sense of respect and make sure that other people know that I have a real, profound sense of respect for where they're coming from.
Amanda: Actually that helped the friendship because I didn't see that [privilege] come out. She was just herself.

Although Cayce links her deference to a mask that she wears, something she does to fit the context, Amanda concentrates on her impression of Cayce as a person who normally approaches people with respect and deference. In this way, to Amanda the *real* Cayce is that deferring, respectful person. Amanda and Cayce's experience highlight how the continued existence of lingering racism does not have to mean that we cannot relate effectively with cross-race colleagues. In fact, our awareness can help us better manage our interactions in our educational settings. We should consider:

- Do you ever consider how our racial history might adversely impact the comfort level of faculty and staff of color in your educational institutions?
- Is it possible that you misattribute your colleagues' behavior as being a product of cultural differences, as opposed to patterns bred from discomfort? Do you share a close enough relationship with your colleagues to engage conversation around these possibilities?
- In what ways are you still holding onto old fears around race, particularly rejection?

"WHERE IS THIS COMING FROM?"
(LEE MUN WAH AND SPENCER)

Lee Mun Wah (Chinese American, producer of *The Color of Fear*) considers himself fortunate that he witnessed his father succeed in business in the face of oppressive whiteness as an adolescent. In contrast to Amanda's experience, Lee Mun Wah recognizes that his family's success helps him overcome some of the silencing messages of limited possibilities that characterize his earlier upbringing. This limiting is similar to Luis and Amanda's battles to overcome the "inferiorizing" effects of whiteness.

Lee Mun Wah spoke at length about the way whiteness is synonymous with loss for people of color, both materially and psychologically.

> So when they took all the lands of the Native Americans, they benefited from the land. When they made sure that only white people got to vote, they all got the offices and all the power. When they hoarded all the resources and took them from other people, they got to build these huge companies. And to this day, the loans are primarily given to white people. So they make sure they have all the money, the material goods, all the land and all the companies, so they can make all the decisions. And so they benefit, and their generations that have passed down also now benefit from all of that. And our loss is passed on to our children. Our feeling second class is passed on to our children. Our restricted dreams are passed on to our children.

As Lee Mun Wah spoke of his own childhood, he described two memorable experiences that brought him into awareness of his status as "other" within the society and the deeply ingrained way this knowledge of difference affects him. One situation involved an ethnic count at his school. His teacher announced that he was incorrect when he raised his hand as an American. She informed him that he was Chinese, not American. The second experience occurred when he got into a fight with a young Black girl and they both used racial slurs against each other. After recounting these stories, Lee Mun Wah offered this statement:

> Just because we don't talk about racism, we internalize it unconsciously somewhere and it comes up when we are scared or angry or afraid. And so those were two very key moments. And then my father told me that he

wanted to expand his restaurant, but that the woman next door who was white said that she would never sell it to a chink. And so I became more and more aware that as my father became more and more wealthy that it did not matter. Money did not change who he was. And that was a very profound lesson for me, because it probably makes me safer. . . . I say safer so I won't hurt myself being in situations where I think I'm just like anyone else.

Although Lee Mun Wah did not mention battling a sense of inferiority, he clearly still approaches life with the sense of being perceived as "different" than American.

Lee Mun Wah now consciously embraces that difference and expresses his pride in his Chinese heritage. Yet he retains a sense that he must be continually aware of his place as "second class" in whites' eyes to maintain safety and avoid emotional risk. Important to highlight is that safety involves remaining conscious of his difference even when he is in teaching situations where he has been invited to speak or run a workshop. His perceived need to be conscious of how white culture views him in order to be "safe" again calls to mind bell hooks' discussion of whiteness as terrorizing.

Unfortunately, quite often, even if white educators consciously attempt to make colleagues of color comfortable in faculty settings, we can do so in offensive and patronizing ways. For this reason, we must keep mining ourselves for our deeper angst and develop conversational skills around this subject. While perhaps obvious to some, this deserves explicit mention: Direct dialogue is generally more effective than well-meaning actions based on assumptions.

Moving forward, Spencer (white, entrepreneur and composer) spoke of how his upbringing remained ingrained within his psyche long after challenging the racism in his cultural surround as a youth:

Now, understand, I still had this underlying face that I was brought up to believe that Black people are scary and don't expect too much out of them. . . . I never questioned it, until I started questioning it. I still couldn't get rid of the voices, the conversations that just came out immediately. Oh there's clouds outside, is it going to rain? There's a Black person, should I cross the street? It was just a gut instant reaction.

This is similar to the "recordings" and "scripts" that Bob mentioned battling against after all these years. Spencer also spoke of the conscious work this struggle requires:

> As I got older and did a whole lot more work on myself, I started questioning all this stuff. Oh, . . . I'm having this reaction. I'm going to stay where I am on the sidewalk. I was challenging all these things that were coming up inside me constantly. This is bullshit. I don't believe this. Where is this coming from?

There is an entire range of experiences whites often face when we become increasingly aware of our racial position and its vast implications. These include guilt and shame, in particular. Their effects are present within some portions of Spencer's dialogue. Spencer does not speak directly of guilt, but he does speak of the shame he feels for both the historic and contemporary forms of racism engaged in by whites, including himself. He recognizes that his behind-the-scenes activities in the social/educational arena are a part of his response to this inner feeling. For this reason, this form of shame should not be seen as a deep, psychological battle, or a negative, pernicious emergence.

This approach stems largely from my perspective that a fair amount of negative affect is a healthy response to a newfound recognition of one's complicity in the contemporary maintenance of racial domination. Yet it is true that continued shame can lead to reactive violence, among other things.[7] For example, guilt can lead us to isolate ourselves from our colleagues of color because we do not want to face people who remind us of those painful feelings. For this reason, the guilt that whites carry needs to be managed and held in balance with an appropriately healthy sense of self.

Yet there is an area where Spencer battles a shame ingrained deep within the psyche, a shame built upon loss and dissociation. In a book titled *Learning to Be White*, Thandeka writes of a systematic conditioning white people experience that results in feeling disconnected from others.[8] She suggests that a deep shame develops wherein whites feel personally flawed. She links this to an inner conflict that results in a simultaneous sense of being better than *and* less than others.

This theory perhaps sheds some light on the challenges Spencer faces regarding his relationship with Native American people:

I always thought that you treated Native Americans with utmost respect. That is my spiritual or religious bent, so . . . I was always removed from it because I always felt that I was one down, you know, I'm not a person of the Earth like they are. I needed to untangle that. . . . I wanted to look equal, but I didn't feel equal.

Spencer's experience highlights the conflicting and contradictory internal conditionings some white folks fight to disentangle. On the one hand, the false messages of inherent goodness and the supremacy of whiteness remain embedded. On the other hand, a deep sense of shame and disconnection can reduce our sense of wholeness and intrinsic value.

Because this project intended to find people who could illustrate a life that appropriately manages guilt and shame, it makes sense that this issue is a small part of the experiences they shared. Yet this painful aspect of perceiving whiteness needs to be present. Guilt and shame are too much a part of the lived experience of white folks' moving through an increase in racial identity to be left out. We now have to stop and ask ourselves:

- How might lingering racism emerge in your educational practice?
- Do feelings of guilt and shame arise when considering your embedded and lingering racism?
- To what degree do you question your self-worth?
- Can you accept the idea that there will always be internal work to do to eliminate racism from your deep psyche?

SEEING IN THE DARK

We must admit to ourselves that no matter how hard we try, and however many years we struggle, racism lingers within us and bumps up against the general "American" sense of "progress" and the "can-do" spirit that many white people carry. We must guard against hopelessness, however. If we can face our deepest shadows, go willingly into the dark night of the new moon when Hecate rules most powerfully, we find that our power grows with increased consciousness.

As they say, knowledge is power, and we have much to offer when we harness our fears, honestly grapple with our internal psyche, and find ways to dialogue about these issues with our cross-race colleagues. True, lingering racism might continue to emerge as recordings or unrecognized blind spots. But as we saw with our storytellers, speaking our concerns aloud, seeking out healing connections, acknowledging the continuing effects, and making use of their messages to inform our actions can help us stay in touch with ourselves and others as we locate the next steps on our path. With this approach, our hopefulness, optimism, dedication, and commitment can truly help us become more successful collaborators and change agents in our educational and organizational settings.

Before closing out this chapter, however, appreciation must be extended to those who took the personal risk to offer such an honest expression of their experiences. Collectively, they offer self-critical and often painful testimony, allowing us to begin to understand the consistent effort necessary to liberate ourselves from lingering racism—in essence, to use bell hooks' phrase, "decolonizing our minds and our imaginations."[9] White folks are purposefully placed within the category of the colonized here, not to equalize the positions, but to reflect how the domination and colonization essential to the development of whiteness depended not only upon lower-class Europeans seeing themselves in terms created by the wealthy elite in order to solidify and protect our capitalistic system but also the development of an inner sense of shame and disconnection.[10]

In this way, part of the movement toward witnessing for white educators includes the decolonization of our own sense of self. This might occur through an honest acknowledgment of the ways that racism remains embedded within our psyches, is unleashed without our conscious attention, and continues to terrorize and shame all of us within our respective institutions. With this acknowledgment, we can work toward becoming challengers to the aspects of our educational systems that perpetuate disconnections and dis-ease.

NOTES

1. Obidah and Teel, *Because of the Kids,* 1.
2. Leonard Pitts Jr., "Crazy Sometimes." In *When Race Becomes Real*, ed. B. Singley (Chicago, IL: Lawrence Hill Books, 2002).

3. b. hooks, *Killing Rage: Ending Racism* (New York: Henry Holt, 1995), 78.

4. Morrison, *Playing in the Dark.*

5. hooks, *Killing Rage*, 37.

6. hooks, *Killing Rage,* 37.

7. J. Gilligan, *Violence: Reflections on a National Epidemic* (New York: Vintage Books, 1996).

8. Thandeka, *Learning to Be White: Money, Race, and God in America* (New York: Continuum, 1999).

9. hooks, *Killing Rage*, 50.

10. Thandeka, *Learning to Be White.*

Part III

THE WORK OF WITNESSING WHITENESS

Chapter Eight

How Do We Witness?

Once educators decide to include taking a stand against racial injustice as part of their practice, the question to ask is, how do we do that? What exactly can we do to effectively witness in our professional and social lives? One key is recognizing that witnessing is a verb, an action. We have to *do* something.

A second key is that we have to become responsible, or better yet, *response-able*. Moving from intellectually understanding racism and white privilege toward developing an educational practice that effectively deals with race requires us to have the *ability* to *respond* to what we see. This type of *response-ability* means engaging the journey toward becoming antiracist activists in both our lives and educational settings. This is required since developing knowledge without a shift in action simply reinforces our role as bystanders. Witnessing, therefore, requires movement, some action that brings us at least one step closer to ally work.

To be realistic, the primary work for educators heading toward ally activities begins with personal investigation, learning, and practice among close relationships, students, and colleagues. As we become increasingly competent, our circle of influence will expand. For this reason, this chapter concentrates on educators' personal development and the initial contacts and supports we need to take our first steps. A level of humility is essential as we enter this dialogue, as is the recognition that most of us have a long way to go before we can confidently and consistently enact an effective antiracist practice. However, as we build our witnessing practice, over time we can become more successful change agents at institutional levels.

To start off, developing the ability to respond to racially loaded situations can be really challenging when newly coming to see the effects of race. If we are going to take a stand, we need to feel prepared to deal with our own sense of discomfort and potential resistance or rejection from others. For this reason, we need an action plan to guide our development. This chapter outlines four main categories of actions educators can take in order to develop and support our efforts at witnessing.

To offer a brief introduction, we need to continue to *build knowledge* and make use of knowledge gained. We have to *build skills*, a set of tools we can use when witnessing either subtle or overt racism. Many of us also feel intense emotions when dealing with issues of race. We must *build capacity* to make use of our skills in the face of our emotions, a process that takes courage and practice. Finally, we need support to continue to practice these skills during moments when we feel confused, disappointed, or frustrated. For this reason, part of witnessing also includes *creating community*, consciously developing a community of people around us who understand our striving, reinspire us when we fail, and celebrate our successful efforts.

This chapter suggests that educators make use of each of these four elements—building knowledge, skills, capacity, and community—in order to transform our teaching practices. I imagine Hecate watching over her cauldron, her magical elixir offering transformative power, insight, and capability. Here, however, I see each educator taking up Hecate's position, creating a personal recipe from the list of essential ingredients offered.

Successfully taking up a witness position requires the addition of each ingredient into the mix of our individual brew. Although tempting to attend to each category in a defined sequence, one after the other, this can lead to difficulty. Especially as educators, we could easily concentrate on building knowledge for an eternity, never feeling ready to take additional action. Therefore, my recommendation is to take up Hecate's position with creativity, working with each element simultaneously. In this way, each aspect supports the work of the other, creating a balanced recipe for the creation of an educational practice that begins to subvert systematic white privilege and racism.

BUILDING KNOWLEDGE

If we do not know much about racism and its relationship to whiteness, then we cannot do much about racism or white-skin privilege. There are several ways to advance our vision regarding these issues, each of which deserves some attention. We can examine the whiteness of our own lives, continue our study, seek diverse informational outlets, and expand our base of experience.

Examining the Whiteness of Our Lives

What do we need to examine? First, we need to notice how deeply our daily experience is embedded within whiteness. This involves questioning where we go, what we encounter, what we fear, what we avoid, and so on. What follows is an initial series of questions that we can ask ourselves to get a sense of how evident racial segregation is in our lives—in essence, how white are our lives? The questions in this section are best used as an activity (with emphasis on the *active* in activity). Take the time to write down the answers to each of the questions in exercise 8.1.

Take a moment and review the answers to the questions in the exercise. Now consider the following questions:

- When do my surroundings inspire me to think about what it means to be part of my racial group?
- When does my environment challenge me about my race?
- Who or what raises questions about race for me?

At this point, we can remember the analogy regarding whether or not fish in a fishbowl notice the water in which they swim. For white educators particularly, if whiteness dominates the majority of our environments, this indicates that we likely have difficulty seeing the whiteness around us. The answers to the previous questions then offer us clues as to the areas in which we may be so thoroughly entrenched within whiteness that we gain a relatively limited perspective.

When reviewing my own answers to the questions above, I noticed that my most segregated environment is my workplace. Although the student body where I teach is extremely diverse, the faculty in my department is composed exclusively of white women. What this means is that even though there are explicitly stated intentions to bring social justice into our program and to be conscious of ourselves as racial beings, I and my colleagues quite likely have blind spots regarding our curriculum and teaching styles.

Exercise 8.1.   How Segregated Is My Life?

- What is the racial makeup of my surroundings?
  - My family?
  - My housing community?
  - My place of employment or educational institution?
  - My place of worship?
  - My various social circles?
  - My favorite entertainment centers?
- Are any facets of my surroundings racially diverse?
  - What makes a place diverse?
    - What percentage of white folks are in these diverse places?
    - What is the percentage of different racial groups in these diverse places?
    - Which racial groups are absent?
  - How often do white people dominate my environment?
    - When do I experience places where 50 percent or more of the population is composed of people of color?
  - Am I ever one of only a few faces in a crowd of my racial background?
    - Where? How often? How do I feel in these situations?
- Are there areas of my city that I avoid?
  - If I do avoid certain areas . . .
    - Why do I avoid these areas?
    - What do I imagine it would be like to live in these areas?
    - Who are the people who live there?
    - Are people who look like me often negatively affected in these areas?
      - How do I know?
      - What sources of information do I rely upon?
    - What do I fear might happen if I go there?
    - Are my fears based on media reports?
    - Am I willing to believe that wonderful events take place in these areas that are worth attending?
  - If I do not avoid certain areas . . .
    - Are there areas of my city that are predominantly populated by people of color?
    - What makes me feel welcomed in these areas?
      Do I know people of color who live in these areas?
    - Does going into areas occupied primarily by people of color affect my perception of the world? If so, how? If not, why not?

Just last year, for example, a workshop at a conference on white privilege alerted me to some problems with a particular text used in one of my courses. Even though I had already noticed enough problems to have carefully picked and chosen the elements used from the book, I now realize that the level of scrutiny needed was beyond my understanding at that time. Since then, I have decided to check in with some of my teacher-friends of color when developing new material. Their eyes bring a different sensibility that might help me increase my own vision regarding these things.

Of course, since segregation still marks many of our work and social spaces, many of us might not have a close colleague to turn to for this kind of help. Building relationships with people willing to serve in this capacity might take significant effort and time, and might not even be available at all. However, we must at least begin by recognizing the importance of making movements toward appreciating the helpful and important nature of feedback from colleagues with different sensibilities.

Another way to examine the whiteness of our lives is by looking critically at ourselves to see how we relate to the various associated meanings of whiteness discussed in chapters 3 and 6. To take but one example, whiteness is often associated with a segregated lifestyle that avoids the struggles faced by many people of color. How true is this for each of us?

Impossible to miss is that many of the questions posed in exercise 8.2 might appear more associated with socioeconomic class than race. But please recall from chapter 1 that whiteness is often associated with achieving middle-class economic status. Separating out the effects of race and class is a real challenge in a society that purposefully enacted racist systems, policies, and procedures in order to concentrate prosperity in the hands of white people. In other words, witnessing racial injustice also includes examining the effects of systems adversely impacting the working poor and impoverished, regardless of race.

Most activists emphasize that working to end one type of oppression requires the common work of challenging all dominating systems. For example, we should know that white folks from lower socioeconomic strata suffer plenty of hardships and that the steps that lead to their advancement can also work to support people of color. However, we can simultaneously recall that this is a society in which a disproportionate number of those at the bottom rungs of prosperity are people of color. The

---

Exercise 8.2.   How Comfortable Are the People in My Life and Myself?

Have I, or anyone I know socially, ever . . .

- Experienced fear-inducing harassment based on race at work or while walking on the street within the last several months?
- Lived in a place for over a year where the majority of people did not speak my or my friend's native language?
- Received an education primarily featuring people of a different race?
- Worked for minimum wage?
- Taken a job illegally paying less than the legal minimum wage?
- Had wages withheld illegally?
- Requested unemployment benefits?
- Applied for public assistance?
- Relied exclusively on public transportation to get around?
- Been unable to acquire health insurance?
- Relied on overcrowded health care facilities?
- Heard gunshots in the night on a regular basis?
- Had a family member impacted by street violence?
- Feared the police, health-care workers, or other public servants?
- Had to appear in court?
- Spent time in prison?

2005 annual report from the Census Bureau on national income data, for example, revealed that 24.9 percent of Blacks live below the poverty line, 21.8 percent of Hispanics, 11.1 percent of Asians, and 8.3 percent of non-Hispanic whites.[1] In essence, we cannot disregard the importance of the above questions simply because they are tied to socioeconomic class since race and class so often go hand in hand.

Yet the importance of linking race and class issues goes beyond simply identifying them as interconnected. Noticing the degree to which our lives shield us from certain difficult experiences is essential in recognizing where our gaps in knowledge may lie. Let me offer an example to illustrate. I recently sat in a meeting with Gloria Killian, a woman who served over 17 1/2 years in prison for a crime she did not commit and whose story and work are featured in the documentary *After Innocence.* Gloria is not a one-sided speaker. She understands why many rules are necessary within institutions and she offers praise for those who treat people fairly. But the story she told detailing the inhumane treatment that often exists in prison, including the recent death of a friend occurring as a result of active neglect, both saddened and horrified me.

Why tell you about this woman upset about the death of another woman in prison? How does hearing her story relate to witnessing racial injustice? Simply, Gloria's story is important in improving our ability to witness racial injustice because she helps us understand the unfair, and sometimes ridiculously inane, treatment and policies encountered within a system that disproportionately impacts people of color. If we do not come into person-to-person contact with someone with her background, we likely would not think of such things. But if our lives include sitting with those who suffer under the weight of troubling systemic policies, we are more likely to feel inspired to support those who do the active work for reform in areas such as criminal justice, health care, education, public transportation, worker's rights, immigration, welfare, etc.

Coming into contact with Gloria did not occur because of my normal work or social routines. In order to look beyond my own diverse classroom environment, I have to go out of my way to attend meetings and events that highlight experiences of people that do not normally enter my networks and social circles. Living in a fairly segregated city, making the time to enter intentional circles where people of different class and race backgrounds come together in dialogue requires effort.

Doing this leads me to listen intently to those who experience the world differently than I do and then to examine myself. This has been invaluable in helping me understand the immediate need for large-scale policy change, changes that go hand in hand with racial justice efforts. With this broad understanding, I am also in a better position to recognize the issues faced by my low-income students and their parents, predominantly people of color, who struggle under the weight of many of the policies currently in force.

Now, let me ask readers this question. As you read about Gloria and pictured her, what image came to your mind? What racial background would you assign to her? Would your reading of the last two paragraphs change if you learned that she is a white woman? Would it make a difference if you learned that her friend who died was also white? Would you be surprised? If so, why? The answers to those questions are extremely important. The answers tell us a lot about how we have been conditioned to see both prisoners and people of color.

One more question. Is it possible that, as bad as Gloria's experience was, it could have been worse had she been a person of color? What if she had *not* been a law school student prior to her incarceration? What if she had *not* had the skills to know how to speak effectively with prison guards and wardens? What if those guards and wardens held racial prejudices? Considering these questions can highlight the ways that someone can sometimes experience disadvantage due to one social position, such as their gender or socioeconomic status, while simultaneously benefiting from white privilege.

Yet, there is more. When Gloria offered feedback regarding my telling of her story, she asked me to include the fact that she was raised in an upper-middle-class family and received a solid education growing up. Important to her is that this text names that she, herself, experienced significant discrimination within the prison because she was seen as a privileged white woman, one who guards saw as needing to be controlled and put in her place. This is not to take away from the questions posed above. Gloria is absolutely clear that racism remains a serious problem. But what she wanted me to highlight is that this experience allowed her to feel "viscerally" what it was like to be abusively discriminated against because of her background. She indicated that most whites do not ever have that opportunity and she said that this experience helps her understand the battle against racism more deeply.

A third way we can examine how our racial position impacts our lives involves honestly reflecting on the ways that our white-dominated social world has played a role in our personal and collective achievements. Since our country tends to operate with an individualistic point of view, we tend to discount or overlook the variety of beneficial influences we receive in our own lives. We need to look at some aspects of privilege that can be so subtle that they commonly go unnoticed, the way our social networks have influenced our accomplishments. Again, slow down and take the time to write down the answers to the questions in exercise 8.3.

An important point to highlight here is that our personal accomplishments are hard-fought and require much effort. Personally, I am very proud of my grade point averages, degrees, awards, and job positions. My successes depended upon my own striving, dedication, and perseverance.

Exercise 8.3.   Who Helped Me Get to Where I Am Today?

- Recall the elders, parent's friends, coworkers, coaches, mentors, teachers, and so on who made a difference in your life.
  - How did these individuals help you? Did anyone . . .
    - Give you a tip regarding a job opportunity?
    - Facilitate you meeting someone in a position of power?
    - Encourage you to complete an application for something?
    - Put in a good word with a boss or advisor?
    - Write you a letter of recommendation?
    - Spend extra time or offer extra attention to help you learn something?
    - Let you know that your accomplishment is important to them?
    - Inspire confidence in your abilities?
    - Get you a good deal on a major purchase?
  - How often was that helpful, supportive person of the same racial background as you?
- Think of the various authority figures that made decisions related to you and your future. Recall the landlords, loan officers, hiring committees, admissions officers, government workers, counselors, and so on.
  - How did their choices affect your life? Were they a part of you . . .
    - Being accepted into an educational program?
    - Contacting college or employment offices?
    - Getting a job?
    - Securing a place to live?
    - Knowing about funding or scholarship opportunities?
    - Moving quickly through a difficult bureaucratic moment?
    - Receiving a loan?
  - How often was that person making decisions of the same race as you?

However, also true is that I am not solely responsible for achieving these things.

Doors swung open for me easily. Beyond my parents, there were many individuals who helped me get to where I now stand. My coaches, teachers, mentors, and friends at various times, and in various ways, helped ensure that hard work did not go without reward. At times, benefits came from those who mentioned that I reminded them of themselves in their younger days. Other times, benefits came from open doors bred from social connections to which many would not have had access.

Further, benefits came from the fact that my entire racial/socioeconomic/cultural background was similar to many of the decision makers in my life, such that I could easily inspire ease and a sense of camaraderie in an interview setting. Again, true, race and class cannot be completely separated. But I benefited from the fact that our white-dominated society often influences people of color, through *internalized racism*, to trust the abilities of white people over those of people of their own background.[2]

I inspired no subtle fear and was not perceived as potentially threatening or challenging by decision makers of any background. No one imagined that my presence might be disruptive or that my personality style might be too bold. To be sure, as our society increasingly sees people of color attaining positions of prominence and power, these disparities also see a shift. But benefits surely came to me due to the entire racist history that portrays whites as more likely holders of knowledge and power.

After all, when looking broadly at the power positions, such as in politics, corporations, organizations, educational institutions, and social support systems, white people continue to occupy high offices at disproportionate levels (exceptions and improvements notwithstanding). It should be no surprise that, in a society based on historic inequality, the benefits white folks derive from social contacts would tend to reinforce already existing power inequities. This social capital need not be transferred consciously.

In fact, quite likely, none of the teachers, mentors, or decision makers in my life consciously tried to reinforce a racially unequal power structure. The reinforcement occurs by default, with white young people far more likely to profit from social networks inhabited by socially powerful adults than young people of color. Recognizing this, we might begin to understand why teachers who make statements referring to a "level playing field" or asking students to "pick yourself up by the bootstraps" can sound more like defensive denials of reality than constructive advice.

Let me reiterate that admitting that I received help in no way takes away from my accomplishments. Rather, examining the full story of how I came to occupy my social positions helps me recognize how racism and whiteness continue to affects people's lives and highlights that there are many who do not enjoy the same help. If this is a difficult thing to admit, we should ask ourselves, why? What does it mean for us if this is true?

Admittedly, examining the role of our racial placement in our lives can sometimes leave us with more questions than answers. What does it mean if the majority of our input comes from segregated experiences? What if our lives do not invite deep connection with people whose stories are significantly different from our own? What if we have developed a rudimentary knowledge of the impacts of race, but do not see how that might alter our own previously held understanding of politics, economics, and so forth? What if the angle of this analysis simply does not satisfy all of the questions inspired? One answer is to seek out additional sources of information.

Continuing Our Study

Books, compact disks, lectures, book talks, videos, documentaries, and periodicals are just some of the ways that we can continue learning about race, whiteness, and their impacts on our psyche, educational practice, and society. This book is meant to open us up to the idea, explain why we have a role to play, and get us started on the path toward witnessing. As a broad introductory text, there are a lot of important subjects that have been either treated rather superficially or skipped altogether. But if we wish to develop a truly comprehensive view, each of us needs to build knowledge on a variety of subtopics. These include:

- Our roots (ethnic, familial histories upon which we can ground our sense of self)
- History of the white supremacist system
- History of resistance against white supremacy
- People's history (multiple threads, many groups, stories white folks generally ignore)
- White privilege (continued investigation into its meanings and manifestations)
- White racial identity
- Interconnections between race, class, gender, and so forth

Locating essential texts in each of the above areas is important in order to avoid a myopic view of how to notice racism and work to counter its effects.

Additionally, what follows is a short list of extremely helpful resources that you might choose in order to advance knowledge building beyond this book.

- *Why Are All the Black Kids Sitting Together in the Cafeteria?* by Beverly Daniel Tatum is a bestseller for a reason. Easy to understand, yet provocative, this book highlights the different paths toward racial understanding taken by various groups, including whites. Do not let the title fool you, however. This text can help white adults understand their own process as much as it informs us about what occurs with young people in schools today.
- *We Can't Teach What We Don't Know*, by Gary Howard. This text is explicitly written for educators and offers a concise and helpful approach to questions of racial identity development for white educators.
- *White Like Me: Reflections on Race from a Privileged Son*, by Tim Wise. This author stands as one of the most well-known and popular speakers on the issue of white privilege in the United States today. His style is easily accessible and he has a keen ability to link personal story with contemporary and historical examples of racism.
- *The Heart of Whiteness: Confronting Race, Racism, and White Privilege*, by Robert Jensen. This short, pocket-sized text offers a critical look at race and racism, using personal narrative to illustrate issues of white privilege and why white folks can benefit from confronting this issue.
- *When Race Becomes Real: Black and White Writers Confront Their Personal Histories*, by Benestine Singley. This collection of short personal narratives by thirty of the best-known authors on race is powerful. Its structure makes it especially useful for those who want to hear from various viewpoints in short intervals.
- *Uprooting Racism: How White People Can Work toward Racial Justice*, by Paul Kivel. This volume is perfect for people who see the need for action and who want more tactics and information on a wide range of specific issues. For example, how can we take a stand on issues such as education, affirmative action, the police, religion, and public policy?

There are also taped lectures or public events where you might continue this aspect of the journey. Internet searches for any of the above authors or subjects quickly put you in touch with a wealth of information. There are also many websites devoted to uncovering racism and white privilege. Most include links and suggested authors and speakers.

Seeking Diverse Informational Outlets

The information received through text, lecture, and audio sources offer a foundational understanding. We then build upon that understanding when we make use of new knowledge to find linkages in our day-to-day world that might affect our student's lives. How are issues of race reflected in our city, state, and country today in ways that might impact our students and colleagues of color? We can then listen to the events in the news with a more critical ear.

For example, witnessing would include taking notice of a story about a car insurance company considering shifting its policies so that the neighborhood in which a driver lives becomes less important than the individual's driving record when determining premium rates. For a long time, those living in poorer neighborhoods with high crime rates have paid higher premiums than those living in wealthier neighborhoods, regardless of driving record. My experience has demonstrated that this can have serious impacts on our school classrooms in that when the students' parents' abilities to purchase car insurance is adversely impacted by such unfair policies, the spiraling consequences of that struggle can be disastrous for the stability of students' lives.

If we are paying attention to that news report about the car insurance rates, we might find out that what is prompting the considered change is pressure from groups claiming that the current policy discriminates against people of color. We might recall that a policy such as this would disproportionately impact people of color since more people of color are concentrated in poorer areas. Then, we might determine that an effort to dismantle one example of white privilege is underway, an issue that although seemingly unrelated is actually very related to the lives and well-being of our students.

We can choose to be a witness to this move and support the change, perhaps writing a letter or making a phone call to add our influence. If we pay close attention to various other items in the news, we might start to see other areas in which policy decisions might have racially discriminatory impacts. Yet, to do this, we might have to investigate further. Mainstream news coverage might not always offer an analysis that allows us to see the racial impacts.

Our regular news sources do not likely offer us a full accounting of how race plays a role in the events portrayed on the news. In fact, given that the vast majority of whites tend to believe that race is an issue of the past, our mainstream media tends not to link the current issues with their relationships to race. Seeking out diverse informational outlets can support our efforts to learn how current issues relate to race. Sources can include people, community leaders, radio news, websites, or news magazines that speak and write from either a social justice or minority perspective. Some examples might include:

- *Multicultural Pavilion* (website)—www.edchange.org/multicultural—a website that offers links to social justice news and other educational related issues.
- *Democracy Now!* (radio program)—www.democracynow.org
- *Counter Spin* (radio program)—www.fair.org—a weekly half-hour show offering a critical look at the issues covered by mainstream media.
- *Global Voices for Justice*—www.globalvoicesonline.org—a news hub where they cover international issues by having reporters from various countries writing about the issues. This is a good international resource to hear about struggles going on globally from folks on the ground.
- *Color Lines*—www.colorlines.com—a magazine that covers progressive activist and organizing focused on people of color issues in the United States.

Certainly, we might not agree with all opinions that come from these programs or websites. That is to be expected. But, hopefully, we know that opening ourselves to see an issue from a different point of view can help us better understand how the policies we vote into law might affect those from whom we are isolated.

Once we expose ourselves to voices often pushed to the margins, we can look at the mainstream media with a slightly different eye. We can then begin to ask ourselves the following series of questions on a regular basis:

- Which racial groups would primarily benefit from a proposed policy, regardless of intention?
- Who are the promoters and decision makers on this issue?
- Are there any subtle allusions to race made using race-neutral speech but racialized images? For example, does the news story make reference to a social problem and link it with images of people of color at the same time?
- Is this issue one that affects primarily whites or people of color? If the issue affects primarily people of color, whose are the dominant voices explaining the situation?

Sitting alone to reflect on these questions might prove ineffective if our knowledge base remains thin. Reading and self-questioning only take us so far. Perhaps the surest way to build knowledge is to get out into the world in a new way and seek out new experiences.

Seeking New Experiences

The suggestion to seek out new experiences also comes with an acknowledgment that not all environments are equally instructive. We would do well to pick our entries into new spaces with some care and attention. To enter any new environment blindly, with assumptions of easy admission, acceptance, and potential learning, actually can be an enactment of privilege in itself. My suggestion, therefore, is to consider environments that offer an instructive, yet provocative, learning space. We might also need to openly ask about the potential for guidance and support. What follows are a set of environments that I have personally found to be most conducive in gaining new knowledge.

Where should we go?

Individuals

Who are the people available in your life? Are there individuals on your campus or in other social groups who might expose you to a new way of seeing that you have previously kept at arm's length? Would you be comfortable telling those persons what you are trying to do and asking for direct assistance? Although there is a definite risk of rejection, sometimes a person will offer the benefit of the doubt, and the result can be beautiful.

Recalling my own experience, about eight years ago I approached a colleague at my school site, an African American woman, and mentioned an issue that perplexed me. Why had I developed deep relationships with men of color, but had no women of color as friends? I shared with her my concern about this and my hope that she might be willing to talk with me. This woman recently told me that she initially found the idea a bit strange but decided that it would not hurt to help out this sincere-appearing white girl. Almost a decade later, she is now one of my best friends and remains a primary collaborator on several educational projects.

Community Events

Where are people of color coming together in your city? What programs are running? Where might there be community displays of art, dance, theater, film, or poetry? My attendance at Voices of Youth events, evenings of poetry put on by youth of color speaking about their experiences surviving inner-city life, have opened up a whole new way of seeing young people. I walk away from those experiences both profoundly saddened by the violence and death that mark their young lives and also inspired by the resilience and courage they display.

Each event inspires more commitment to supporting programs offering young people opportunities and second chances. If you have never heard inner-city youth speak out about their experiences, you are missing something profound. Depending upon your location, there might also be social justice-oriented educational gatherings that intend to raise awareness for those in attendance. Do not be shy. Ask someone there to explain something you find confusing. More often than not, those who attend these events are more than willing to offer some information, especially if you share your interest.

Museums, Art Displays

Exhibits and programs that concentrate on evaluating or displaying the history of a particular group of people of color can also be an important vehicle for filling in our knowledge gaps. Our learning in these spaces largely depends on our approach. Do we take someone with us with whom we can discuss what we see? Or do we simply observe images and displays allowing us to see the history of other's experiences? If we choose this forum, we can challenge ourselves to keep this question at the forefront of our minds: How does this particular history inform the present?

Workshops/Retreats/Classes/Speakers

There are a number of groups offering workshops specifically oriented around raising awareness related to white privilege and racism. Colleges might offer classes, and smaller bookstores often host guest speakers. The trick is keeping our eyes out for these opportunities. There are also retreats that bring together diverse groups in an effort to find essential connections as they simultaneously face social divisions and inequities. For men, Mosaic Multicultural Foundation's annual six-day retreat is a great example. For women, Unity Bridges, a young, grassroots group in Los Angeles, produces three-day retreats on a biannual basis. These retreat spaces generally draw approximately 80 to 100 people per event.

Conferences

Larger, more formal conference spaces can also offer educators a great source of new learning. As more and more people recognize the need to confront issues of white privilege, more educational conferences related to social justice that specifically deal with race and whiteness have developed. A favorite is the White Privilege Conference, which is held near the last weekend in April each year. This conference brings together upwards of 800 people per year. The keynote speakers are generally some of the best-known thinkers and writers on the subject of race, and their insights can propel a year's worth of study and investigation.

Faculty Development

If the local community does not offer sufficient opportunities, and traveling to a conference is impossible due to cost and time constraints, another option is to advocate for faculty development experiences to be held in your district or on your campus. There are plenty of speakers and facilitators who offer workshops about race and privilege designed specifically for educators. Speaking with other faculty and approaching your administrator as a team and offering a clear vision for the needs, purpose, and goals for the workshop might help facilitate bringing resources to you.

What Makes a Good Learning Space?

To be honest, learning about racism can invite painful experiences. White folks' long history of ignorance and neglect on this topic rightly infuriates many. It is only fair to acknowledge that white folks are likely to run across people who are ready to share their pain and anger in ways that inspire discomfort for many of the white people in the room. Although it can be healthy to confront feelings of guilt and emotional pain as we move into a deep recognition of our collective history, we might want to check that the environments we choose have an understanding that awareness and healing are some of the goals.

People of any background should be on the lookout for a stated purpose when choosing new learning spaces. What is the shared intention for people coming together? Are the people you speak with in tune with that purpose? If activists are planning the event, to what degree do they recognize that race is not the only lens worth utilizing?

What follows is an example of the types of explicitly stated purposes that readers might look for when choosing a class, workshop, or conference. This list comes directly from the advertisement material related to the White Privilege Conference, and demonstrates the clear thinking and acknowledgments that help to bring together a collection of people who are invested in challenging the status quo, learning, and healing.

1. It is not a conference designed to attack, degrade, or beat up on white folks.
2. It is not a conference designed to rally white supremacist groups.
3. It is not a conference just for white folks; WPC is open to everyone.
4. WPC is grounded in the historical premise that since America was founded for and by white people, white privilege is a historical and current reality.
5. WPC is a conference designed to examine issues of privilege beyond skin color. WPC includes diverse voices and perspectives to

provide a comprehensive look at issues of privilege, including race, gender, class, sexuality, disability, and so on—the ways we all experience some form of privilege, and how we're all affected by that privilege.

6. WPC is an exciting conference that examines the challenging concepts of privilege and oppression and offers solutions and team-building strategies to work toward a more equitable world.

7. WPC attracts students, professionals, activists, parents, and community leaders/members from diverse perspectives. WPC welcomes folks with varying levels of experience addressing issues of diversity, cultural competency, and multiculturalism.

8. WPC is committed to a philosophy of "understanding, respecting, and connecting."

Building our knowledge base requires us to *look within* to examine how often white spaces dominate our lives and *look without* in order to seek out new sources of information and experiences. If the thought of attending a class, lecture, workshop, or conference on this topic inspires reticence, we should ask ourselves why. What do we have to lose? Book learning alone, with no action, simply does not move us any closer to healing ourselves and deepening our relationships with cross-race students and colleagues. True, we might feel nervous because we do not yet have the skills to engage in dialogue. Knowledge without skills does not do us much good. So building skills is another ingredient we must add to our mix.

BUILDING SKILLS

Once educators see the issues surrounding racially loaded situations more clearly, what do we do? How do we put our learning into action? How do we speak to our students, family, friends, colleagues, acquaintances, and strangers who do not recognize that our racial placement is meaningful, racism continues, white-skin privilege exists, and racist jokes are problematic? How do we conduct ourselves with students and colleagues with whom we would like to talk about race? In essence, what tools can we use in anxiety-provoking moments? This section focuses on two main areas of concern. One, we need to have some practiced options to use when speaking with our students, friends, family, and colleagues. Two, white educators need to find ways to learn from people of color without reenacting white privilege.

Speak Up—Naming the Problem

There is just no way around the fact that witnessing requires us to use our voices. If we see racism, we have to name racism. There is also no doubt that, for most of us, this is easier said than done. They are bystander moments, times when we get caught off guard by some comment that we cannot believe we just heard. At the same moment, we might be trying to sort through (1) What are the issues surrounding what this person is saying? (2) Do I feel safe enough to say or do something? And if so, (3) How should I respond?

All of these questions are important, but they can also immobilize us within the conversation or situation. We can get caught like a deer in the headlights. We sometimes become still, mouth agape, so confused that we often end up simply smiling strangely, perhaps muttering some type of disagreement under our breath, but otherwise just trying to get past that uncomfortable moment. These moments can also occur very rapidly, which only adds to the difficulty.

One of my most remarkable bystander moments occurred while I was in Washington, D.C., to conduct interviews with Katie and Lorraine. The diversity of the city impressed me. For the first time in my life, I ate at a fancy restaurant that catered to a relatively affluent, African American clientele. I have yet to see this at home in Los Angeles. One evening during the trip, on my way down to meet Katie in the hotel lobby, I entered the elevator, scooted around a few people and positioned myself near the back. An Asian American man was at one side and five or six white folks were in the center.

Apparently, I entered in the middle of an ongoing conversation because one of the men said to another couple, "Well, it is just nice to be with white people again. I mean, it's like you can't get away from them here. They're everywhere." He went on to say a few more rather objectionable things that I cannot recall. But, by the time I got my head wrapped around what he was really saying, the "ding" sounded, the elevator stopped, and the man and his group walked out. The couple the man had addressed said something about how the man using offensive speech must have been drinking and just as soon as they made their comment, they walked out of the elevator. The Asian American man had slipped by me quickly as well. I then stood there, alone, not quite sure what to do. Katie stood before the open elevator doors, and I just slowly walked out and said, "I can't believe what just happened."

The entire event surely took less than 30 seconds. Easy consolation comes by saying that there had not been enough time to say anything. And true, the situation did happen rapidly. But it is also true that a practiced repertoire of responses would have allowed me to be less immobilized and more able to say something to bear witness to the racism before me. Even though the man might not have dialogued with me further, the racism present in that moment could have been named.

The next section offers a set of approaches we can practice to develop responses to moments such as these. Moments where something really ought to be said can occur anywhere: at home, at school, at work, with friends, at parties, at church, out for coffee, in a restaurant, on the bus, in airports. Really, anywhere can be a place to let someone know that something said or done is mired in some level of racism or privilege. We might struggle with how to do this at first. But as my father always says, practice makes perfect. Besides, the more we practice in our day-to-day lives and in our classrooms, the easier it becomes to take action with the officials in our educational institutions where the personal stakes might be higher.

Practiced Responses to Racism

Here, we concentrate on person-to-person contact. Some might consider this a more basic form of witnessing than writing a letter to a supervisor or calling an administrator to complain about discriminatory practices. However, witnessing racism in front of another individual, even a student, can be far more daunting for many people. For that reason, we really do have to ask, how do we respond when faced with racially loaded comments or jokes that we recognize as objectionable? What follows are a series of effective strategies that we can practice.

Questioning

This approach asks us to speak in a way that gives people the benefit of the doubt, acting as though they could not possibly mean what they appear to be saying. For example, when a person offers an analysis that appears either subtly or overtly racist, we might respond with a question such as, "When you say _____, it sounds like you are saying that _____, but I am not sure if this is what you mean?" This offers the person an opportunity to reflect and perhaps alter his or her speech.

If the person truly believes in prejudiced ideas, this approach surely will not change his or her point of view—but at least it might disrupt the conversation enough for the speaker to find out that prejudice is not welcomed or acceptable in your presence. This pattern can continue as needed, with the questions becoming more explicitly challenging. We might actually have to say, "I'm sorry, but that sounds rather prejudiced. Are you comfortable with sounding that way?" The essential idea is simply that we act a bit dense, as though we simply cannot believe that an intelligent person would ever say something with such obvious racial overtones.

Educating

This approach asks us to make use of the knowledge that we gain and try to inform the people around us why their statements are troubling for us. Note that this approach is not called lecturing. Instead, we can make short statements, such as, "You know, when I hear what you are saying, it reminds of when I thought something similar. But then I read something that made me realize that _____." Or, we might say something like, "Hey, I know sometimes the media makes it seem like that, but I found out recently that _____." In both of these sample statements, we avoid directly naming either the person or his or her speech as involving racist elements.

Depending upon the need and our own comfort, we can go father. We can say, "Hey, I am sure you don't mean it this way, but it sounds like that idea comes from a perspective that can be seen as pretty racist." With this approach, the words we say may or may not be heard. The person may or may not continue with the subject, stick around to continue the dialogue, or feel comfortable with us. But, whatever the result, we have let that person know that we are not someone with whom he or she can safely speak using racially derogatory speech.

Express Personal Emotional Reaction

This approach asks us to tell a person making racist comments or jokes what it is like for us to hear those things. By letting the person know how we feel, we are avoiding directly challenging the content of what is being said, but instead asking the person to respect who we are and notice that his or her speech is not OK with us. We might say something like, "When you say that, I feel _____ and that makes it hard for me to be here with you." This approach can be especially effective with people close to us because we are not directly challenging the content of what the person is saying as much as the level of respect existing within the relationship. If these folks care about us, won't they want to make sure that we feel good about spending time with them? At least, that is the question we can ask to try and get the person to shift his or her use of language.

Empathetic Relating

This approach asks us to invite the person speaking to imagine how he or she would feel if a similar negative statement were applied to him or her. We might respond to a racist comment or joke by saying, "Wow, when you say that, I can't help but imagine what those folks would feel if they heard that. Can you imagine what it would feel like if people were sitting around talking about us like that? What if they were teasing about the way we . . . ?" (Here, we might include something that we sense might be a meaningful stereotype that is used to injure). We can then ask, "Wow, how would that make you feel?"

Repeated Opportunities

Even with these strategies, we might not always respond perfectly. Some-times we still might get confounded. Other times we might feel unsafe. Still other times, we might realize that we are up against a losing battle. There may be some serious power issues at play. Are we willing to challenge our senior colleagues or administrators in our workplaces? Of course, if we are serious about this, we would like to find some way to do this. However, the degree to which we respond always depends on the context, who is there, the relationship we have with the person, and how much time we have at that moment. However, when we do see an opening, having some options to draw upon can help.

Lastly, we also can give ourselves permission to return to a person once the situation has shifted and deal with the issue at a later time. For example, we might return to a student or colleague and say, "You know, yesterday (or last week) you said _____, and I just want to ask you what you meant. I felt _____ hearing it and wanted to check in with you about it." We can choose to question, empathize, educate, or express our own feeling. But this way, even if we miss a moment, we still see that there might be a chance to respond once we have developed more clarity about the issue and a plan of approach.

Important to acknowledge is that these approaches are not necessarily designed to change the mind of the person with whom we are interacting. A person we challenge might develop a new awareness depending on our ability to explain ourselves, the openness of the person, and a myriad of other factors. But this is not a how-to-change-people's-hearts-and-minds guide. The effort here is about naming what we see out loud in front of our close family, friends, students, and colleagues so that we at least offer everyone the *opportunity* to see things in a different way.

Going Deep in Conversation

Speaking up in front of family, friends, students, and colleagues can often be the most challenging situation. If we enjoy dialogues full of debate, confrontation, and open acknowledgments of feelings, we likely struggle less. However, many white folks have been trained to be rather reticent to express the types of difficult emotions and pains that disrupt the status quo. As painful as it is to admit, I know this is true not only within my own family but within the majority of my white friends' families as well. Also, recall that some of those interviewed spoke of their white families needing everything to stay "tidy," "neat," and "sanitized." To the degree that we feel this to be true of our own relationships, we might struggle more to witness in front of the white folks in our lives. To get a sense of this, we might want to ask ourselves these questions:

- Do you fear that confronting and/or discussing racism and white privilege within your family or on your campus will cause you to be treated differently?
- Will your family shut you down if you start talking about race at a family dinner?
- Can you already imagine the kind of negative responses you might face?
- Do you fear that you will lose your standing with some of your friends if you challenge their racism or unrecognized white privilege?

Our intuition and fears might tell us a lot about our potential to deal honestly with this subject. On the other hand, they might not. If we have never engaged in this type of conversation, armed with our newly acquired knowledge and skills, how do we really know that we will not be heard? Perhaps we can invite the dialogue in a way that reveals more possibility than we currently imagine. This is perhaps the most essentially personal area. No one knows our relationships better than we do. Each of us needs to evaluate the possibilities for ourselves and follow the path that feels right. Yet we should not rest too comfortably before at least attempting to push the margins a little bit to investigate areas where there might be an opening. Here are a few ideas to consider when witnessing within our closest familial, teaching, and collegial relationships:

- *Begin slowly.* No need to speak out on every new piece of knowledge all at one time if our friends or family are not asking for more. These are our closest relationships. We have plenty of time to initiate these folks into this way of seeing the world. Besides, jumping in too quickly might very likely only push them away.
- *Speak from the heart.* Refer to recently acquired information and how it has been personally affecting. Ask only for them to listen and to try and understand why you feel as you do.
- *Demonstrate excitement.* If we offer some of our new realizations with excitement and interest, we stand a better chance of getting peo-

ple on board. A sudden shift into anger alienates and makes our journey less appealing.

- *Challenge sensitively*. Using the previously described strategy of expressing our personal emotional reaction to statements can be extremely helpful when we need to challenge something said within a dialogue.
- *Be humble*. Becoming angry with our families, students, and colleagues for not seeing issues of race as you do is a sure way to get shut down and turn them off.
- *Pick battles carefully*. Some people just are not ready to hear what we have to say. Reserve energy for moments when our efforts can make a difference. Retreat and come back a different day, or a different year, depending upon the individual.
- *Plant seeds*. Know that we plant seeds every time we witness actively. We might not see immediate results, but some new epiphany might be growing in someone that will someday emerge, even if we never see the tangible results.
- *Extend the invitation*. Invite family, friends, students, and colleagues to join this journey with you. Give this book as a present to someone. Ask someone to watch a movie that features a racially provocative theme with you. Invite someone to attend a culturally or racially diverse art show, musical performance, or other event with you. Find a way to both follow your teaching standards *and* deal with race simultaneously. Ask questions and prompt conversation to see what people are thinking.

My hope is that these strategies for engaging people in dialogue and ideas for how to witness within our most sensitive relationships empower each reader to make the material in this text come alive. Even if we begin with fits and starts, as we continue to practice standing up against racism, we internalize these skills and make them our own. Once this occurs, our ability to explain how being part of our racial group makes a difference in our lives improves and, simultaneously, so does the effectiveness of our explanations.

I remember the time period when deciding that whiteness would be the focus of my dissertation. One night I sat at a family dinner absolutely petrified that either my parents or our family friends would ask about my topic. They did, and I blushed and blundered, saying as little as possible to keep from having to say more. Since no one knew anything about the topic anyway, they all let it drop, probably glad that they were not mixed up in that type of academic pursuit. That was only five years ago. Things are markedly different today. Speaking about issues of race and white privilege now feel natural. My parents even consented to be editors on this project, and my father now brings up examples of white privilege he notices. The next time our family friends question me about my work, they will get a more confident and extensive explanation.

This practice with my closest family, friends, students, and colleagues has now expanded such that I no longer suffer any discomfort when race becomes a topic of conversation at my school. This level of ease with the subject is directly related to the amount of effort made when *not* at my school. In this way, witnessing is *not* simply about our educational practice. Witnessing is a comprehensive approach to our lives that *improves* our educational practice. But at the same time that my ability to talk with white folks needed improvement, there has also been a long road traveled to improve my ability to interact successfully with my cross-race students and colleagues.

Listen Up—Inviting Dialogue in Diversity

Some of us enjoy a diverse set of teaching and collegial relationships. Perhaps we discuss race on a regular basis, but perhaps we do not. Others of us have never had real, honest, and professional relationships with anyone but other white people. For those of us in this position, we might be more nervous about trying to start a conversation about race with someone we only know on a professional or surface level. Wherever each of us lies on this vast spectrum of experience, hopefully at least some of what follows will prove helpful.

This book generalizes what it means to be white in order to create a picture of a certain reality to which white folks are generally oblivious. My hope is that the white folks reading this are now able to at least see the outline of how being white benefits us and are motivated to spend additional time seeing ourselves through this racial lens. For us, this is usually a departure from the norm, and we can readily return to our vision of ourselves as individuals without a stake in racial identity.

On the other hand, society regularly pushes people of color to see life through a racial lens. If white educators take up our efforts at witnessing in ways that reinforce that push, we further the problem rather than act as part of the solution. In other words, white educators will do a better job witnessing our whiteness if we examine ourselves in terms of some generalized patterns of behavior common to many white folks. Here are a few things we should know about how our group is experienced:

White People Can Be Incredibly Rude

How would you feel if a stranger walked up to you, began to touch your hair, and asked you how it got that way? Most people I know would be outraged at the audacity of someone disrespecting their personal space and asking personal questions without permission. Unfortunately, white folks regularly offend people with these sorts of approaches. Not too long ago, one of my Black female friends called me to ask, "What would make this white woman feel that she had the right to touch me like that?" She had been in a campus bookstore waiting to pay for an item when a white woman approached her from behind and began to touch her hair. My friend was honestly perplexed, outraged, and a bit hurt, and hoped that I could help her understand the behavior of this white woman.

The sad part is that this white woman probably thought that she was simply demonstrating her acceptance and interest. Unfortunately, what we really reveal in these moments is our ignorance, disrespect, and privilege. We have to really question ourselves about how we approach people. Can we see how our approach might unwittingly dehumanize? Are we conscious of the degree to which we ask people we hardly know to trust and accept us? Do we ask permission before we attempt to enter a personal, racially loaded dialogue?

White People Can Be Too Self-Focused

Many of us have so much hidden anxiety and emotion over race that we sometimes try to push relationships too quickly. When my collegial relationship with three Black teachers at my school initially formed, I was thrilled. I enjoyed their company and was honored that they invited me to join their monthly gatherings. However, at our monthly dinners, one of the women hardly looked at me when she spoke. During those moments, I felt invisible and wondered if she did this consciously. I took it rather personally and almost decided to end my participation until one of the women prompted me to just relax and let the trust build slowly. As it turned out, as my sincerity and interest were demonstrated over time, the relationship became stronger.

White folks can all too often get stuck in our own heads and forget that the people we are building relationships with might also be moving through difficult territory. We have to be ready for someone to say "No thanks" to our collaborative efforts without feeling personally insulted. History has given a lot of people good reason to be wary of white folks, especially as it relates to social and racial justice work. If we can get out of our own head for a while and see that we are not the only ones taking risks, we stand a better chance of getting through the rough spots.

White People Often Treat People of Color Like Objects

When we become oversensitive to race issues, we run the risk of treating people more like racial beings than human beings. There are two aspects to this difficulty to which we need to pay attention. First, we must be careful not to turn people into representatives for their race. If we are curious about an issue, we can consciously ask the question, "How do you feel about this issue?" or "Would you be willing to share how this issue has affected you?" instead of "How do people of color feel about this issue?" Although seemingly simple, this is the type of thing we can forget about when our own anxiety gets the better of us.

There is also nothing wrong with telling a person that we are a bit embarrassed or feel nervous about admitting our lack of knowledge or experience on certain topics and are looking for a different viewpoint. The essential point is to remember that at the same time that we recognize that living in the United States offers different experiences for people of color and white people, each of us also has a unique experience that must be honored.

A second aspect to which white folks ought to be attentive is that we should assume nothing about another person's experience. At times, my group of white colleagues, in our attempts at subverting racism, can sometimes drift into assuming how our students or colleagues of color will feel in a certain situation and alter our behavior in an attempt to solve a problem that we do not even really know exists! My suggestion is that we need to use our sensitivity to raise questions that we then check out with people, instead of imagining that we already know how another person feels. Basically, we should check in with individual people to find out if what we imagine is true for that particular person. Doing this can help us avoid a tendency to enact a type of caretaking for others in a patronizing way that disrespects people's personal power and decision making.

White People Can Be Both Vulnerable and Strong

Sometimes white folks have to extend our hand and keep it humbly extended in the face of refusal. After first meeting Jennifer Obidah, the African American professor who co-authored *Because of the Kids*, years before inviting her to be a part of my dissertation project, she chose not to participate in a dialogue series on which I was working. She said that it did not fit with her interests at that time. I accepted her refusal without question. However, that did not stop me from recognizing what an amazing source of feedback she might be.

Although Jennifer thought that her critiques would frighten me off, I returned and asked her to speak with me at a later time, admitted my sense of inadequacy, and stated out loud both my hopes and my fears. I asked her for her guidance and named my interest in hearing the truth, even if it would be challenging. Over time, a relationship grew so that she is now not only a mentor but also a friend. When we meet, our conversations around issues of racial work are part of our personal sharing, incidental to our relationship, no longer primary. Showing my vulnerability to her while demonstrating my resolve to stay with the issue helped build the trust we share.

The above set of suggestions can hopefully help those of us without much experience move into respectful dialogues with diverse groups within our classrooms and educational institutions. But being actively engaged with the people in our lives sometimes requires additional skills. The most essential skill is listening. We have to listen deeply. There are two key aspects that might make our listening more effective. However, developing our capacity to really enact these suggestions follows in the next section. Briefly, if we choose to engage people in dialogue regarding their experience with race and white privilege, we can do the following:

First, white folks need to *dismiss the devil's advocate*. I still fight this one. Just months ago when going out to dinner with one of my teacher-friends, she took offense to the behavior of our waitress, interpreting her actions as racist. I did not. As my colleague described her interpretation of the situation, I found myself trying to poke holes in her theory and challenging her view. In truth, there is no reason to believe that her explanation is not accurate. There are no facts that can offer conclusive evidence. My only honest argument against her interpretation is that if I were that waitress, I might have mistakenly done the same thing out of a misinterpretation of the situation.

In other words, my questioning of my colleague stemmed from my identification with the white waitress. In defending her, I defended my imagination of myself acting in her place. Thankfully, I am now at least semi-attuned to this process and stopped myself before doing serious damage to our relationship and was able to shift my approach to ask my friend to elaborate on her felt sense of the situation. From my experience thus far, arguing facts and possible misinterpretations gets us nowhere. Listening to the felt experience of our students and close colleagues is far more important.

Second, white folks need to *value new information*. Hearing critical feedback is not easy for any of us. When I first got challenged about the ways my lingering racism emerged in my conversations and behaviors at school, my frustration emerged on a regular basis. Sometimes it felt as though I was walking on eggshells because everything I said or did seemed like a problem. Looking back at that time period, I am really happy that I stayed in those difficult conversations and tried to find the truth in the critique. Even when I wanted desperately to dismiss opinions that did not resonate for me, I could not escape the fact that my colleagues were telling me that I was acting similarly to the majority of white educators they encountered. I can now see how that information is priceless. If we can sit with new information about ourselves and soak it up even when personally offended, we can learn so much more.

Developing these skills is essential. And yet, there may well be times when our own capacity to sit in the moment to absorb the information offered will be challenged. It is during those times that we will rely on the various ways we can build our internal capacity.

BUILDING CAPACITY

Take a moment to imagine a time when someone verbally challenged you. Sit for a minute and reflect on how the scene played out. Did you feel anxious, stressed, confused, or angry? What did you do with your feelings? Did you express them in the moment? Did you start to concentrate on the feelings more than what the person was saying? How did you overtly respond? Did you argue back, seek the nearest escape route, or complain to a supervisor, colleague, or friend? Or, did you instead simply dismiss the criticism in favor of labeling the person crazy? Were you able to stand in that moment and calmly hear what was being said? Did you have the capacity to listen attentively, offer some type of apology as needed, and dialogue about how you both could resolve the situation?

Now imagine a conflict that involves a high level of intensity (if the previously imagined situation did not). How would you respond if the person displayed a lot of emotion and raised his or her voice? Have you ever been in a situation where the criticism became generalized so that the person suggested that you *always* make this mistake, and not only that, but *everyone* like you does the same thing? Has critique ever started to feel not only uncomfortable but also unfair?

Personally, my immediate tendency is to want to escape and then dismiss the critique. In my better moments, I can approach the person later and admit where I see the truth in what he or she said. But my defensiveness arises rather easily. Managing my inclination toward avoidance takes a lot of effort. On the other hand, one of my teacher-friends is spectacular at standing in front of angry colleagues, remaining calm, searching for a common goal, and moving things forward in a way that acknowledges everyone's emotions and reactions. She is a sight to behold, her emotional maturity offering me a valuable model.

Please take note that none of this necessarily involves race. Emotional maturity is a hard-fought commodity for anyone, regardless of race, class, age, or culture. We should reflect on the answers to the above questions in order to locate the areas in which we need growth. This internal work is essential if we are going to be successful when we (1) teach in diverse classrooms and (2) engage in cross-race collaborations with some of our colleagues. Here is why.

If we already know that we have difficulty handling conflict, how much more difficult might it be for us when we add to the above scenario the simultaneous pushing of all of our emotional hot buttons regarding race? Since white folks have overwhelmingly been able to avoid facing race issues in the past, there are a lot of emotionally charged, unreleased, unheard, unwitnessed emotions just waiting for us when we invite dialogue with people regularly brutalized by racism in this country.

Our ability to move toward better cross-race teaching and collaborative relationships depends on our capacity to witness the angst, really pay attention to it, even if it appears personally undeserved at times. Ultimately, as a group, white folks have been protected for so long from certain types of critiques that our skin can be rather thin. In this respect, witnessing asks us to develop some coping strategies so that we can handle tough situations.

The essential question dealt with in this section on capacity building is, *how can we develop the ability to stay receptive during moments of challenge?* None of us is perfect, and inevitably, we will make missteps that call for critique. To the extent that we develop relationships with students and colleagues of color who are highly perceptive and sensitive about race issues, we will find ourselves taking some heat. Depending upon the level of pain or anger and personality style of the person with whom we share relationship, we might receive more direct and fiery heat than we are comfortable handling.

We need to be able to withstand these difficult moments in order to (1) respect the relationship, (2) put our skills to good use, (3) learn something new about ourselves, and (4) become witnesses to the anger, frustration, and pain that eats at many people of color in this country. Let me restate, in case this point is not clear: Building our capacity to witness is as much about our own education and growth as it is about being helpful contributors to larger, collaborative educational reform efforts. My deepest hope is that when white educators increasingly witness the expression of people of color's rage and grief, something positive can result for each side. What follows is a personal story illustrating my increasing capacity to withstand the heat of challenge.

Creating a Strong, Healthy, and Permeable Sense of Self

A recent experience helped me clarify areas of additional internal work. This is a story about a dinner among colleagues. The hostess, Ms. Moussa, is an African American elementary school teacher who lives in Los Angeles. She is maternal, strong, savvy, and a veteran teacher who carries an authority about her that people respect. Near the end of winter in 2005, Ms. Moussa invited a group of three younger African American teachers over for dinner, former colleagues from the elementary school where she teaches. Among them were Keisha and two of my best teacher-friends. Since I had also taught alongside all four women years earlier and got along with each of them, my friends invited me along, with Ms. Moussa's permission. We met on a Friday evening after school.

Conversation flowed easily throughout dinner, as we each spoke of our current projects, school, life changes, and future collaborative ideas. To some degree, there was a feeling of homecoming for me, not having been with some of the women for several years. The mood was jovial and warm. After dinner, we settled in on Ms. Moussa's long black leather couch to watch an *Oprah* episode featuring members from the cast of the movie *Crash*. After the show ended, dialogue began and my friends and former colleagues offered commentary on pieces that they found either interesting or troubling, and how they related it to their experience of the world. I participated, and then went one step further.

I began to offer criticism regarding the show featuring only the African American and white cast members, noting that race issues in the United States often wrongly become dichotomized in this way. One of my friends gently reminded me that Oprah is not a political figure and that she simply featured the most well-known celebrities. Instead of letting the point drop, I continued to speak on an area I considered problematic about the movie itself. In a city where approximately 40 percent of the population is Latino/a, to have only one rather thinly developed character representing that population seemed an area worthy of critique.

Without awareness or intention, I had stepped all over some deeply felt opinions and feelings within my former colleagues. Ms. Moussa began to instruct me about how African American issues are, in her opinion, the most important ones upon which we ought to focus due to the intensity of the history between African Americans and whites and its long-standing and continuing ramifications. For a while, I tried to explain myself, offering reasons for why I said what I did. I tried to speak about the need for each group to work together for the benefit of the whole. As I continued, Ms. Moussa's responses became more personally revealing, at times showing anger and frustration. Finally, Ms. Moussa made it clear that she is really primarily interested in working with her African American community. That is her focus because that is where there is the most intense need.

In this situation, my critique demonstrated my ignorance of the intensity of this need. Simultaneously, my critique of the show's guests had unwittingly stepped all over Ms. Moussa's sense of purpose in the world. Realizing this, I tried to explain *my* intentions in the world, my hope to raise awareness within white folks to battle racism and that in order to do that my orientation was best served by having a broader focus. As we continued talking, my sense was that we seemed to reach a mutual understanding, perhaps hard-fought, but respected.

Keisha also took issue with what I said and spoke on a more deeply personal level of the suffering she sees around her on a daily basis, the pain she experiences firsthand, and the inescapable tragedy continually swirling around her. For what seemed like a very long time, Keisha spoke of experiences that I knew nothing about, pressures and pains that cut her to the core, and how my perspective reminded her of the inequity and injustice that surrounded it all. There was nothing for me to say. I sat, listened, and nodded in agreement.

Throughout it all, my two best friends sat silent. Throughout it all, I wanted desperately to escape. Throughout it all, however, I also knew that something really important was happening. I had to sit there and listen as best as I could even if I did not feel good about everything in the moment. Time would give me the chance to evaluate things, but in that moment, my job was to stick it out and soak up whatever was offered. The evening came to a close with hugs all around and the extension of another invitation to return the following month.

I went home with my head spinning, both kicking myself for starting what to me had felt like an argument, and yet pleased that I had not let my emotions get the better of me. The following day one of my friends called to offer me praise for sitting through it, offering her opinion that I had not necessarily deserved all of the force that came at me. A few days later, my other friend also talked with me about the evening and said something rather similar. We then talked about what I learned from that experience.

There are a number of important lessons that can be learned from that evening's dialogue. Hovering around each element is the global recognition that white people need to develop a strong, healthy, and permeable sense of self if we are going to be effective witnesses. Included underneath that wide umbrella are the following associated capacities. We should be able to:

Take Responsibility

Great importance lies in me admitting that I began the dialogue that ultimately brought tears to Keisha's eyes. Although I am not directly related to the source of her pain, my comments steered the conversational flow. Had my presence and my commentary not been present, the groups' post-Oprah dialogue surely would not have ended with Keisha wiped out and exhausted. My lack of awareness due to my privilege led to the pain she experienced that night. I have to take responsibility for the role I played in moving the dialogue in that direction.

What can we all take from this? First, we do a better job witnessing if we accept responsibility for triggering emotional upset. Exactly what pulled the trigger is not as important as how we respond. Perhaps we enacted our privilege or displayed our ignorance. Perhaps a person feeds off of the response of another. Ultimately, the fact that we did not intend to create emotional upset means little. Even if the emotion that comes up stems from an entire history of experience, if we help stir up the emotion in someone, we should have to sit and deal with the emotion alongside him or her.

Second, my two friends sat quietly because their job in that moment was to bear witness to the situation at hand, not to rescue me. In essence, we should take up our responsibility, the *ability* to *respond*, by sitting in the fires we set for ourselves without either (1) judging the person reacting as "overly emotional," which white folks tend to do, or (2) expecting to be rescued from the fiery heat.

Accept Multiple Truths

Also important for me to recognize is that my critique of the television episode appeared as a statement of fact. This manner of speaking is related to my upbringing within white society. White folks regularly learn to speak as though our thoughts contain absolute truth, even when we are novices within a subject area. We can magnify this for those of us who are also used to being in positions of authority as teachers! "The problem with the show is that . . ." I sat on Ms. Moussa's couch and offered my best, professional analysis of race issues facing the United States with no qualifier, no sense of humility, and no questioning stance. No wonder the dialogue took on the tone of a debate.

There are several things we can take from this. First, we would do well to consider to what degree we believe that we are holders of the truth. Part of white privilege involves many of us white folks being trained to assume that our opinions should be accepted or, at least, politely received and debated. Life outside of white circles often does not work this way. Second, purposefully qualifying our statements about loaded topics with openers such as, "From what I know so far . . ." or "It seems to me that . . ." might help. While a subtle shift, this language conveys the message that we recognize the difference between our *personal truth* and *absolute truth*. Finally, the more we remember to do this, the easier it becomes to remain conscious that we also should accept that other people's experiences have led them to different truths about the world.

Demonstrate Dedication

With Ms. Moussa, there was no need for me to abandon my orientation when discussing my approach to race issues. Nor was she going to abandon hers. Although starting from very different points of view, we found a place of mutual understanding. How? First, being able to describe why my approach makes sense when talking with white folks helped. Even as I went back and forth with Ms. Moussa, the thought came to me that even six months previously, I would not have had the clarity of understanding to stand so strongly in my position. Nor would my dedication to my position have been warranted. My continuing efforts to learn as much as possible about these issues supported me.

Second, my expression was not detached from emotion. Ours was not an intellectual debate. The honest truth—that I am wholly committed to, passionate about, and invested in advancing racial justice—was evident. For those of us who end up sitting within uncomfortable conversations, the ability to choose wisely which positions to hold with strength becomes paramount. My strength in this setting was not out of defensiveness; the position held had been deeply considered. When we have put in the work to truly understand something deeply, we do not have to abandon that orientation. However, we will be more successful if we hold our position tenderly and simultaneously work to understand why others feel differently.

Stick with It

The desire to flee the scene enveloped me for a good portion of the time that I sat in witness to Keisha's outpouring. Yet leaving was not an option. Staying required me to rely on some personal coping strategies. Yes, I actually counted to ten at one point. Yes, I actually concentrated on my breathing. Yes, I actually used some visual imagery. From what my friends told me later, this helped me to remain visibly calm and hide the fact that internally my heart was beating at twice its normal rate, my stomach was in knots, and I was sweating profusely.

What learning can we take from this? I know that I am not the only one who experiences this type of anxious reaction. For those of us who (1) have not spent a lot of time in dialogue over issues of race, (2) avoid conflict as a general rule, and (3) realize that our privilege makes our staying in the fire a choice, sticking with it requires a great amount of courage. But if we can develop some coping strategies to calm ourselves so that we can really be present in the experience, great learning can result.

Draw Upon Our Knowledge Base

As Ms. Moussa began to more pointedly express the reasons why she disagreed with my position, I began to recall the different statuses of racial identity development outlined within Dr. Beverly Daniel Tatum's book, *Why Are All the Black Kids Sitting Together in the Cafeteria?* I took note that Ms. Moussa and I were speaking out of different statuses. Neither status is to be seen as higher or lower, but simply different orientations. I then recalled an article I read during my doctoral research regarding conversation patterns among people utilizing different status positions. Yes, these things did actually flash into my mind during the most heated moments of the conversation. Was my mind drifting? No. Rather, I was trying desperately to find the best way through the experience and to understand the situation fully.

Drawing on the knowledge gained from those texts helped me see that any attempt by either of us to alter each other's positions was going to be futile, not because anyone was more stubborn than the other but because we were both operating out of radically different racial identity statuses. What can we learn from this? Knowledge is power, and the more we know, the more effective we can be at judging the situation and moving forward.

Depersonalize Appropriately

In the room that evening, I started out sitting as a white woman at ease with four Black women, talking about race, acting knowledgeable, assuming my opinions would do no harm. I then sparked a furious condemnation of how ignorant white folks are regarding the pain of Black America. I witnessed the depth of Keisha's anger at white America. That evening I *became* white America: past, present, and future.

I represented the entire history of my race, its blindness in the face of injustice, and its refusals to face the enduring legacy of trauma. Keisha let me have it, verbally. However, Keisha also knew that the fullness of her verbal expression, though directed at me, was not all about me. She even said so at one point. I knew it, too, and that made it tremendously difficult for me to sit and take it in. And that is exactly what I learned from this. If we take it *into* ourselves, take it personally, and hold it, we are more likely to either explode or run away.

On the other hand, if we know that the rage, although directed at us, is not for us alone, we can see it as a wind that can blow *through* us. I literally sat and visualized the emotion moving through my body, letting it freely move past me. This allowed me to really listen to Keisha, really witness her describe the deep pain held by her community, appear calm, and refrain from cutting her off. Had I shut her down, white America would simply have injured her all over again. If we are to witness, we have to be permeable.

Appreciate the Intimacy of Conflict

One of the thoughts that crossed my mind as I tried to survive my own anxiety that evening was that I was sure that I would never be invited back to the house again. My assumption was that I had ruined my colleagues' evening. Not only that, but I was sure that whatever closeness our mutual past as teaching colleagues offered was also dissolving. To my great surprise, these women did not seem to hold anything against me and I have since been invited back for many dinners, lunches, and gatherings.

Upon reflection, I see how much I relate to Karen and Bob's stories about relationships always needing to be polite and without difficulty. Clearly, my own whiteness emerged in this moment. I could not see that their dedication to staying in the conflict was actually a testament to their investment in the relationship. They were taking the time and effort to teach me. Instead, I feared the conflict signaled the end.

Recognizing this, I can understand why an experience such as this can be absolutely overwhelming to a white person like myself but hardly memorable for someone else more comfortable managing conflict. Perhaps this is why one of my Black friends now can hardly recall the evening's events. The point for us, however, is that our ability to see our own whiteness can help us refrain from overreacting to conflict, and prematurely and unwittingly ending a collegial relationship that might not only be life enhancing but also rich with collaborative potential.

Recognize the Value of Releasing Rage

Finally, were it not for moments like those with Ms. Moussa and Keisha, I might not be as aware as I am regarding the extent of the trauma suffered by people of color in this country. One thing I also realized is that rage does not have to be destructive. Psychologists know the value of having a witness after a traumatic injury. For someone who feels injured in some way, having someone there who can *honestly* say, "Yes, I hear you, I can see what you mean" can make a difference. Our nation as a whole requires healing. Our shared history is rife with violence done to all of our spirits. People of color have had to turn to each other with their pain long enough. Growth and healing cannot be complete until white folks learn how to witness the constructive rage that awaits us—if only we can stay open.

Surely, white educators should *not* try to elicit rage and difficult emotion from our students and colleagues. But if we are going to attempt to develop meaningful relationships, it is likely that we might unwittingly do so anyway. Essential is that we recognize that our capacity to bear witness to the pain residing in our students and collaborative partners is instrumental in developing trust and demonstrating our dedication and commitment to our internal work. This is one of the keys that can help solidify teaching relationships and collaborative relationships, thereby enhancing what we can accomplish within our classrooms and furthering the reform and diversity work we intend to do together in our schools.

Developing a sense of self that is strong and healthy enough to withstand rage yet permeable enough to let the fire pass through us takes a lot of work. Yet this capacity is not uniquely applicable to racially loaded situations. Our practice can begin any time conflict emerges in our lives. The more we can develop our emotional maturity, the better we can witness. However, for those like me who avoid conflict like the plague, we might not create many opportunities for this type of practice. We also might be overwhelmed at the thought of even entering the room when we sense deep anger present, much less sitting through the type of conversation described in this text. This is where our final ingredient requires addition. We need to build a community that can help us sort through our feelings, propel us forward, and support us as we figure out our next step.

CREATING COMMUNITY

Dialogue on race is on the tip of my tongue just about all of the time. No surprise, then, that my college courses often involve conversations on race issues. One semester one of my students, an assistant principal at a Catholic high school who also has a legal background, spoke up and mentioned his early training's emphasis in critical race theory. He later talked with me on our way out of class and told me that he knew what I was trying to do, respected my efforts, had already gone through it, and was a bit uncomfortable being dragged back into a conversation on race. After a lengthy discussion, I asked him to consider that perhaps his discomfort with the subject indicated that there might be some room for additional personal work.

During one of the many conversations we had that semester, this student asked me, "So, how long will you be into this?" Essentially, he saw working on race issues as a phase that would ultimately lead to burn out. I responded that this feels like lifelong work. What makes my experience different from his? Our academic programs had led us to very similar perspectives on systems of inequity and white privilege. But why did he experience a focus on race as an intellectual pursuit that translated into being a "phase," while I see it more as a lifelong commitment?

After class later in the semester, standing in the parking lot near our cars, this student spoke about the pressure he received from others to "stop making everything about race." His colleagues, mainly folks of color, were tired of being reminded about race. But this left him without anywhere to share his continuing thoughts and feelings regarding how he relates to being white and how to battle against the white privilege and racism he sees around him. In response, he shut down and went on with his day-to-day work.

I then told him about a community of white anti-racists of which I am a part, why we meet, and how it is helping me to form an explicitly anti-racist, Radical White Identity. Upon hearing my explanation, my student asked me to repeat something I had said, excitedly telling me that he needed a self-validating affirmation, something that he could tell himself on a daily basis to reinforce what he truly believed deep down.

This is what I said that struck him. "It is okay to still concentrate on race. There is a lot of work still to be done, and our work to end racism is a lifelong journey." Although simple, this kind of validation does not generally come from our white community. And, as we discussed in chapter 2, communities of color have carried the weight of supporting white folks for a long, long time. No wonder that my student's colleagues wanted him to stop analyzing race around them. They needed a break themselves.

The important question for this section is, *in the face of pressures to stop concentrating on race, how can we make witnessing a lifelong commitment?*

The AWARE-LA Community: Who, What, and Why

For the past several years, my participation in a group called AWARE-LA, an Alliance of White Anti-Racists Everywhere-Los Angeles, has offered me validation, inspiration, comfort, support, challenge, knowledge, skills, a space for reflection, and above all, a sense of belonging. Knowing that I am not alone keeps me hopeful and motivated. I attended the first AWARE meeting. There were about six of us. One of the founders of the group came to tears that day as he reflected on the multiple efforts he had made previously to get a group like this going. This time a continuing group began, successfully creating a community from which many of us benefit. The group list now includes over 300 individuals, about 60 of whom attend meetings regularly. Who are the people who come? What do we do? And why is a group like this beneficial and necessary?

A main part of AWARE is its Saturday Dialogues. These are monthly meetings for white folks who are interested in (1) developing a Radical White Identity, (2) challenging and supporting each other to see our privilege more clearly, and (3) learning skills to act against racism. Some people who come are just starting to hear phrases like *white privilege*, while others are practicing social justice activists who want to investigate how their work relates to their whiteness. A large proportion of our group members are educators, teaching at the elementary, high school, or college levels. We come together to learn how to better navigate our own diverse educational settings as well as more thoughtfully develop our curricula. As we have grown over the past four years, we have also invited some of our high school and college students and faculty colleagues into the group.

The entire Saturday Dialogue project is built upon AWARE's model of Radical White Identity. This model essentially involves recognizing that white antiracists need a healthy, explicit white identity that involves investigating our (1) roots, (2) history, (3) privilege, and (4) organizing potential. Yes, we work on building knowledge, skills, capacity, and community. But, first and foremost, we recognize that we need to have a healthy sense of racial identity for any of our knowledge, skills, and capacities to be enacted well.

For me, this is the space where white folks work together without requiring people of color to be our teachers. We work to heal ourselves.

We admit our resistances, question our actions, support each other's growth, and challenge each other to desegregate our lives. We see our work on Saturdays as instrumental in supporting our ability to do the real work of witnessing, which is to be in continued relationship with people of color, working together toward increased racial and social justice, and combating the continuation of white privilege.

What do we do during our dialogues? A facilitation team develops an agenda for each monthly meeting. Each dialogue begins with a check-in. We discuss our "homework" and the ways race has played a role in our lives the previous month. Meetings also include an orientation for new folks, a thematic topic for the day, exercises to help us relate to the idea, small and large group dialogues, and role-playing activities.

Some topics we explore include the interaction between race and various other social positions, such as gender, class, sexual orientation, religion, age, and education. We also discuss issues such as immigration, cultural appropriation, gentrification, and interracial relationships. Some of the questions we might ask in relationship to any of these issues include the following:

- Where do racism and/or white privilege play out within this issue?
- How do we feel about this issue and our role as white people in it?
- How can we challenge the racism and/or white privilege?
- What capacities do we need to develop to effectively challenge the racism and/or white privilege?

We brainstorm together, each of us adding our knowledge, and each of us contributing to each other's toolkit for how to respond to racially loaded situations.

Why is a white antiracist community so helpful and necessary? As essentially social creatures, humans benefit from validating experiences. Whether that validation comes from parents, teachers, friends, colleagues, or administrators, we all want to know that our contributions are valued. When white educators take up witnessing, we need people around us who understand our striving and can support us.

Given our history, the more that white educators can become supportive witnesses for other white folks, the less we need to seek validation from people of color. For me, I know that being a part of a white antiracist community has helped me become less needy in my interactions with colleagues and students of color. Only a few years ago, I needed my colleagues of color to tell me I was doing a good job in order to feel like I was one of the "good white people." But now I confer with people of color on a more equal footing, checking in to remain accountable and gain additional insight, but without the psychological need to be validated.

Also, recall from chapter 2 that when white educators move into community work without working through issues of guilt, we can often act out of a savior complex. There is nothing wrong with wanting to make a difference in a person's life. However, quite often, we go about this work in order to fill a hole within ourselves. We *need* to make a difference because of the guilt that eats away at us from within. My approach to people at my school shifted as a result of feeling connected to a group of white people who support and challenge me.

For example, there was a time when I felt that my dedicated efforts to teach inner-city students of color were my way of redeeming myself in the world. Being the vehicle for a student to extend beyond the boundaries in view made me feel good in the world and gave my life meaning. I needed the students to need me. Since deepening my relationships with AWARE, my approach has changed in a very subtle but meaningful way.

I noticed the change upon my return to my former middle school site to visit a colleague. While waiting for her, I happened upon a former student, Jesse, a stocky kid with a shaved head and an infectious grin. We sat to talk and he shared his most recent experiences with me, including the ones that had removed him from my classroom just a few months prior. He showed me his bullet wounds, talked about the reach of the Mexican Mafia, and how he saw little hope of escape. We talked about his future and mine, his continuation in school, and my outline for this book. We talked about his fears and my hopes. I talked about groups who have effectively gotten youth out of the reach of gangs to ensure their safety.

By the end of a lengthy conversation, Jesse had my phone number with explicit instructions to call me if he ever needed someone to come get him out of the area. I reinforced my belief that his life is important and that I would do whatever was in my power to see that he stayed alive. He then left for home, indicating his need to walk with his friends so as not to be alone on the streets. I have not seen or heard from him since.

Later, I thought about my role in that situation. Was I responding to an internal savior complex? We both recognized and spoke about the fact that I was quite literally trying to save his life. That is absolutely true. But reflecting inward, I noticed a subtle yet important difference. I did not need Jesse that day to make me feel better about myself. Offering him support did not make me feel like a better person than anybody else.

Sure, the connection and ability to be of potential aid offered a good feeling. And perhaps there is still more of the savior complex deep down for me to explore, more work to be done. However, my internal sense shifted. No longer did I need Jesse to validate me in the world. The skills and validation gained through my work with the other antiracist white folks helped me approach Jesse with more awareness, less superiority, less pride, and an increased ability to hear his concerns. Being less full of myself, I was more available to just *be* with Jesse.

Although the AWARE meeting space has helped me tremendously, there are many people who understandably distrust any group of white people meeting without any people of color present. Many believe that white folks cannot be trusted without being either monitored or guided by people of color when it comes to dealing with racism. Simply, many believe that white folks alone together always indicate racism in action.

White educators do need to be in consistent and meaningful relationships with people of color in ways that allow us to see ourselves more clearly, especially when we are trying to do ally work. It is also certainly true that for as much internal work as AWARE members have accomplished, we likely regularly miss things, essentially taking one step back for every few steps forward. On the other hand, we do not deny this reality, and experience with this group has convinced me that we do end up farther ahead in the end.

Additionally, AWARE's work is largely concentrated on investigating ourselves as white people and developing the kinds of skills that are commonly referred to as part of an "accountability" practice. We learn to listen, recognize the emergence of our privilege, and confront our defensiveness on many subjects. To be even clearer, this means that AWARE Saturday Dialogues are *not* used to plan advocacy or activist work in the service of communities of color. Instead, the AWARE meetings are about investigating ourselves so that we can be more (1) just within our day-to-day diverse settings and (2) useful to multiracial collaborations working for educational, social, racial, economic, and environmental justice.

What it boils down to is that, just as sometimes men and women need separate spaces in which to do their own particular gendered work, so white folks need a space in which we can move through our own learning process. In this way, we see our group of antiracist white folks as a *community of necessity*, an essential and temporary creation, as we work toward the abolition of all remnants of white supremacy and its historic privileges.

Of course, this work cannot be conducted wholly in isolation. The movement is a breathing process. We move in and then out. We come together and we go into our multiracial spaces. Back and forth, together and apart, learning and sharing each step of the way. With this frame, a sense of community among whites working at witnessing offers validation for efforts made without draining people of color's energy. To be sure, the goal is to recover from this social construction called race so that we exist primarily in integrated spaces. However, creating witnessing communities may be a necessary intermediary step.

Building a Community of Witnesses

Although AWARE works as a racially caucused group, that does not mean that witnessing groups cannot be multiracial. The concept of witnessing can be used by anyone of any background. The essential idea, though, is that educators developing a witnessing practice might look to create a community that can help them stay focused on learning how to notice racism and white privilege, develop practical skills, and do the internal work of capacity building. Anyone motivated to be part of that conversation should be welcomed. Certainly, starting by inviting fellow educators (and possibly students, depending on circumstances) makes sense. But effective work can also happen when our community of witnesses includes people from a wide array of experiences.

If we as educators develop a core group of people around ourselves to help with this process, we can avoid the isolation that many people feel when they begin to speak out regarding racism and white privilege. Then, as we combat loneliness through the development of a supportive community, our witnessing is more likely to become a lifelong dedication. Keep in mind that AWARE began with a small circle of people. Even if we have no intention of developing a large group, what can we do for ourselves to stay motivated?

- *Start small.* Speak to people you already know who might be open to a conversation on race. Perhaps you begin with two or three people. Expand as your ability to initiate the dialogue increases.
- *Create a book club.* If you find this book helpful, move through it with others. Invite your most trusted colleagues and friends (again, possibly students) to become part of your process. Talk about each chapter, what feelings you have about it, what is meaningful, and how it motivates you to take action.
- *Create an intentional community.* Determine the purpose of why you meet and what you would like to accomplish in general.
- *Set goals.* Look at each of the four aspects of how to witness: building knowledge, skills, capacities, and community. Decide which actions you plan to take and hold each other accountable.
- *Create shared agreements.* Talk about how you can support each other. What are the avenues for challenge? How are you responsible to each other for following through with the goals that you set?
- *Move outside of yourselves.* Open dialogue about your experiences within the diverse spaces you inhabit. Be sure to explore how racism or white privilege might exist there. If there are no multiracial spaces in your lives, brainstorm how to expand your lives to experience more diversity.

Sharing this work with friends and colleagues (and perhaps even students) can help make the suggestions offered in this text come alive. Also, putting these ideas into action can help avoid overintellectualizing the journey. Even if the idea of convincing others to take up this work may sound daunting, you might be surprised. If you have found the ideas and suggestions within this text motivating, someone else might as well. It is worth a try. Not only that, but for the sake of our larger effort at reducing racism's effects in our schools, we really have to make this effort.

MOVING FORWARD—IMAGINING
POSSIBILITIES FOR ALLY WORK

The more white educators put understanding and skills into action, the more we might find ourselves invested in becoming part of a larger network. If we become so inspired, we can seek out other social-justice-oriented education organizations and we might come into contact with many wonderful people with plenty of good advice about how we can increasingly take on ally work. Most of them are just a Web search away. The possibilities are endless, and the need is great.

During my third year with the AWARE group, I found myself increasingly invested in attending political events, leadership meetings, and development opportunities. What drives this higher level of commitment and activity? Is it my increased knowledge? Yes. Is it the increased confidence in my ability to enact skills learned? Sure. But, in addition to that, I like spending time with these new friend-colleagues. They are there when I am confused. They support and challenge me when I make mistakes. They push me to take another step forward. They accept that we might disagree on some political issues. However, we are on the same page regarding our efforts to work toward personal and collective understanding and transforming our education system into one that is more equitable and humane.

Ultimately, I feel good when I am around AWARE members. My journey into witnessing is not a lonely one. I am connected to a larger body of people, a collective movement of people who are willing to respond to the call to witness. This collective movement comes with tremendous possibility. Ultimately, when enough educators make this shift and begin to influence their students, colleagues, families, and peer networks, I believe the culture can transform as well.

NOTES

1. Joel Havemann and Ricardo Alonso-Zaldivar, "Middle-Class Workers Ailing in Census Checkup," *Los Angeles Times*, August 30, 2006. Also see, Income, Poverty, and Health Insurance Coverage in the US: 2005 (external link, pdf), available at www.radicalmath.org/browse_category.php?cat = data

2. This abbreviated definition for *internalized racism* is taken from Donna Bivens, "Internalized Racism: A Definition," Women's Theological Center, 1995. A more complete explanation can be found at www.evaluationtoolsfor racialequity.org/termRacial.htm

> Internalized racism is the situation that occurs in a racist system when a racial group oppressed by racism supports the supremacy and dominance of the dominating group by maintaining or participating in the set of attitudes, behaviors, social structures and ideologies that undergird the dominating group's power.
>
> It involves four essential and interconnected elements: decision making, resources, standards, and naming the problem.

Chapter Nine

How Can We Create a Witnessing Culture?

Did you ever have a teacher or mentor who dared you to dream bigger than you might have on your own? Was there ever a figure in your life who challenged you to make a grand leap and fulfill a vision you held dear? This chapter is dedicated to the educators in our lives who have asked us to see beyond ourselves, follow our numinous dreams, and live them as if they were already reality. In other words, this chapter is dedicated to those who modeled for us what it truly means to educate. For me, this includes two fierce women professors who bridge the soul and the world, linking deep psychology with social justice.

Whereas chapter 8 is a call to individual reflection and action, this final chapter asks readers to join in a collective dreamlike pursuit to dig deep down into our cultural soul and imagine our way through to a different way of being in the community. This chapter asks us to see ourselves not only as teachers, professors, administrators, mentors, or trainers but also as cultural workers. Bringing this dream to manifestation requires all of us to expand ourselves, our educational practices, and the scope and reach of our work. What follows is intended to invite a broad, deep, and uplifting reflection. Ultimately, the vision offered reflects my grandest hope for our country.

The goal: Transform the current, dominant form of white culture into an antiracist white culture that regularly names and dismantles racism and white privilege. This work may be started at home, extended into our classrooms, and infused into our work settings. This is long-range work. Transforming familial and school culture understandably requires much time and collective effort. But, in the midst of that individual struggle, we must simultaneously hold a larger view of our collective role. This work must also extend outward into the various reaches of our influence, community groups, religious/spiritual affiliations, and social networks. Yes, we may start this work with a small circle of friends, family, students, and colleagues. However, our ultimate goal must remain the transformation of white culture overall.

Since the existence of "white culture" is in itself contested, let me be really specific. What we need to transform is the white culture people speak of that is associated with segregated social lives, isolation, disconnection, individualism, sanitization, arrogance, obliviousness, entitlement, unrecognized privileges, the avoidance of social concerns faced by disproportionate numbers of people of color, the sense of self as normal, innocent, and unaffected by race, and the acceptance of Western ideals as universal and the only valid way of seeing the world.

The caveats: First, each of us has a different relationship to the features of whiteness listed above, and therefore the amount of personal change required necessarily differs. However, for white educators who are part of this group working toward cultural transformation, we need to recognize the broad parameters so that we can locate ourselves within the shifting terrain.

Second, the beginning of anything is often the hardest part. We face a fairly steep learning curve so that our first attempts may be clumsy. Thankfully, there is a history of antiracism on which to build. Foundations have been laid demonstrating how to do the work of witnessing. There are also groups of antiracist educators already living out witnessing practices for us to relate to and with whom we can build community.

Third, cultural shifts generally take place within a complete alteration of worldview. Is reading this one book sufficiently provocative to alter an educator's entire view of the world? Perhaps the answer is no. However, continued increases in our knowledge base, social connections, and experiences can support movement in that direction.

Finally, choosing to dedicate our time to a new effort in addition to our regular, daily responsibilities can be extremely difficult. For white folks, we have the privilege to choose whether or not to take up a witnessing role. No one will force us. We have to be intrinsically motivated to make this shift.

The motivation: In the face of our constraints and resistances, what can prompt white educators to give energy to a witnessing practice on a regular basis, both within and without classroom settings? We must have a vision, some imagination of how our life will improve. This idea of creating a witnessing culture has just such a vision. At its core, this is a vision of our own healing, the creation of a healthier sense of self for white educators particularly, who can then guide others beyond the dis-ease most white folks feel regarding race issues.

This imagined reality includes educators forming enough communities of witnesses that perceiving racism and privilege becomes the norm for white educators as well as their colleagues, families, students, and social networks. In this vision, attending to the effects of race is such a regular part of life that white folks in general become skilled at giving voice to race realities. This is one way white folks can earn a positive sense of our racial selves, standing proud in our antiracism practice, knowing that we are truly working toward developing a culture around challenging the dominating whiteness that has injured our collective spirit for too long.

How to effectively make this cultural shift happen on a wide scale understandably raises many questions. This last chapter imagines the answers to the following: What will it take for educators to begin to transform white culture? What values are essential within a witnessing culture? And is it really possible for a witnessing culture to exist in the United States?

A HOPEFUL, EXPANDING, STRATEGIC COMMUNITY

The truth is that the problems we face regarding race are huge. In the face of the overwhelming challenges, we need both a sense of hope and a strategic approach. The fact that many educators already feel overwhelmed by just the *thought* of speaking up and taking action in regards to race issues is a serious problem. Although true that many people feel hopeless in the face of our history and its effects, another truth is that many people feel powerless in general when it comes to our social, economic, and educational institutions. This lack of perceived power runs so deep that we see it in our responses to movies and advertising.

The reactions I heard to the film *Minority Report* can serve as an example. There is a scene within the film in which the main character, played by Tom Cruise, moves through a high-tech mall. Cameras recognize each customer by name, calling out to each with a welcome and an invitation to purchase. Just imagining that as a possible future horrified me. However, a deeper distress emerged as several white acquaintances and colleagues proclaimed that the scene displayed our future as though it were an already foregone conclusion. Did they like that future? They all agreed that the vision offered within the film was bothersome to say the least, and some called it frightening. However, they all appeared to submit to the eventuality of its impending reality. Why?

These reactions speak to a pervasive problem. Many of us believe that we lack personal power within our collective world, regardless of whether or not the subject is race related. Hopelessness emerges when we take in other people's visions for our future as though we have no say. With this as a starting point, the reader might rightly ask, from whence can come a sense of hope? How can we hope for widespread change in the face of this lack of social agency?

My relentless hope comes, in part, from my own recognition of the limitless creative potential within each of us. We hold enormous possibility within ourselves, and this expands exponentially when we come together in community. Our future is ours to create together, and when we create shared agreements about how we wish to live, how we intend to be in relationships, and what values we hope to display and instill in our youth, the strength of those social contracts creates unseen movement.

This internal sense receives external support in the book *The Cultural Creatives: How 50 Million People Are Changing the World*, by Paul Ray and Sherry Ruth Anderson. This text draws upon 13 years of survey research conducted with over 100,000 U.S. Americans. So, what do the authors mean when they speak of the Cultural Creatives? They write,

> Since the 1960s, 26 percent of the adults in the United States—50 million people—have made a comprehensive shift in their worldview, values, and way of life—their culture, in short. These creative, optimistic millions are at the leading edge of several kinds of cultural change, deeply affecting not only their own lives but our larger society as well. We call them the Cultural Creatives because, innovation by innovation, they are shaping a new kind of American culture for the twenty-first century.[1]

The call to transform our culture into a witnessing culture aligns with this movement. In this way, those of us responding to the call to witness racism and white privilege are engaged in a similarly directed track with those who push for social and ecological change in other ways.

According to the authors of *The Cultural Creatives*, this movement is largely unnoticed by many people. Yet they also offer impressive evidence that a cultural wave is already taking shape that can alter the economic realities and political dialogue of this country. Some of our students and colleagues may already be influenced by the cultural shifts in play. As our voices strengthen and our economic choices and demands follow, businesses and institutions are increasingly forced to pay attention.

Recognizing that we are a part of a larger wave of movement offers hope because although *The Cultural Creatives* focuses on people involved with movements oriented around ecological sustainability, healthy living, and psychological/spiritual development, part of this emerging group also works toward a more equitable and cross-cultural world. Of those defined as "core" Cultural Creatives, approximately half, 24 million, are said to be concerned simultaneously with both social justice *and* personal growth, rejecting the notion that they are mutually exclusive.[2]

This core of the Cultural Creatives is the group with whom I feel myself most aligned. (Although there is no breakdown to suggest how many of these 24 million people are white, we can at least conservatively imagine that the number is substantial.) This group recognizes that there is a large matrix of issues, interconnected and mutually reinforcing, each of which requires its own efforts. Working on each can simultaneously work to support the others. Coalition building between educational reform, social justice, and ecological groups naturally emerges with this understanding.

As educators, we can play a particularly important role in helping our students see how seemingly disparate groups have connections and mutual interests. True, not all of the 24 million are currently concerned with race issues in particular at this time. But their current interests are likely to make them more open to the concerns raised within this text, more likely to fold the ideas contained in this text into their awareness of other issues, perhaps then witnessing injustice and the effects of whiteness on multiple levels. In this way, our role as educators also expands such that we can take up responsibility to educate those outside of our classrooms regarding how to witness whiteness, thereby expanding our communities of witnesses.

If these Cultural Creatives are already creating new forms of culture, what is it about contemporary American culture that they reject? Among other things, they reject "materialism, greed, me-firstism, status display, glaring social inequalities of race and class, society's failure to care adequately for elders, women, and children, . . . and intolerance and narrowness of social conservatives and the Religious Right."[3] True enough, this list hardly mirrors the above list regarding what a witnessing culture might work against. However, some linkages are there. These folks have the potential to become a wave of cultural transformers that expand a community of witnesses. In this possible field of witnessing agents there is a place of beginning and a wellspring of hope.

Ray and Anderson's conclusion offers an explicit vision for what Cultural Creatives seek, and it deserves a full reading:

> There is nothing inevitable about the kind of life we have now in modern society, and nothing inevitable about the kind of future that lies before us. Cultural Creatives are quite clear that they do not want to live in an alienated, disconnected world. Their guiding images refer again and again to a sense of wholeness. They say that each of us is a living system within a greater living system, connected to each other in more ways than we can fathom. If we focus on that wholeness, we can begin to imagine a culture that can heal the fragmentation and destructiveness of our time.
>
> The appearance of the Cultural Creatives, we suggest, represents a promise that a creative vision of the future is growing. It is a resurgence of hope, of imagination, of willingness to act for the sake of a better civilization. The work toward a reintegration of, and design for, a new culture can have great power in our collective imagination. What we want and what we choose can shape our future.[4]

True, not all Cultural Creatives are witnesses for racial justice . . . yet. But they might become witnesses if educators begin to let them know how essentially linked racial justice and identity issues are with environmental equity, healing, and psychological development efforts. We can start there.

Another reason that a hopeful stance makes realistic sense comes from the analysis offered within *The Tipping Point: How Little Things Can*

Make a Big Difference, by Malcolm Gladwell.[5] We can learn a lot from this text, taking its suggestions and using them to propel real movement. A main premise is that big changes come from small events. This energizes when we see how the wave of Cultural Creatives might become the critical mass necessary to allow our message to take off and inspire both local and multinational businesses and politicians to respond.

The Tipping Point also offers strategies that can help make our efforts more successful. For example, the book explains three types of people whom educators can target with our messages regarding witnessing. We need to locate the connectors, those who walk in many worlds, know many people, and link communities. Second, we can bring our message to the knowers, those who act as the voices of expertise in particular areas. These are the people who others seek out to find out if a product or message is valid and valuable. The knowers act as our consumer controls. They are socially invested and want people to know the truth about things. If we can get them on board, others will follow. Finally, we know the persuaders when we see them. They are the folks who can sell us anything. Their charisma precedes them. If we can convince them of the importance of witnessing, they will convince others.

Taking a strategic approach to our witnessing work, both personally and as an educational community, might help us reach the point where our message sticks. Also important is that *The Tipping Point* describes what is called the *Rule of 150*.[6] Apparently, the best-functioning groups within organizations are those that do not grow past this crucial number. The key element for success over time appears to be community, the sense of knowing the various people in various roles and feeling a sense of personal accountability to the individuals that make up the team.

If educators begin to construct witnessing groups to keep us accountable to each other as regards the development of our antiracist practice, the potential for growth and expansion increases. Our self-identity becomes involved and we experience increased motivation and dedication. In sum, the messages within these two texts, *The Cultural Creatives* and *The Tipping Point*, offer us a realistic and well-researched vision of a group of people likely to be open to the development of a witnessing culture and some strategies to help us develop the necessary communities. The beauty here is that there is no reason to feel alone and powerless. Educators have concrete steps to take that can connect us with a movement of people. We can capitalize on the massive wave of change already underway, albeit seemingly hidden from view.

CULTURAL VALUES OF WITNESSING

In truth, a good number of educators and students are part of the wave of cultural transformation taking place and already promote many of the values that run counter to the dominant forms of white culture listed above. It would make sense that many educators reading this text might already be somewhat aligned with the 24 million core Cultural Creatives mentioned in the previous section. Still, we cannot simply reject the dominant form of white culture without defining specific alternatives. If we are to turn away from some attributes of white culture, what alternatives do we seek? What are the values that a witnessing culture might display?

To start this imaginative process, I returned to Kelly Oliver's philosophical text, *Witnessing: Beyond Recognition*, for inspiration.[7] This investigation also draws upon the countless conversations I have had with other people regarding what helps frame their perspective regarding race issues. Surely this chapter does not offer a complete list of what is possible or desired. But for the sake of beginning, a culture of witnessing would value multiplicity, interconnection, passion, obligation, vigilance, accountability, historical memory, and reconciliation. Let us look at each one to see how it supports a cultural practice of witnessing whiteness.

Multiplicity

Most elementary and high school curriculums include mythology to some degree or another. Although we recognize the importance of the stories, there is something more that educators can take from the genre. Even if the level of analysis that follows seems removed from our classrooms as written, let us delve into a mytho-psychological framework for a bit in order to see how the essence of the ideas absolutely has a place within our educational and witnessing practices.

When we look at ancient myths across cultures we find that their power lies in their portrayal of essentially human themes. Regardless of the culture of origin, within myth we meet characters, both human and divine, that struggle as we struggle. We find that our ancestors grappled with the same troubles and joys we meet today. We confront conflict, greed, generosity, envy, pride, love, heroism, sacrifice, fear, arrogance, friendship, death, and initiation, to name just a few. Within mythological realms, all of these energetic forces, these characters or gods that personify human characteristics, have a respected and honored place.

In depth psychological terms, these energies are the multitude of archetypes that exist as part of the foundation of our consciousness. We understand what it means to be a hero because that archetype already exists within our deepest psyche. In the same way, we have the capacity for greed, spite, and maliciousness as much as we do for love, sacrifice, and devotion. We recognize the wise mother and the lover just as we recognize death and the thief.

The innumerable qualities that live within the depths of our psyches, taken together, are what are referred to as the *multiplicity of the psyche*. Essentially, we are fragmented to the core and we have the capacity to act out of any of the various archetypes imaginable. Bits and pieces often emerge without our control, which can leave us feeling confused, lost, and in pain. However, our inner aspects in combination, fully accepted, also offer us a sense of wholeness. Nothing is left out. All energetic forces have a place within our deepest selves

If taken seriously, the recognition that even the most obscene action has its roots in an energetic, archetypal force that lies hidden deep within each of us asks us to begin to approach the world differently. True, our upbringing often stops us from enacting certain behaviors. True, our own personality styles inhibit us. True, our cultural framework and environmental influences have shaped our tendencies and conscious restraints. And yet, if we are really honest with ourselves, we should be able to imagine that if our social conditionings were completely stripped away, if crisis befell us and our stable sense of self, place, and safety fell away, none of us really knows what we might draw on to survive.

Important shifts in thinking occur when we see the truth of our inner multiplicity. First, we can more readily move beyond the *either/or* dichotomy of the modern worldview and, instead, increasingly take the position of *both/and*. Can two things be true at the same time? we begin to ask. Might something be both horrible and profoundly educational? This shift is essential as white folks reconsider our sense of identity and what characteristics we hope to exemplify.

Recall that part of the historic development of white identity included demonizing certain ways of being and excluding them from our sense of self. From a mythic perspective, this is tantamount to banishing a divine energy from the pantheon of the gods. Part of healing from dissociated white culture involves white people reimagining ourselves so that we make room for what, historically, has been split off from the white self. For example, white folks traditionally claimed the energy of Productivity while demonizing what the modern world sees as the opposite, Laziness.

The use of capitalization asks us to imagine Productivity and Laziness as archetypal deities. Just for a moment, let us note that each attribute, or mythic deity, might associate or conspire with others. For example, we can see that Laziness in our culture is generally doomed to existence as the jailor of Ambition. Spending hours sitting under a tree watching the birds and feeling the caress of the wind or filming the twists and turns of a plastic bag dancing in the breeze are things that would generally be seen as nonproductive.

Yet, in this judgment we also dismiss the importance of Laziness' possible co-conspirators, the Calm, Receptive, and Subtle, the moments that touch our Soul. From this point of view, is it possible that what we might sometimes call Laziness can be a partner to that which invites Soul into our world? Is it possible that our white culture's loss of meaning, in part, stems from our inability to stop and wait patiently for the world to tell us something essential about life?

Valuing our multiplicity can help us reclaim the soulfulness that many white folks feel is missing in our lives. Following this logic, we might also find the deep benefits that come from sitting in extended, diverse dialogues and deepening our sense of self in the world. This means that we would value taking time to truly connect with others in ways that satisfy our soul, but appear less productive to a largely isolated, segregated white culture.

Further, we can examine the contemporary cultural myths and stories prevalent in the United States. We might consider how stories pertaining to cowboys, explorers of all sorts, and heroes, to mention just a few, reinforce a particular set of values. We can ask how the cultural stories and myths we grew up with reflect and reinforce problematic aspects of white culture. How do we continue to condition ourselves to see people as either all good or all bad through our storytelling and interpretations of events? Then we might imagine, what might be the new stories that would promote the values of a witnessing culture? The collective answer will emerge as we each make choices regarding how we interpret events, which stories we decide are worth repeating, and how we tell the tales.

Another shift that comes with valuing multiplicity is that this perspective helps us tap into our deep sense that we are neither more nor less human than anyone else. People's actions spring from a well of possibility that exists simultaneously within each of us. No longer can we point to a few bad apples or name someone a monster in order to disconnect from the uncomfortable reality that our own humanity, our own culture, requires serious work.

Instead of looking at *those racists over there*, an appreciation of multiplicity prompts us to self-identify in an effort to locate where that disturbing conditioning exists in us, our teaching practice, and the systems we inhabit. In so doing, we see the blood on our own hands as humans struggling to better deal with the same old themes that our ancestors faced, the disconnections between peoples and the efforts to move beyond blindness to self and prejudice toward others.

Ultimately, truly recognizing the multiplicity of our deepest selves helps us see our personal responsibility for the development and evolution of our culture and our humanity. As such, we can consider the following:

- In what ways is the value of multiplicity already expressed in your interactions and/or practice with students, colleagues, family, and friends?
- Where do you see openings to infuse this idea more fully in your teaching practice?
- How might you advance this value within your educational setting?

Interconnection

About as far as public education generally goes on the subject of interconnection is that new technologies have radically advanced our ability to connect with people across the globe. We might also teach that if one country pollutes the Earth that the rest of the planet's population eventually suffers. Some courses might even highlight how communities affect each other through their economic or political systems. Overall, though, our education and culture tends to push us to see ourselves as individuals first and community members second. Our approaches to school and student evaluation only serve to reinforce this individualized orientation.

Important to recall from chapter 3 is that the individualistic perspective depends upon the conception of the self as autonomous, independent, self-determining, unique, separate, and free. Remember that this orientation matches the modern worldview, which is also associated with being Western and white for many people.[8] Witnessing ourselves asks us to take a hard look at the degree to which we value this type of *individualism* and imagine moving in a different direction.

In general, white culture teaches us that we exist as separate bodies, islands without obvious and imperative connections to others. We often link this sense of individualism with the glory of independence and freedom. In many ways, these have become gods in the mythological sense. Yet there is a price paid for this stance. The mythological gods are constantly entwined in complex relationships. Independence and Freedom do not travel alone. With them can come Separation, Isolation, Alienation, and Loneliness.

Bowling Alone, by Robert Putman, offers a complex view of the increased lack of social engagement evident in our society over the past several decades.[9] That millions of Americans feel this alienation is indisputable in a gated-community culture with an epidemic rate of depression and self-medication. While this connection oversimplifies the torment of depression and addiction, there is something real about how our individualistic, independent self frequently feels misunderstood, fearful, and alone in the world.

As mirror images and complements, some type of Imprisonment arrives with the heralding of unrestrained personal Freedom. We somehow become trapped within our selves, our desires, and our individual destinies. Our isolated achievements become objects of envy, inspiring the need for better personal protection and security. We build more gates. Our Independence can thus invite the sorrow of someone free to feel . . . alone.

With all of the beauties and benefits that Independence does bring, the image of ourselves as islands in a vast sea not only ignores the deep, underlying connectedness of our common ground beneath the water; it also fails to value equally the shared ocean and our mutual dependence upon the sun, the salt, the water, and the wind. Educators who advance a witnessing culture would challenge the way individualism leads to isolation and segregation, naming its associations and problems.

Unfortunately, the suggestion that educators need to challenge individualism can be easily misunderstood and resisted. This occurs because many confuse individualism with the job of becoming an individual. These are two completely different ways of relating to the world. The modern, white self who subscribes to *rugged individualism* risks becoming isolated, disconnected, and competitive. On the other hand, Carl Jung, one of the fathers of depth psychology, offers us a different way of seeing the self as an individual. He describes *individuated* people as those who are conscious of the way that familial, societal, and cultural factors shape them.

The *individuation process* includes becoming aware of our groups' influences and evaluating ourselves against them.[10] As part of this process, white educators would ask, do the white social norms listed above reflect how we wish to be in the world? We can then make our own choices regarding how we want to relate to our society's value system. The degree to which we are able to consciously choose is the degree to which we are actually free. If we do not even know how our social conditioning affects our day-to-day lives, how in the world can we consider our choices freely made?

Important to note is that the individuation process cannot be completed within one workshop, retreat, year, or even one life stage. This is a lifelong effort. Even the most sophisticated people still have blind spots regarding the ways culture impacts their decision making. Most of us white folks have hardly even begun considering how being white shapes perceptions, attitudes, and behaviors. For white educators to create a witnessing culture, we need to open our minds to the possibility that what we see as simply our individual personality is also reflective of white culture.

In my opinion, one of the most beautiful ideas within Jung's vision is that the individuation process is one that ties us back to the social collective. Interconnection is not forgotten. The price we pay for separating ourselves out of the group for a time through our self-reflection process is that we must return with our newly acquired wisdom.[11] In this way, becoming a true individual requires us to find the divine within our deep self, discover our intrinsic relationship with the collective, and offer something beneficial back to society. In this way, our sense of self develops along with our sense of connection with others.[12]

Particularly important is that this approach helps us see that we can give up *individualism* without sacrificing our sense of *individuality*. We can develop our internal sense of value and personal destiny while simultaneously recognizing our essential interconnection. Witnessing ourselves then becomes both personally liberating *and* socially transforming.

Given that white folks are generally extremely unconscious regarding how our racial placement affects us, we really need a majority of white educators to start delving into this question and then return to teach others. Although emerging from a psychological orientation, educators need to serve as illustrative models of this individuation process in order for it to become widely understood and engaged as part of the development of a witnessing culture. We also should consider:

- In what ways is the value of interconnection already expressed in your interactions and/or practice with students, colleagues, family, and friends?
- How might you encourage students to develop a sense of self as individuals without promoting individualism?
- How can a form of critical pedagogy that invites students to analyze the societal influences inherent in text and curricular materials become part of your practice?

Passion

Passionate teachers have been the subject of texts and movies for years for very good reason. Passion penetrates, persuades, and inspires. From our experience, each of us can reflect on lessons delivered well, recalling the spark that gains interest. Similarly, we know when we fall flat, when the emotion evaporates and a cold, dry feeling pervades the classroom. If educators are going to successfully initiate a shift in our cultural frame, we have to come to that work with the same kind of passion we bring to our best teaching moments. In other words, we must witness as passionately as we teach.

Part of approaching race work with passion, though, involves healing from our cultural splits wherein our history has encouraged us to value the head, mind, and rational over the heart, body, and emotional. To be sure, men have suffered under the pressure not to display emotion, and women have suffered by being portrayed as overly emotional. Thankfully, the past several decades have involved significant shifts in these historic patterns. And yet, unfortunately, these patterns do continue and our witnessing practice benefits if we confront their effects in a few different ways.

First, we might need to become more sensitive in order to (1) notice the emotions that arise within us and (2) pay attention to that feeling-knowledge. In uncomfortable situations, when race issues come to the foreground, we need to attend to the sensations flowing from our heart and stomach. If we can notice the aches and pains that come with witnessing something challenging, we can use that information to name our own resistance, defensiveness, and discomfort. This is essential because dominant white culture's love of rationality supports our tendency to act as distanced spectators. It is much easier to watch, analyze, and judge. But when we invite our hearts to be part of our process we can stop acting like experts all of the time, engage in a way that admits when we are unclear or unsure, and acknowledge our vulnerabilities.

A second way that white educators might need to alter our relationship to passion involves breaking through the sanitized and controlled way many of us deal with difficulty. To truly be passionate, we have to reconcile our need to be neat and tidy all of the time. When we go back to the etymological roots of passion, we find it linked with being pathetic. Are we ready to be pathetic for racial justice? Will we risk standing up in front of our students and colleagues and be perceived as the fool? Can we allow ourselves to break down in order to build ourselves back up anew? This may require small, initial steps, but we will all benefit profoundly if this level of honest expression becomes a cultural norm.

A third way that our relationship to emotion and passion needs to shift involves accepting the importance of feeling-oriented knowledge that comes from others. We may trust what our gut or heart is telling us, but there often remains a strong tendency to discount this kind of knowing from someone else. The repeating pattern I have observed is that we may become passionate about issues close to our hearts, but we can become

cold in the face of others' concerns. We might listen, but we often intellec-
tualize the issues.

From a symbolic point of view, this might have to do with the way our
socialization into individualism has allowed us to see our cardiac system
as a closed circuit of energy. If our heart remains closed, passion cannot
fill us. Compassion then becomes impossible. My suggestion is that a necessary cultural shift involves letting our hearts become more than simple
pumps. Instead of seeing the heart as an empty vessel used to move
energy around within ourselves, we can recognize the heart as an organ of
perception.[13] When our hearts see and hear concerns raised, our *response-
ability* then can kick in.

If we combine an open-hearted and passionate perception with a sense
of interconnection, then we can move a long way toward reducing the percepticide we may have fallen into over the course of our lives. When we
see how the myriad social justice issues actually make a real difference in
our students' lives, we are more likely to express our witnessing with the
kind of infectious passion that can influence others to join us in taking a
stand to make necessary systemic changes. We can also think about the
following:

- In what ways is passion already expressed in your interactions and/
  or practice with students, colleagues, family, and friends?
- Where do you see openings to infuse passionate dialogues about race
  in your teaching practice?
- How might you need to open your heart further in order to better
  hear concerns raised by students and fellow colleagues?

Obligation

A sense of obligation is not a foreign value to educators. We regularly
obligate ourselves to our students, families, friends, and so on. In this way,
there is already something essential we understand and value about obligation as part of our culture. Yet a witnessing culture would require us to
extend our sense of obligation. Instead of only having an obligation to do
our best for a select few in our lives, we also need to feel an *obligation to
the social collective*.

When we truly recognize the interconnections between us all, we see that we truly are all one people and that our obligation to one another must increase. This suggestion also mirrors what Robert Putnam calls for in *Bowling Alone*, as he imagines what is required for our society to remake the social glue that keeps us together.[14] Without an increase in the type of civic engagement that both binds us and creates bridges between groups, our country will move toward increased divisions.

For white educators, being obligated to the social collective means three things, which have been discussed in previous chapters. First, we must choose to regularly and purposefully face the privilege we benefit from in this white-dominated society. Second, we have to challenge ourselves to act against racism and white privilege in spite of our freedom *not* to act. Third, for a witnessing culture to emerge, white folks have to support each other's work to end systematic racism and white dominance.

Racism is far more entrenched within our systems and institutions than we generally like to admit. Although essential to take up our task of thoroughly looking at ourselves to find remnants of racism and how we benefit from whiteness, we also are obligated to recognize that large-scale, systemic change only occurs when large numbers of people begin to support an issue. In this way, to have a witnessing culture, we would need to be ready to extend the messages of social justice activists and support their efforts with our votes and donations.

When white folks feel obligated to witness for social justice, we might find that the conversations between Cultural Creatives can also expand. For example, efforts toward environmental sustainability are tremendously important. A witnessing culture would ensure that corresponding issues of environmental racism also make it onto the discussion table. Linking our work with spiritual and psychological healing movements is also essential. A witnessing culture will ask these movements to see how taking issues of race into account can actually increase self-awareness and add a grounded, soulful element to spiritual growth.

For me, it also comes down to a basic premise that we cannot simply ignore the struggles of those around us and enjoy psychological health. The trend toward healthy living, then, is a dedicated effort toward increasing the health and well-being of our collective. Surely becoming aware of how race impacts our lives should be part of that healing effort. In the end, the degree to which educators feel inclined to take up a witnessing stance with a sense of obligation will be the deciding factor in whether or not we reach enough people to inspire a real movement of change. We have to ask ourselves:

- In what ways does obligation to the social collective already find expression in your interactions and/or practice with students, colleagues, family, and friends?
- Where do you see openings to link race issues with other social justice concerns within your teaching practice?
- To what degree do you feel obligated to work on racial/social justice concerns outside of your teaching practice and educational setting?

Vigilance

Educators know how easy it is for students to disengage from a lesson or task. We offer specific guidelines and timeframes, checking in regularly to make sure that an assignment does not get lost among a hundred other possible things our students might choose to do. We do this when we are invested in the outcome. Similarly, witnessing whiteness can be seen as an important, ongoing task, an assignment that we choose to work on that requires oversight in order that it does not become lost in the flow of our lives. For this reason, educators need to value the ways that vigilance would play an essential role in maintaining a witnessing practice.

Given that the predominant cultural norm for white folks is to turn away from race, the decision to witness involves a dramatic reversal of perspective. Developing a sufficient number of people dedicated to witnessing requires a cultural shift that supports vigilance in several areas. We need to (1) break through percepticide, (2) commit to the long-term nature of the effort, (3) build a collective process, and (4) continually seek out feedback.

First, valuing vigilance means that white educators confront our long history of collective *percepticide*.[15] What are all of the various ways we have killed off our own perceptions? For a long time, percepticide has been one way that white people have denied evidence that we are unintentionally complicit in systemic injustice. Valuing vigilance means stripping ourselves of this defensive pattern on a day-to-day basis. The benefit for white folks is that this vigilance offers us a viable path away from our reliance on a false sense of innocence. Instead of depending upon a sense of inherent goodness for a positive sense of self, we can start to feel proud of our efforts to face our history and dismantle white privilege.

Second, valuing vigilance means that white educators thoroughly understand the long-term nature of the commitment to witnessing. As discussed in chapter 8, we have to guard against the belief that our internal journey to excise racism from our psyches will ever be completed. At precisely the moments when we become comfortable, we are really ready for our next breakthrough. That is when the next layer of our psyche is ready to be peeled back. In this way, our relationship to witnessing racism and the ways it embeds itself in our psyches is like peeling an onion. There are layers upon layers upon layers.

For us to have a witnessing culture, we have to be consistently on guard. Yes, we need to appreciate our progress. At the same time, we also need to appreciate the depth of challenge we face. It will be important to avoid beating ourselves up mercilessly when we encounter our blind spots. Continued self-flagellation only makes us want to give up and retreat into a privileged disconnection. That is why our vigilance is so important. Dedicating ourselves to a lifelong effort of uncovering blind spots, although painful at times, also can bring feelings of pride that keep us moving forward.

Third, valuing vigilance as part of a witnessing culture requires building a collective effort. To do this, white educators have to interrogate the way that the vestiges of our individualism can influence what we imagine it means to be vigilant. When we think of someone on guard, we might imagine that person alone, the only one up late at night. This is a really hard position. If we imagine that we are going to be the only one on watch for an extended period of time, we are likely not to want to sign up for the job.

Part of our ability to stay vigilant depends on educators creating a community where members keep each other awake. We need the rejuvenation that comes with camaraderie. In the darkest hours, we need people around us who are equally committed to keeping watch with us. A witnessing culture's vigilance, then, goes hand in hand with a rejection of the ideal of the lone hero who shoulders the weight of the world in isolation.

Finally, part of valuing vigilance involves white educators continually searching for feedback. True, we are generally correct in believing that we know ourselves better than anyone else. However, when it comes to the way that our behavior betrays our socialization into white culture, white folks are generally hopelessly inept. After years of inquiry, we are still likely to miss subtle areas. If we are really going to remain vigilant, we need to open ourselves to taking in information from those who have spent their lives trying to move effectively within white spaces. In other words, we are likely never to be as sensitive to issues of white privilege as a person of color, and therefore part of our vigilance involves us seeking feedback from willing contributors.

To the degree that we value vigilance, we continue to do the work of increasing the skills, knowledge, and capacities that enable us to respond to all that we see within our classrooms, schools, and social lives. We can then begin to inspire vigilance in others. Some things we ought to consider include:

- What are the challenges that can get in the way of our intended vigilance?
- In the face of our challenges, what supportive structures can we create to help keep us engaged?
- Specifically, who can help ensure that we stay engaged in our witnessing work with . . .
  - students?
  - colleagues?
  - the extended social/racial justice community?

Accountability

Whether in our classrooms, at our school sites, or within a larger community context, when we increasingly notice racism and white privilege and employ active responses, our witnessing can quite organically lead us toward what many consider "ally" work. The possibility that our witnessing might be confused with ally work is a good thing. That would mean that we are really making great strides. One thing we would have to prepare for, however, is that discussions involving the word "ally" usually include the word "accountability."

Since accountability is a concept that a witnessing culture must value, there are several questions we ought to at least briefly discuss. What does being accountable mean? Why should white educators value this concept? And how does this term relate to some difficulties white educators may run into when developing witnessing communities?

A primary requirement of accountability is that white folks do not create collective actions against racism without including people of color. This is essential because too many white activists have rallied together and set out to battle racism without listening to the folks of color impacted by such racism. Given our relative ignorance of the subtleties of the issues, white folks acting against racism are highly susceptible to error. Therefore, we *require* assistance from people of color invested in antiracism work.

Additionally, a witnessing culture valuing accountability recognizes that although we, as white educators, do this work for our own humanity, we are not the only ones invested in the outcome. We must ask questions and listen. For example, there is no way that I would have written this book without checking in with people of color. Problematic issues both of content and style emerged that I would never have noticed on my own. The contributions of people of color have been essential in making this text what it is.

The idea of being accountable can raise complicated questions, however. What exactly might accountability look like? Does it mean that white educators need to take a backseat to people of color and be told what to do? Does it mean that we cannot use our own voices to offer opinions? The honest answer is that it depends on the context: the situation, the people involved, our knowledge base, and our experience. Sometimes we will need to simply take directions. Other times we might be asked to be in the lead. Still other times we will be full, equitable partners. These are questions that can only be answered within our cross-race relationships with collaborative partners.

As we move more fully into the work of witnessing and become increasingly seen as allies, the development of accountability guidelines becomes essential. These guidelines can be really valuable. For example, being accountable can help us troubleshoot so that we save ourselves the pain of messing up badly on a larger stage. Second, setting up accountability measures for our witnessing work also helps us develop nonoppressive communication skills that can help us create multiracial dialogue spaces where relationships can deepen.

As discussed in chapter 8, white educators will likely run into critical questions if creating witnessing communities that include only white people. We may find ourselves in a bit of a catch-22. On one hand, we know that white educators need to talk to white students and colleagues about these issues, work together to advance our own understanding, and take up some of the burden that has fallen upon the shoulders of people of color for far too long. In this way, we know that these may be seen as *communities of necessity* and, ultimately, we have been asked to do this work by people of color. On the other hand, our lack of experience and collective history of making inappropriate decisions when operating on our own makes us understandably untrustworthy in regards to this work. Where does that leave us?

My answer is that white educators can, and should, do both. We can struggle together as white folks to understand our own identity process, our pains, guilt, and fears. A witnessing space filled with white folks doing this work together is where we can share our successes, failures, and emotions in a community that encourages us to keep moving forward. When we realize that we are doing this for our own humanity, we have an invested interest in this, regardless of whether there are many people of color in our immediate environments.

However, we also have to ensure that we do not reinforce our own isolation. White educators must be part of communities that include people of color who are invited to comment on what they see as either beneficial or problematic about our process. We can use that feedback to improve our own internal process with white folks. In the end, the white space should exist solely for the purpose of helping us (1) learn about ourselves, (2) better sustain and participate in multiracial spaces, and (3) develop our witnessing practice. Healthy, sustainable integration in a just society is the larger goal!

- Are there any people in your life who might be willing to offer you feedback regarding your witnessing efforts?
- What type of witnessing community are you most likely to form: racially caucused, multiracial, or both? Why?
- How will you make sure that your work with white people does not unintentionally reinforce problematic aspects of racism or white privilege?

Historical Memory

Most educators appreciate the idea of learning from the past. For those of us who teach history or social studies, we try to convince our students that we can avoid tragic errors by attending to past events and applying the lessons learned in our present. However, *historical memory* refers to something different. Historical memory refers to the way that the past is in evidence in the present and requires attention for the sake of our future.

If we appreciate the strength of historical memory as part of our witnessing, we need to develop our vision from at least three different angles. These include recognizing (1) the way that our socio/political/economic history influences what we see in society today, (2) how historical memory is passed down through generations of families and communities, and (3) from a decidedly non-Western point of view, we need to imagine how our unhealed ancestors continue to require attention in order for personal and community healing to occur.

First, we can ask, how does our country's history play out in the present? The last section of chapter 3 offers some examples of how the historical development of whiteness has shaped some contemporary issues in schools today. However, when we expand our view we can begin to recognize how our history of racism contributes to each of our sociological patterns and institutions.

To take but one example to illustrate a much more expansive reality, how do we explain the great concentrations of African Americans living within inner cities and the preponderance of whites living in predominantly segregated small towns and suburbs across our nation? I recall wondering about this myself years back. My ignorance led me to draw upon stereotypes to surmise that African Americans either simply chose to coalesce together out of a felt sense of familiarity, did not have enough money to move, or perhaps, since I live in Los Angeles, did not want to go somewhere with a cold climate. These explanations are rather common among white folks. I knew nothing about Sundown Towns. Most white folks have not heard of them either.

James Loewen's book, *Sundown Towns: A Hidden Dimension of American Racism*, details how at least 1,000 towns and/or suburbs went "sundown" between 1890 and 1968.[16] A sundown town is defined as "any organized jurisdiction that for decades kept out African Americans (or others)."[17] Many of these towns are still exclusively white today. An initial reaction might be to assume that this simply meant not selling property to prospective African American homeowners. This would be wrong.

Loewen offers, in painstaking detail, the various ways that communities of Black and other minority families were removed from towns, sometimes within one night! He discusses middle-of-the-night violence, threats, the rise of the KKK *after* 1915, ordinances, and official government action. These towns often posted signs that read, literally, *N——.* *Don't let the sun set on you in* _____. Until you have read this book, you have no idea how close this might hit to your own hometown. I was personally affected as I read that Long Beach, California, the city where both of my parents grew up, had been one of the more vicious sundown towns in my state.

The issue here, beyond our need to learn about this history, is that white folks generally have a lot of opinions about why things are the way they are. We do this within a society that encourages us *not* to see how our history of racism is a key factor. Educators then teach from this perspective. The new mantra is that class and personal choice are largely to blame for our contemporary segregation. But Loewen offers evidence to support the conclusion that "racial and religious exclusion came first, not class,"[18] and he treats the various explanations whites usually offer to excuse ourselves from our role as the protectors of this pattern.

If, as we build our knowledge base, we look for books on just about any of our social systems and institutions, we find that racism set patterns in place that continue today. Unless active work is engaged to disrupt these cycles, they will not stop. A witnessing culture has to be knowledgeable enough to (1) see through conversations and curricular materials that continue to ignore the effects of unjust social structures that white people put in place and (2) offer our students an education that does not sidestep the impacts of our racial history. We then also have to do something about the unjust social structures.

A second way to appreciate the strength of historical memory is to see how earlier generations' experiences are passed down to subsequent generations. Elders regularly teach their children and grandchildren coping mechanisms and strategies to deal with social stressors present in earlier years. If the external influences change markedly, the young ones might cast off those increasingly unnecessary skills and strategies. However, if the environment appears to stay the same, we should not be surprised that new generations carry their elders' messages of how they should expect to be perceived and treated and how to navigate their way through a society marked by racism.

This pattern extends far beyond familial relationships. Generational transmission of a person's sense of possibility and place occur wherever a young person walks in society. Youth learn from authority figures, other community members, and media sources. We have a duty to look really carefully at the messages young people receive from society these days, both about themselves and their opportunities. This transmission of historical memory is a little discussed but gigantic issue within our schools. The more we can understand the messages our students receive and why, the more we can appreciate the issues they face and the work we must do to facilitate a different experience of the world for them. Only by eliminating enactments of racism and white privilege can we convince our students that a different world is possible.

A third way that we can understand the idea of historical memory involves the spiritual viewpoint that our ancestors remain connected to our world in ways that continue to affect us. If we can extend ourselves out of Western, modernist thought, we can see this as a metaphysical reality wherein the unhealed ancestors of our traumatic history continue to require healing. Most white folks I know pretty much shut down at this concept. Our Western conceptions often cannot imagine that the anguish of someone killed years ago would haunt our present reality.

However, there are also many who understand that the blood spilt on this country's ground reflects deep, unhealed wounds and that the spirits of those who participated and died require healing gestures before any of us can move on. If you have ever sat with someone who appears to actually tap into the pain of his or her ancestors, you might understand what I am saying. Figuring out how to honor that pain and anguish so that we might build a better future together requires us to recognize the reality of this historical memory and value reconciliation gestures. As educators, we need to ask:

- In what ways does your teaching practice take historical memory into account?

- Where in your teaching might the impacts of our racist history go unrecognized?
- What messages do your students receive regarding how they need to act in the world in order to navigate distrusted systems?

Reconciliation

Starting as early as preschool, educators impart the message that when someone does something to injure another person, a sincere and meaningful apology must follow. We know this as a deep truth. But that is often as far as we go in considering the role of reconciliation efforts. Playground traumas and adolescent slights are primary. Yet there is a completely other type of effort we can begin to consider, an altogether different level of healing process. When we expand our understanding of generational injury and recognize the strength of historical memory, we might be able to better appreciate that reconciliation efforts that come generations after an original injury are also legitimate and necessary.

In refusing to attend to the wounds of the past, the majority of the white population generally pushes forward believing in the old adage that time heals all wounds. Although possible that time does heal, an important factor is what we do during that time. Do we turn a blind eye to what caused the wounds in the first place? Or do we seek a deeper understanding and a way through to a different life? Overall, the United States has not set a good example of how to recover from crimes against humanity.

When Dr. Roberto Cabrera spoke of reconciliation processes and peace building in a lecture in Belfast in 1998, he posed the question, "Should we remember?" Even though he was speaking of reconciliation processes in Guatemala after the 36-year internal war, his fundamental question seems equally applicable to issues surrounding race relations in the United States. In response to that first question he then asked, "Has any victim forgotten?"

Dr. Cabrera suggests that we consider the following: Who benefits if the atrocities of the past are forgotten? He goes on to say that, "Most of the excuses not to remember say that it must not reopen the wounds of the past. I can certainly say, that denying the past will never lead to the closing of wounds. They are there, fresh and painful, unless the society as a whole [does] something to heal them."[19]

What might efforts at reconciliation look like in our classrooms, schools, and communities? There are more possibilities than I can even imagine. They might involve whole group dialogues, class art projects, or written expressions at a school level. Or they may look like truth and reconciliation panels at a local level. They could involve community gatherings and dialogues, public apologies, affirmative action policies, reparations, political activity, and so forth. The point is not to suggest any particular form. More important is conveying the idea that each person might be inspired to offer something back in his or her own way. When that happens, and if the effort is sincere, we can be supportive of that effort.

For example, Andrew Hawkins, a descendant of Sir John Hawkins, and a group of his friends recently traveled to The Gambia, knelt in chains in front of 25,000 Africans and asked for forgiveness for the sins of his direct forefathers. Perhaps not surprisingly, the group's "reconciliation walk" did not impress some of the village elders they passed. However, the elders' attitudes reportedly changed after they engaged in dialogue with the British group. Andrew Hawkins stated that, "I think they wanted to see an emotional connection from us, and to see that we had gone there in humility. All I could say was that we have got to do more listening and learning."[20]

Regardless of whether or not you would ever imagine being part of a gesture of that sort, the question is, how would you respond to Andrew Hawkins? At this point, the dominant white culture holds distain for his actions, wondering how someone can apologize for a past action in which he did not directly take part. A culture that witnesses whiteness does two things. First, a witnessing culture supports those who have the courage to step out of our collective denial and irresponsibility in order to stand up for the sake of healing old wounds, for the sake of healing our historical, ancestral memory. Thankfully, there are some U.S. states that very recently officially apologized for their role in our collective history of slavery. This is a start.

Second, a witnessing culture ensures that if and when we ever decide to participate in a healing ritual of any kind that we first check our level of sincerity. As a spiritual move, that would surely make all the difference in the world. Here, it also bears repeating that any move in that direction would surely warrant a checking in with those who would hold us accountable so that we can ensure that our efforts are as effective as possible.

Lastly, one of the participants in the original research project leading toward this book, Michael Meade, spoke rather eloquently on the topic of trauma, healing, and ancestral memory during our interview process. As a community educator who incorporates healing rituals into his work, Michael combines his love of symbolism and ancient wisdom to capture some ideas that offer an image to work toward without glossing over the horrors of our past. His thoughts deserve a full reading.

I think America is an experiment in trauma as much as an experiment in freedom. I think America is a traumatic collision of people pitched into, dragged into, escaping into a place which becomes an aggregation of historical trauma. And if there's an American dream, and I think there is, it's that a nightmare could become a dream, not in some naïve way, but in the sense of an awakening to a healing ground where historical and even ancestral trauma could be worked on.

That view comes out of a little vision born of working with diverse groups of people in ways that allow distinct medicines to come out. Just as there are literal medicines that come from roots in the Amazon, there are certain medicines that can come out of old Europe, medicines from Africa, medicines from each land.

Like if you were above the Earth looking at all the trauma and all the wounds in all the peoples, you might also see the medicines in all the different places as well. Then, if all the people meeting in a given place brought the medicines from their backgrounds and their root forms of knowledge, the trading of these medicines might induce a mutual healing. That's the best image of America I've ever had.

Ultimately, people have to learn to trust in people unlike themselves because the difference, the Otherness, is also the medicine for the illness one inherits. That's how I see it. People unlike oneself turn out to be carrying the medicines one's own tribe doesn't have or else has lost . . . some of the best healing I've found for those wounds have been with people from other cultures dealing with similar damages. Mutual healing is the hope that I have for America; but it depends upon cracking the white shell, the shell of "white thinking."

If you go into African cosmology, white is associated with bones, shells, stones, ash, and salt. . . . Some of the essential symbolic associations include deep memory, ancestral connection, language, stories, poems, met-

aphorical shapes for rich communication. So what I think has to happen . . .
is that the deeper memory that is ancestral to humans has to awaken. Not,
the Balkanized level of tribal memory, that's the traumatic layer that
requires great healing, but below that the deep medicine of the Old Mind,
the ancestral mind and soul that is the inheritance of all humanity.[21]

Take special notice that the ability for us to get to this level of healing,
where the various medicines residing within each cultural group can be
offered and accepted, depends on our ability to break through whiteness.
As educators, we need to take time to reflect on how this deep message
might find translation into our teaching practices:

- Is there room in your educational practice to promote the value of
  reconciliation efforts?
- What might it look like to have students participate in a reconciliation gesture where they acknowledge the deep wounds of our
  country?
- What type of dialogue among staff and faculty might be required to
  create a sense of appreciation for the reconciliation efforts you might
  support?

To conclude, each of the eight values discussed—multiplicity, interconnection, obligation, passion, vigilance, accountability, historical memory,
and reconciliation—all combine to invite us to move away from the dominant forms of white culture so prevalent at the beginning of this twenty-
first century. If educators (1) choose to collectively express the values
described above and (2) entice others who are invested in creating a new
culture to attend to the effects of race, we can create a witnessing culture
that might make a real difference in our society.

JOINING THE HIDDEN AMERICA

The final question for us to consider is whether or not a witnessing culture
can exist within the United States. The answer is that yes, assuredly it can.
The truth is that a witnessing culture has always been here, hidden under

the surface, just waiting for enough of us to notice and grab hold. The culture of witnessing has a long history. It is a culture with well-worn paths, albeit not ones that are well publicized. For those who are most active, the path can be rocky and appear treacherous at its beginning. Following it to its end, one enters the world of the allies. For those who speak of this way of being, they often include the recognition that it is a different world. In a letter to antiracist activist Anne Braden, William Patterson, an African American activist, offers that

> You don't have to be part of the world of the lynchers. You do have a choice. You can join the other America. The other America has always been here. From the time the first slave ship arrived. It is the people who fought against slavery. Against injustice. The people who fought for humanity. It was Black and it was white.[22]

This "other America" is home for those who witness actively, those who might someday be considered allies.

This is the hidden America, an America that strengthens and supports all of her residents, an America that includes rather than excludes, and an America that fulfills its deepest purpose. This America has so far existed in the shadows. If educators en masse join this other America in the spirit of witnessing, we can heal the dis-ease we feel about race. In our healing, we can help make America what it has never been for so many, the America of our ideals. This is the American dream many of us hold in our hearts. So, really, the question is, will enough of us stand up and witness so that America's dream can come true?

NOTES

1. P. H. Ray and S. R. Anderson, *The Cultural Creatives: How 50 Million People Are Changing the World* (New York: Harmony Books, 2000), 4.

2. Ray and Anderson, *The Cultural Creatives*, 15.

3. Ray and Anderson, *The Cultural Creatives*, 17

4. Ray and Anderson, *The Cultural Creatives*, 341.

5. M. Gladwell, *The Tipping Point: How Little Things Can Make a Big Difference* (New York: Back Bay Books, 2000).

6. Gladwell, *The Tipping Point*, 179.

7. Oliver, *Witnessing: Beyond Recognition.*

8. Tarnas, *The Passion of the Western Mind.*

9. Putnam, *Bowling Alone.*

10. C. G. Jung, "Conscious, Unconscious, and Individuation," in *The Collected Works of C. G. Jung*, vol. 9, trans. R. F. C. Hull (Princeton, NJ: Princeton University Press, 1969), 275; original work published in 1939.

11. C. G. Jung, "Adaptation, Individuation, Collectivity," in *The Collected Works of C. G. Jung*, vol. 18, trans. R. F. C. Hull (Princeton, NJ: Princeton University Press, 1969), 451; original work published in 1970.

12. C. G. Jung, "On the Nature of the Psyche," in *The Collected Works of C. G. Jung*, vol. 8, trans. R. F. C. Hull (Princeton, NJ: Princeton University Press, 1969), 226; original work published in 1947.

13. Romanyshyn, *Ways of the Heart.*

14. Putnam, *Bowling Alone*, 400, 404, and 411.

15. Lorenz and Watkins, "Silenced Knowings, Forgotten Springs," 3. The concept of "percepticide" is taken from Taylor, *Disappearing Acts.*

16. J. Loewen, *Sundown Towns: A Hidden Dimension of American Racism* (New York: New Press, 2005), 80.

17. Loewen, *Sundown Towns*, 213.

18. Loewen, *Sundown Towns*, 145.

19. R. Cabrera, "Should We Remember? Recovering Historical Memory in Guatemala," 1998, www.brandonhamber.com/publications/Chap%203%20 %20Guatemala%20Roberto%2 0Cabrer a.pdf

20. Alan Hamilton, "Slaver's Descendant Begs Forgiveness," *The Times Online*, June 22, 2006, http://www.timesonline.co.uk/article/0,,3–2236871, 00.html

21. Thompson, *A Promise and a Way of Life*, 52.

Bibliography

Allen, T. W. 1997. *The Invention of the White Race*. New York: Verso.

Allen, T. W. n.d. Summary of the Argument of *The Invention of the White Race*. Part Two. Available at http://clogic.eserver.org/1-2/allen2.html.

Alonso-Zaldivar, R., and J. Merl. 2004. Booklet That Upset Mrs. Cheney Is History. *Los Angeles Times*, October 8, A1.

American Anthropological Association. 1998. *Statement on "Race."* May 17, 1998. Available at http://www.aaanet.org/stmts/racepp.htm.

Association for Supervision and Curriculum Development. 2003. *Closing the Achievement Gap: A Vision for Changing Beliefs and Practices*, ed. B. Williams. Alexandria, VA: ASCD.

Ayvazian, A., and B. D. Tatum. 1994. Women, Race, and Racism: A Dialogue in Black and White. *Work in Progress*, No. 68. Wellesley, MA: Wellesley College, Center for Research on Women.

Better, S. 2002. *Institutional Racism: A Primer on Theory and Strategies for Social Change*. Chicago, IL: Burnham.

Bigelow, B., B. Harvey, S. Karp, and L. Miller, eds. 2001. *Rethinking Our Classrooms*, vol. 2: *Teaching for Equity and Justice*. Milwaukee, WI: Rethinking Schools.

Bivens, D. "Internalized Racism: A Definition." Women's Theological Center. A more complete explanation can be located at www.evaluationtoolsforracialequity.org/term Racial.htm.

Brown, M. 1991. *Race, Money, and the American Welfare State*. Ithaca, NY: Cornell University Press.

Bruce, P. A. 1902. *Social Life in Virginia in the Seventeenth Century: An Inquiry into the Origins of the Higher Planting Class, Together with an Account of the Habits, Customs, and Diversions of the People*. Richmond, VA: Whittet & Shepperson.

Cabrera, R. 1998. Should We Remember? Recovering Historical Memory in Guatemala. Available at www.brandonhamber.com/publications/Chap%203%20-%20Guatemala% 20Roberto%2 0Cabrera.pdf

Coll, C. G., R. Cook-Nobles, and J. L. Surrey. 1997. Building Connection through Diversity. In *Women's Growth in Diversity: More Writings from the Stone Center*, ed. J. V. Jordan, 176–98. New York: Guilford Press.

Crass, C. 2004. Beyond Welfare Queens: Developing a Race, Class and Gender Analysis of Welfare and Welfare Reform. *Infoshop.org*. Available at www.infoshop.org/texts/welfare.html.

Cushman, P. 1995. *Constructing the Self, Constructing America: A Cultural History of Psychotherapy*. New York: Addison-Wesley.

DeGruy Leary, J. 2005. *PostTraumatic Slave Syndrome*. Milwaukie, OR: Uptone Press.

Festinger, L., S. Schacter, and K. Black. 1950. *Social Pressures in Informal Groups: A Study of Human Factors in Housing*. Oxford: Harper.

Frankenberg, R. 1993. *The Social Construction of Whiteness: White Women, Race Matters*. Minneapolis: University of Minnesota Press.

———. 1997. Introduction. Local Whitenesses, Localizing Whiteness. In *Displacing Whiteness: Essays in Social and Cultural Criticism*, ed. R. Frankenberg, 1–34. Durham, NC: Duke University Press.

Gilligan, J. 1996. *Violence: Reflections on a National Epidemic*. New York: Vintage Books.

Giroux, H. A. 1992. Postcolonial Ruptures/Democratic Possibilities. In *Border Crossings: Cultural Workers and the Politics of Education*, ed. H. Giroux, 19–38. New York: Routledge.

Gladwell, M. 2000. *The Tipping Point: How Little Things Can Make a Big Difference*. New York: Back Bay Books.

Hamilton, A. 2006. Slaver's Descendant Begs Forgiveness. *The Times Online*, June 22. Available at http://www.timesonline.co.uk/article/0,,3-2236871,00.html.

Haney Lopez, I. F. 1995. White by Law. In *Critical Race Theory: The Cutting Edge*, ed. R. Delgado, 542–50. Philadelphia: Temple University Press.

———. 1996. *White by Law: The Legal Construction of Race*. New York: New York University Press.

Hartigan, J., Jr. 1997. Locating White Detroit. In *Displacing Whiteness: Essays in Social and Cultural Criticism*, ed. R. Frankenberg, 180–213. Durham, NC: Duke University Press.

Havemann, J., and R. Alonso-Zaldivar. 2006. Middle-Class Workers Ailing in Census Checkup. *Los Angeles Times*, August 30.

Helms, J. E. 1992. A Race Is a Nice Thing to Have: A Guide to Being a White Person or Understanding the White Persons in Your Life. Topeka, KS: Content Communications.

———. 1995. An Update of Helms's White and People of Color Racial Identity Models. In *Handbook of Multicultural Counseling*, ed. J. Ponterotto, J. Casas, L. Suzuki, and C. Alexander, 181–98. Thousand Oaks, CA: Sage.

Hillman, J. 1983. *Healing Fiction*. Woodstock, CT: Spring.

———. 1986. Notes on White Supremacy: Essaying an Archetypal Account of Historical Events. *Spring* 46:29–58.

HistoricalDocuments.com. n.d. The Immigration Act of 1924. Available at http://www.historicaldocuments.com/ImmigrationActof1924.htm.

hooks, b. 1995. *Killing Rage: Ending Racism*. New York: Henry Holt.

Howard, G. 2006. *We Can't Teach What We Don't Know*. New York: Teachers College

Hughes, L. 1994. Let America Be America Again. In *The Collected Poems of Langston Hughes*, ed. A. Rampersad and D. Roessel. New York: Alfred A. Knopf.

Ignatiev, N. 1995. *How the Irish Became White*. New York: Routledge.

Jackman, M. R., and M. C. Crane. 1986. "Some of My Best Friends Are Black . . .":

Interracial Friendship and Whites' Racial Attitudes. *Public Opinion Quarterly* 50:459–86.

Jay, G. 1998. Who Invented White People? A Talk on the Occasion of Martin Luther King Jr. Day, 1998. Available at www.uwm.edu/~gjay/Whiteness/Whitenesstalk.html.

Jensen, R. 2005. *The Heart of Whiteness: Confronting Race, Racism, and White Privilege.* San Francisco: City Lights.

Jordan, W. D. 1969. *White over Black.* Baltimore, MD: Penguin Books.

Jung, C. G. 1969a. Conscious, Unconscious, and Individuation. In *The Collected Works of C. G. Jung*, vol. 9, trans. R. F. C. Hull. Princeton, NJ: Princeton University Press. (Original work published 1939)

———. 1969b. On the Nature of the Psyche. In *The Collected Works of C. G. Jung*, vol. 8, trans. R. F. C. Hull. Princeton, NJ: Princeton University Press (Original work published 1947).

———. 1970. Adaptation, Individuation, Collectivity. In *The Collected Works of C. G. Jung*, vol. 18, trans. R. F. C. Hull. Princeton, NJ: Princeton University Press (Original work published 1970).

Kendall, F. 2006. *Understanding White Privilege.* New York: Routledge.

Kivel, P. 1996 *Uprooting Racism: How White People Can Work toward Racial Justice.* Gabriola Island, BC: New Society.

Kozol, J. 1992. *Savage Inequalities: Children in America's Schools.* New York: Harper Perennial.

Lipsitz, G. 1998. *The Possessive Investment in Whiteness: How White People Profit from Identity Politics.* Philadelphia: Temple University Press.

Loewen, J. 1996. *Lies My Teacher Told Me: Everything Your History Textbook Got Wrong.* New York: New Press.

———. 2005. *Sundown Towns: A Hidden Dimension of American Racism.* New York: New Press.

Lorenz, H. S., and M. Watkins. 2001. Silenced Knowings, Forgotten Springs: Paths to Healing in the Wake of Colonialism. *Radical Psychology* 2, no. 2. Available at www.rad psynet.org/journal/v012-2/lorenz-watkins.html.

———. 2003. Depth Psychology and Colonialism: Individuation, Seeing Through, and Liberation. *Quadrant* 33, no. 1:11–32.

Mahoney, M. R. 1997. Segregation, Whiteness, and Transformation. In *Critical White Studies*, edited by R. Delgado and J. Stefancic, 654–57. Philadelphia: Temple University Press.

McIntosh, P. 1989. White Privilege: Unpacking the Invisible Knapsack. *Peace and Freedom*. Philadelphia, PA: Women's International League for Peace and Freedom.

Meade, M. 1993. *Men and the Water of Life.* New York: HarperCollins.

Mennott, M. 2005. Spotlight Skips Cases of Missing Minorities. *USA Today*, June 12.

Moore, S., and R. Fields. 2002. The Great "White" Influx. *LA Times Online*, July 31, 2002. Available at www.uwm.edu/%7Egjay/Whiteness/latimesarticle.htm.

Morales, A. L. 1998. *Medicine Stories: History, Culture and the Politics of Integrity.* Cambridge, MA: South End Press.

Morgan, E. S. 1975. *American Slavery, American Freedom: The Ordeal of Colonial Virginia.* New York: Norton.

Morrison, T. 1992. *Playing in the Dark: Whiteness and the Literary Imagination.* New York: Vintage Books.

Obidah, J. E., and K. M. Teel. 2001. *Because of the Kids: Facing Racial and Cultural Differences in Schools.* New York: Teachers College Press.

O'Connor, A. M. 2006. Diverse Realities of Mysteries. *Los Angeles Times,* July 5.

Oliver, K. 2001. *Witnessing: Beyond Recognition.* Minneapolis: University of Minnesota Press.

Olson, R. A., 1998. White Privilege in Schools. In *Beyond Heroes and Holidays: A Practical Guide to Anti-Racist, Multicultural Education and Staff Development,* ed. E. Lee, D. Menkart, and M. Okazawa-Rey, 83–84. Washington, DC: Network of Educators on the Americas.

Omi, M., and H. Winant. 1994. *Racial Formation in the United States.* New York: Routledge.

Parvez, Z. F. 2002. Women, Poverty, and Welfare Reform. *Sociologists for Women in Society.* Available at www.socwomen.org/socactivism/factwelfare.pdf.

Pitts, L., Jr. 2002. Crazy Sometimes. In *When Race Becomes Real,* ed. B. Singley. Chicago, IL: Lawrence Hill Books.

Putnam, R. 2000. *Bowling Alone: The Collapse and Revival of American Community.* New York: Simon & Schuster.

Race, Place, and Segregation: Redrawing the Color Line in Our Nation's Metros. 2002. *The Civil Rights Project,* Harvard University. Available at www.civilrightsproject.harvard.edu/research/metro/three_metros.php.

Ray, P. H., and S. R. Anderson. 2000. *The Cultural Creatives: How 50 Million People Are Changing the World.* New York: Harmony Books.

Roberts, R. 2003. *My Soul Said to Me.* Deerfield Beach, FL: Health Communications.

Robinson, E. 2005. (White) Women We Love. *Washington Post,* June 10, A23.

Rodriguez, L. 1993. *Always Running: Gang Days in L.A.* Willimantic, CT: Curbstone Press.

Roediger, D. R. 1991. *Wages of Whiteness: Race and the Making of the American Working Class.* New York: Verso.

———. 2002. *Colored White: Transcending the Racial Past.* Los Angeles: University of California Press.

Romanyshyn, R. 2002. *Ways of the Heart: Essays toward an Imaginal Psychology.* Pittsburgh, PA: Trivium.

Sentilles, S. 2005. *Taught by America: A Struggle of Struggle and Hope in Compton.* Boston: Beacon Press.

Singley, B. 2002. *When Race Becomes Real.* Chicago, IL: Lawrence Hill Books.

Tarnas, R. 1991. *The Passion of the Western Mind: Understanding the Ideas That Have Shaped Our World View.* New York: Ballantine Books.

Tatum, B. D. 1992. Talking about Race, Learning about Racism: An Application of Racial Identity Development Theory in the Classroom. *Harvard Educational Review* 62, no. 1:1–24.

———. 1994. Teaching White Students about Racism: The Search for White Allies and the Restoration of Hope. *Teachers College Record* 95, no. 4:462–77.

———. 1997. Racial Identity Development and Relational Theory: The Case of a Black Woman in White Communities. In *Women's Growth in Diversity: More Writings from the Stone Center,* ed. J. V. Jordan, 91–106. New York: Guilford Press.

———. 1999. *Why Are All the Black Kids Sitting Together in the Cafeteria?* New York: Basic Books.

Taylor, D. 1997. *Disappearing Acts*. Durham, NC: Duke University Press.

Thandeka 1999. *Learning to Be White: Money, Race, and God in America*. New York: Continuum.

Thompson, B. 2001. *A Promise and a Way of Life: White Antiracist Activism*. Minneapolis: University of Minnesota Press.

Twine, F. W. 1997. Brown-skinned White Girls: Class, Culture, and the Construction of White Identity in Suburban Communities. In *Displacing Whiteness: Essays in Social and Cultural Criticism*, ed. R. Frankenberg, 214–43. Durham, NC: Duke University Press.

Vanderryn, J. H. M. 1993. *A Qualitative Analysis of the Meaning of Being White American*. PhD dissertation, University of Colorado, Boulder, 1994.

Wertenbaker, T. J. 1959. *Patrician and Plebeian in Virginia*. New York: Russell & Russell.

Zinn, H. 1980. *A People's History of the United States*. New York: Harper & Row.

———. n.d. History Is a Weapon: Drawing the Color Line. Available at http://www.history isaweapon.com/defcon1/zinncolorline.html.

Index

abolitionist, 65–67, 69

accountability, 294, 318–19

Allen, Theodore, 77–83, 104–7, 207

ally:

  activities, 68–69, 104, 249, 294, 297, 318

  model of white, 66–67

American:

  as a new identity, 83–89, 91–92, 98, 102n42

  use of term, 107n44

  values, 88–89

ancestors, 77, 87, 198, 207, 307, 309, 321–23

Anderson, Sherry Ruth, 302, 304, 328, 334

anecdotes by author:

  conflict with a mentor/friend, 145

  growing up with ethnocentric education, 73

  liberal approach to student discipline, 64

  racist treatment of parents in schools, 61, 102

  relating with students without neediness, 293–94

antiracist practice, ix, 8, 212, 305

  elements of, 267, 250, 280, 289

  techniques, 268–74

antiracist white culture, 299

appropriation, cultural, 42–43, 292

assimilation:

  effects of, 35, 38, 43, 68, 83, 88–89

  in schools, 102

AWARE-LA, 8, 67 68, 161, 291–97

becoming white, *See* American as a new identity

Better, Shirley, 21, 31, 181, 219

Bowling Alone, 196, 310, 315

Brewer, Spencer, 122–25, 148–49, 163–73, 186–90, 192, 194, 240–43

Brown, Michael, 28

Cabrera, Roberto, 324

Calloway, Casey, 136–41, 186, 188, 192, 197, 202–4, 233, 236–39

capitalization of Black and white, viii–ix

Cole, Lorraine, 131, 133–36, 186, 222–29, 237, 268

Color of Fear, 122, 124, 163, 166, 240

colorblindness, 15, 26, 43–44, 53, 137

About the Author

Shelly Tochluk is an educator with a background in psychology, and she spent ten years as a researcher, counselor, and teacher in California's public schools. She now trains teachers to work with Los Angeles' diverse school population as an assistant professor of education at Mount St. Mary's College. Tochluk also strives to build community across race, culture, age, sexual orientation, and ability as she co-produces multicultural women's retreats through Unity Bridges, the nonprofit organization she co-founded.

Shelly's personal dedication to confront issues of race developed first through her participation with UCLA's NCAA Division-I All-American Track and Field 4X400 meter relay team and later through her inner-city teaching experiences. Shelly serves on the leadership team of AWARE-LA (Alliance of White Anti-Racists Everywhere–Los Angeles). She also co-created a workshop series that leads white people into a deeper understanding of their personal relationship to race, white privilege, and systemic racism. Tochluk has presented at the White Privilege Conference and is committed to speaking at community forums whenever possible to highlight issues of white racial identity.